ADVANCES IN HUMOR AND PSYCHOTHERAPY

Edited by
William F. Fry, Jr., MD
Waleed A. Salameh, PhD

Professional Resource Press
Sarasota, Florida

Published by Professional Resource Press
(An imprint of Professional Resource Exchange, Inc.)
Post Office Box 15560
Sarasota, FL 34277-1560

The copy editor for this book was Patricia Hammond, the managing editor was Debra Fink, the production coordinator was Laurie Girsch, and Jami's Graphic Design created the cover.

Library of Congress Cataloging-in-Publication Data

Advances in humor and psychotherapy / edited by William F. Fry, Jr.,
    and Waleed A. Salameh.
            p.   cm.
        Includes bibliographical references and index.
        ISBN 0-943158-78-8
        1. Wit and humor--Therapeutic use. 2. Psychotherapy. I. Fry,
    William F.   II. Salameh, Waleed A.
    RC489.H85A34   1993
    616.89'14--dc20
                                    93-17202
                                    CIP

Dedication

I dedicate this volume to the pioneers of all human ventures - wandering, discovering, curious, restlessly exploring new worlds and prospects.

William F. Fry, Jr.

I dedicate this book to the Goddess of Writing, my salvation, my inspiration, and my ultimate sanctuary. This book is also dedicated to the memory of my grandmother, Tamem Catrib, who taught me much more than I first realized.

Waleed A. Salameh

Foreword

The *Upanishads* already mentions what for us therapists seems to be at the root of human problems - namely that all suffering is due to the painful contradiction between the way the world *is* and the way it *should be*. And for Mani, the founder of Manicheism, reality is the painful, inescapable, uncompromising fight between the forces of light and of darkness which - in the distant future - will be resolved by the total victory of light. Aristotle is similarly outspoken: The world is a dichotomy of true and false - *"tertium non datur,"* there is no third.

A basically similar reality is created by political and ideological propaganda: "Who is not for us, is against us" - there is no third.

Very much the same seems to hold for our so-called patients - caught as they are in the traps of irrationality, only insight into the real causes of their predicament can bring about change.

And yet, the "third" seems to exist: It is the *joke*. Jokes have a disrespectful ability to make light of seemingly monolithic world orders.

In his talks, Viktor Frankl occasionally mentions such an example: In the First World War an aristocratic colonel and his regimental medical officer, a Jew, are sitting in their dugout under heavy Russian shelling. The colonel looks at the doctor and says half-condescendingly, half-compassionately, "Well, admit that you are scared. It just goes to show the inferiority of the Jewish race." The little doctor replies, "Yes, I am really scared. But what that proves about races, I don't know. Because if you, colonel, were as scared as I am, you would be running for dear life."

From our work we know that people are half over their emotional problems once they manage to laugh at their predicament. "He laughed to free his mind from his mind's bondage," we read in *Ulysses*. And after his odyssey through the Magic Theater, the hero in Hermann Hesse's *Steppenwolf* laughs out loud as he realizes that reality is nothing but the free choice of one of many doors that are open at all times. And something similar happens to Zen pupils at the moment of enlightenment - they burst out laughing.

The authors of this book are to be commended for their numerous, fascinating, and enjoyably unorthodox contributions to the role of humor in psychotherapy. May this book find the recognition that it richly deserves!

Paul Watzlawick
Mental Research Institute
Palo Alto, California
March 18, 1993

Preface

The production of this volume can be recognized as a testimony to significant development in at least a segment of our world culture. That development has taken place in just these past few years. Our first volume of edited chapters on the roles of humor, mirth, and laughter in psychologic health and therapy, *Handbook of Humor and Psychotherapy: Advances in the Clinical Use of Humor*, was a bold, somewhat iconoclastic adventure in 1987. It was innovative; it dared to present views of the relations between humor and psychotherapy, which were not widely held or approved, and were even denounced in some quarters. The chapters of that volume were largely contributed by professionals who had worked with this collaboration of forces (humor and psychotherapy) as pioneers, even "mavericks" in some instances.

Individually, each of the present contributors is no less adventuresome, creative, and progress-oriented. But the adventure and daring which they have dreamed and performed has gained an acceptance and respect which did not previously exist. The therapeutic world has become a different environment. It is our full expectation that their presentations in this new publication will augment and further the cultural advance indicated in this progression. These authors have been carefully chosen to contribute their ideas and experiences, not only for their considerable communicational skills and high professional quality, but also to indicate the wide range of professional activities and disciplines participating in this cultural progression.

This present publication clearly states, in its very being, that traditions have changed; humor has begun to receive recognition and acceptance as a valuable adjunctive force in the important segment of our culture which is dedicated to mental and emotional health and health care. But we do not offer this volume to its readership as simply a shrine to mark historic evolution. We have intended, and the chapter authors have masterfully responded to our intention, that this volume provide stimulation of a specific and practical nature. We believe that this stimulation is derived from experiences offered by these chapters and the wisdom of observations detailed and explained by their authors.

It is, therefore, with appreciation and respect that we offer our first acknowledgment in this volume to the scientists and other professionals who have shared with us all, in each chapter, their intelligence and guiding experience. They have been hardworking and dedicated in their efforts for this book. They have been effective and creative. We fully anticipate that their works will make important contributions to increasingly valuable efforts at making the rich human resource which is found in humor, mirth, and laughter more and more useful in mental health care.

In the wake of this second volume, we would like to sincerely acknowledge others who have provided us with enormously helpful material assistance and/or moral support during this thrilling adventure. William F. Fry would like to thank family members, including Mrs. Elizabeth S. Fry. Waleed A. Salameh would like to acknowledge the support of his mother, Mrs. Espérance Salameh, and his aunt, Mrs. Rajaa Ghorayeb, for helping keep a smile on his face during the preparation of this manuscript. Gratitude is expressed to Dr. Michael Titze, Dr. Bernard Tétreau, Father Robert Daigle, Dr. Wael Salameh, Dr. Donald Pollie, Dr. Alfred Raphelson, Mr. Morton Grabel, Mr. Albert Zerka, Mr. Alfred Ghorayeb, Mr. Imad Ghorayeb, and Mr. Jihad Catrib, for their unique senses of humor and their friendship. Appreciation is also expressed by Waleed Salameh to Dr. Robert Horowitz and other colleagues who shared their therapy jokes and clinical experiences. Other friends whose support and exceptional senses of humor have made a difference include Dr. Jack Barakat, Dr. Nabil Kanbar, Dr. Riyad Nassar, Uncle Jack Hamady, and Omar Helaihel.

Editing was significantly aided by the generous secretarial assistance of Mrs. Elizabeth S. Fry, Mrs. Dolores Espinoza, and Ms. Barbara Laundrie. We further wish to express appreciation to our publishers at Professional Resource Press, Drs. Lawrence G. Ritt and Peter A. Keller. Our final acknowledgment is not the least of all in any sense. It is to the remarkable skill, patience, diplomacy, and creativity of the Professional Resource Press staff, particularly Debbie Fink (who always seems to be in the office, no matter when we phone) and her dedicated assistant, Laurie Girsch.

W. F. F. and W. A. S.
March 1993

Table of Contents

Introduction

THEORY AND SCIENTIFIC DYNAMISMS

In the "Conclusion" section of our first book (*Handbook of Humor and Psychotherapy: Advances in the Clinical Use of Humor*) of this series of edited volumes on the values and uses of humor in psychotherapy, Dr. Salameh and I speculated that "subsequent" volumes might ensue. That was not a particularly wild speculation, but it was courageous. After all, there had been that tradition of decades (centuries?) expounding against any mixing of humor into professional mental health therapeutics. I had been trained specifically in that tradition during my psychiatric education. It was only after I became involved in family therapy research at the Mental Research Institute (MRI) in Palo Alto, California, that I began to recognize the rather amazing absurdity of the absolutist stricture against humor in therapy transactions. But, of course, recent openings of therapeutic avenues in many areas - not only family therapy - has had a marvelously creative impact on the mental health field in many regards. These new openings have enlarged our understanding in many areas, not simply in discovering the heady truth of valuable roles which can be taken by humor in the therapeutic process.

I feel quite comfortable in stating that the generally accepted therapeutic model of 30 years ago was a pallid, even drab, ancestor of what pertains in this present "enlightened" time. During the odd quiet moment, from time to time, I blush to think of the wooden, artificial, and stuffy image I must have projected to some of my early therapy participants - as was the style prescribed by tradition. Not that I am deeply humiliated or seized by guilt by those memories, but they remind me of former insecurity-driven rigidities and sophomoric naïveté. And these were certainly not my most gloriously laudable attributes.

It is sometimes appropriate to question whether there ever is *real* progress in human ventures, or whether that impression is illusionary. In many instances, it is truly appropriate to question progress; the question is not simply the mouthing of kitchen cynicism. One can easily bring up examples relating to the various short-sighted ways in which human advances in technology have served to diminish, rather than enhance, quality of life on our spaceship planet. And each of us can think of some further instances of the image of "progress" having glimmered away and been revealed as failed.

But, surely, this illusoriness cannot be universal. There certainly are instances in which benefits have not been defeated or compromised by grossly undesirable consequences of the actions that were deemed necessary to produce benefits. I will affirm that, if not in any other province, at least there has been real progress in advances of psychotherapy during the recent decades. The realization of the values of humor in psychotherapy is one important such advance.

Nevertheless, the restrictive tradition against humor in psychotherapy has been firmly ensconced in the professions. Although the tradition was showing extensive fading at the edges in 1987 (*Handbook of Humor and Psychotherapy* publication year), it still *was* - and had the power of being the word of archetypal elders. In that context, against that background, it was a courageous suggestion that interest in this subject could be of any degree sufficient as to warrant consideration of producing further volumes in the same general field.

The argument might have been, "It will only be the young turks, those who are more daring, more impatient, more willing to take risks, and concerned to try new approaches in patient care; only those could be interested in additional information and exchange on this controversial subject of humor and psychotherapy." Well, either there has developed a very large proportion of young turks in the present therapeutic population, or the proposed argument was faulty at its core. It seems more likely that the latter is the correct explanation.

It has been quite stunning to discover the extent of interest in the therapeutic values of humor. This interest is shown in book sales and individual enthusiasm expressed by a surprisingly large

number of mental health practitioners at all levels of
of a broad range of disciplines and theoretic persuasi
terest is also indicated by the relatively large numbe
and skilled practitioners manifesting enthusiasm f
chapters for "forthcoming volumes." This enthusiasm ...
vided further verification of broad-based interest in the subject. It
also insures that the considerable audience for this information
will be served amply and well. High quality is assured by the
mental vitality indicated in writer enthusiasm for contributing material to successive volumes and by the spirited dedication evidenced in author willingness to move against convention and
commit oneself in publication to a new prospect.

What is particularly stunning to me is the range of theory and
discipline represented by individuals who have informed us of
their enthusiasm for being published in our subject. As you will
discover in examining the biographical data about the authors in
this book, this range is impressively wide. Additional author interest has been made known to us that is sufficient for a third
volume, and perhaps even a core for yet a fourth volume in this
series, with continuing richness in orientation and style.

This wide range is very interesting to me for two reasons.
The first lies in the fact that during recent decades, a great deal of
ferment and change has taken place in the psychotherapy field.
The entire professional discipline has undergone massive expansion and extension. There are now effectively practiced disciplines of therapy not even imagined 30 years ago. The various
forms of therapy represented in this new blend are practiced by tal-
ented and energetic professionals. It is reasonable, and exciting,
to observe this vigorous response from pioneers of many varied
orientations and schools.

A second reason to thrill at this diversity of origin is much
more complex and is bound up in the importance of the word
homeostasis. This is a word with a distinguished history that has
come to have wide application in science. It was originally derived in the first half of this century by the renowned Harvard
University physiologist, Walter Cannon, to designate a balanced
physiologic state of biologic entities (such as human beings).
Cannon considered that this balanced state is necessary for successful biologic functioning. He proposed that balance is obtained and maintained by various physiologic "homeostatic
mechanisms," some of which have developed exclusively with
that function, through evolutionary selection processes.

Cannon's theory was an extension of earlier formulations presented by the famous 19th-century French physiologist, Claude Bernard, who came to understand the necessity of recognizing an interior presence, or "reality," or biological "beingness" of creatures. He came to understand that there is a great deal going on in interior functioning, with very complex presences and interrelationships. He presented the phrase "milieu intérieur" (in contrast to "milieu extérieur") to designate an internal environment in which an amazing pageant of physical and electrochemical events takes place, representing life processes of the creature. In discovering "the milieu intérieur," Bernard created the scientific stage on which most of the advances of the biologic sciences of the past 150 years have been developed. In absence of that insight, very little in terms of understanding the biologic realities of life would be possible.

Cannon's great contribution in this regard was in recognizing that the milieu intérieur must be kept in a state of functional efficiency and coordination. He understood that the various components of the milieu could not just be independently doing their own physiologic thing, without interaction with all other components of the milieu: A system of biologically effective interrelationships must be present to avoid functional chaos. *Homeostasis* was the crucial element of that picture, with many "homeostatic mechanisms" continuously operating in coordination, insuring systematic maintenance of interior balance of biologic function, making it physiologically possible for the milieu intérieur to be continuously ordered, avoiding chaos and confusion. Thus, the word *homeostasis* is not intended to indicate a particulate component of physiology, but rather a general characteristic of physiology as it has developed over the eons.

The use of *homeostasis* has been extended far beyond the origin of its meaning in physiology. *Homeostasis* of psychological adjustment has been introduced into our parlance. *Homeostasis* of group interaction is examined and discussed. Corporate *homeostasis* is considered a desirable quality of business entities. *Homeostasis* is described in other scientific provinces than physiology - such as geology, ecology, political science, climatology, botany, and volcanology. The *homeostasis* of many nonbiological entities is studied, including glacier movement and structure, ozone concentrations, chemical content of water, population statistics, national and international economies, sports and other recreation statistics, temperature and water content variations, and chemical composition or thermodynamics of stars. The concept of *homeostasis* has made powerful contributions to human understanding and analysis of the world and ourselves. It has provided illumination of many previously obscure aspects of the universe.

The relevance of all this important history to the issue of great variety in the theoretical and practice orientations of professionals who have indicated their enthusiasm for writing about humor in psychotherapy is derived from the fact that *homeostasis* has become an anachronism. That is, the word no longer has fundamental significance, as a result of what we have recently learned about the previously unrecognized enormous complexity of physiology. The image of physiologic *stasis* being attained, and maintained, in any fashion other than simply being a theoretical model, or "for the sake of argument," is revealed as a vast oversimplification, as a result of our new knowledge of physiologic complexity. We have come to realize that there is no *stasis* in the milieu intérieur. The interior state is not static; it is not steady; it is not even in balance - except in a macro-macrofunctional fashion. The physiologic systems and their various modalities and components are in constant flux, with variations, modifications, changes, fluctuations, and alterations going on constantly - in all interactive systems, at all times. The milieu intérieur is in a constant condition of dynamic flux.

I have proposed the word *homeodynamics* in several places and at several times as the more proper term to identify this impressive complexity we observe in biologic functioning. *Homeostasis* is a misnomer for what we now recognize as taking place - continuously, throughout life - in the physiology of living creatures. *Dynamics* is what truly happens in physiology. *Stasis* is incorrect; it artificially freezes the function and distorts reality. *Homeodynamics* conveys the more correct picture of interrelationship, complexity, constant fluctuation and adjustment - the continuous seeking and modifying and altering that characterizes the life process.

There is nothing static about the functioning of an organism. Physiology is a continuously dynamic process, complexly and inextricably interrelated. The body is no quiet pond, kept in steady state by effective, relatively ponderous compensatory mechanisms. The more proper metaphor is that of a powerful dashing stream, in continuous activity and variation. Like a free-running stream, it is ever changing; it is never the same. The body state never returns exactly to what existed before. It is like the Zen koan: One can never put one's hand in the same stream twice. And it is never over; this dynamism never stops until a final dissolution.

My recognition of the much greater appropriateness of the word *homeodynamics* for describing physiologic functioning gives clear evidence of the development of my familiarity with the dynamic character of physiology. That familiarity has become a source of fascination and conviction for me. It also is what brings me back to my original topic of the recently discovered wide range of interest in humor among professionals and scientists. My familiarity with physiologic dynamics was developed to a large degree through my studies of humor physiology, initiated in 1968 and reported in sporadically published articles. Humor physiology is so dynamic and so complex that one must be looking the other way to miss its homeodynamic nature.

This busyness of biologic process, this *homeodynamics*, can be sighted through other windows besides that of humor physiology. It can be observed in cardiac activity, in immune functioning, in the physiology of sleep, central nervous system activity, cellular metabolism, and elsewhere. But the contours are sharper, the details are more intensely defined, when observed through humor physiology.

Fine compatibility is demonstrated in these issues. Complexity and dynamism are demonstrated in humor physiology, and are found in the diversity of professional interest in humor's roles in psychotherapy. Complexity and dynamism also are found in the energetic response of professionals, of a wide range of theoretical origins and traditions, to the opportunity of sharing experiences regarding humor in psychotherapy. It is my impression that this compatibility and the prevalence of complexity and dynamism reflect the richness of the lode which is being mined by the authors of the chapters that we are privileged to present in this volume. Waleed Salameh and I are delighted with the wonderful opportunity to extend in this volume new information about our topic of interest and thus make further contribution to the advancement of our professions and of our deep enthusiasm - humor in psychotherapy.

William F. Fry, Jr.

ON THERAPEUTIC ICONS AND
THERAPEUTIC PERSONAE

We have come a long way! When William Fry and I launched our first ship into the sea of humor with the publication of the *Handbook of Humor and Psychotherapy* in 1987, little did we know where our ship would travel or how it would fare in its professional voyage. At that time, we did not realize that we were helping to launch a new movement, a movement that included both sophisticated and beginning psychotherapists looking for different ways of doing psychotherapy through the key of humor. As we now launch this second publication, I am struck by the continuing constructive feedback I have received regarding the first volume. Professional reviews have been as positive as is possible within the context of conventional journals. Clinical feedback, which is the genre of feedback that I personally value most, has been consistently positive.

Nevertheless, I would like to use the present introduction as a vehicle for further exploring concerns I share with numerous other colleagues regarding the meanings and purpose of psychotherapy and how these meanings would relate to humor. I have come to believe that psychotherapists as a group suffer from occasional existential inquietude. And how can we not suffer from such inquietude? As clinical psychotherapists, we are routinely assailed by having to attend to the headache-producing business aspects of our practice, dealing with patient difficulties, and not getting consistently clear feedback on the validity and importance of our work. Psychotherapy is a very intimate experience, and this epithet has both positive and not-so-positive aspects.

The intimacy, confidentiality, and privacy of psychotherapy provides a nurturing atmosphere, a womb within which the patient can unfold his or her issues. However, for the therapist, the restriction of privacy and confidentiality can backfire as he or she needs to restrict numerous reactions in order to attend to the patient. Many complex factors enter into psychotherapy.

As therapists, we must continuously struggle to give our patients the very best we have to offer while simultaneously not expecting them to lend their constructive motivation to the therapeutic process. We are restricted in the ways we express our dissatisfactions and feelings regarding negative factors - such as some patients' manipulations, improper terminations, unjustified complaints, unrealistic demands, or unwarranted questioning of our work. Our dissatisfactions need to be muted. The privacy provided by the psychotherapeutic context is believed to be beneficial to patients, yet it exacts a heavy price from therapists. Such privacy and its accompanying emotional muffling can sometimes be suffocating for the therapist. Therapist wear and tear may result from a stifling cycle of unvoiced dissatisfactions. The literature often addresses the abuse of patients by therapists, yet the topic of therapists being abused by some of their patients is seldom, if ever, addressed. We are told that good superman/bionic woman therapists can, and indeed should, "take it." Let us examine the following examples of therapist abuse by patients that have been shared with me by several colleagues:

- A patient angrily and prematurely quits individual psychotherapy, accusing the therapist of encouraging him to leave his girlfriend. This causes distress to the therapist. Three months later, the patient calls the therapist for an emergency appointment. He shows up with a bandaged, partially excised index finger. He reports that he had a fight with his girlfriend and that she attacked him with a butcher knife and excised part of his index finger as he was trying to protect himself.
- A patient who owes a large balance of fees to his therapist for professional therapeutic services goes to jail for rape. As of the last reading, he has not yet paid his bill.
- A patient who was helped back from the brink of psychotic disintegration over a 3-year period appropriately terminates treatment, having made good progress and holding a good job. She then refuses to pay her outstanding balance for professional services rendered by her therapist, despite the fact that the therapist had seen her numerous times on a pro bono basis when she clearly needed but could not afford therapeutic care.
- A borderline patient who was seen by a therapist for 2 months terminates treatment by her choice and files numerous complaints against the therapist for having provided "a substandard quality of care" when the patient had actually made reasonable progress during the brief period the therapist was able to work with her. Despite the fact that the patient's complaints were completely unfounded, that she had voiced various complaints about nearly all her previous therapists, and that the complaints were psychodynamically related to the patient's manipulative character pathology and unresolved rage

at several abusive figures in her life, the therapist still had to expend a sizable amount of costs in legal defense fees. The patient's deceitful complaints to different bodies lasted approximately 3 years and ended up nowhere while costing the therapist time, distress, and money. During the same period, the patient kept mailing the therapist harassing letters, threatening, among other things, to come to the therapist's office and kill her. Although the patient's letters contained numerous disparaging comments about the therapist, she was legally advised not to respond to the letters. Although she won the complaints battle, the therapist retained anger, sadness, anxiety, and a persisting bitter aftertaste regarding the ordeal.

- A patient who was helped during 6 arduous months of treatment to obtain disability status stemming from a chronic head injury calls after a 3-month treatment hiatus and asks his therapist to fill out a detailed form regarding the patient's mental status. When the therapist explains to the patient that he has not seen him for 3 months and needs to have an evaluation session with him to reevaluate his condition prior to filling out any forms, the patient responds, "Everybody wants money from me" and hangs up the phone on the therapist.

- A litigious and hateful patient on whom a therapist had completed a psychological evaluation refuses to pay for his share of the evaluation fees. When the therapist refers his bill to collections following a long period of unresponsiveness to billings, the patient becomes very angry and sneakily obtains the therapist's home address from the Department of Motor Vehicles, thus allowing him to further scare and harass his therapist. He accuses the therapist of being involved in a motor vehicle accident with him, and initiates a series of baseless complaints regarding the therapist with several agencies.

- A patient signs an agreement regarding specific therapy fees with his therapist, then ends up partially reneging on his agreement to pay. He calls the therapist with expectations that the remaining fees for his sessions be waived as a professional courtesy, while readily acknowledging that he has significantly benefited from treatment.

- Following her return to work after a lengthy illness, a therapist gives a patient she worked with prior to her illness the choice of either continuing psychotherapy with herself or obtaining referrals to other therapists. The patient states that she would like to come in for an evaluation session to make a decision regarding treatment. She subsequently cancels two consecutive appointments within 1 month, which prompts the therapist to call her as a last-ditch effort to clarify the nature of the therapeutic relationship. The patient then writes a letter accusing the therapist of "threatening" her because the therapist had responsibly attempted to end the state of limbo regarding the patient's treatment.

- A patient who was referred by an emergency hotline for clear suicidal intent, including a specific suicidal plan, engages in an hour-long verbal diatribe with the therapist returning her telephone call to the effect that she does not need hospitalization. She states to the therapist that "You do not know what you are talking about!" and that she would kill herself whenever she wanted to. The therapist compassionately listens to the patient's ravings, only to feel helpless and worried about her.

- A patient interprets a therapist's medical illness of which he was informed as an abandonment of him during a critical phase of his life and threatens to complain about the therapist's absence from work.

- The attorney husband of a female patient gets quite angry that his wife is becoming less passive and more assertive as a result of her psychotherapeutic treatment. He begins to send threatening legal letters to his wife's therapist. On one occasion, during the Christmas season, he sends the therapist a "booby-trapped" letter containing a frightening noise system triggered by the therapist opening the envelope containing the husband's letter. The timing of the letter at Christmas time, combined with the mischievousness of the patient's husband, puts a damper on the therapist's Christmas season as well as the subsequent months.

- A patient being treated for alcoholism is loyally supported by her therapist through a difficult hospitalization and subsequent recovery from her alcohol addiction. She suddenly decides to get a new job and move to another city without paying the outstanding balance due for the therapist's professional services. The therapist later learns that the patient had relapsed after she moved out of town, which results in anger and sadness on the therapist's part.

- A patient who was seen for an initial evaluation by a therapist decides not to pursue treatment and refuses to pay her bill.

Three months later the therapist receives a subpoena for the patient's records because she is involved in litigation and has apparently used her unpaid-for evaluation with the therapist as a substantiation of her claim for psychiatric damages against another party. The therapist feels manipulated and angry.

- After 3 years of hard work in psychotherapy, a patient reaches a good level of improvement allowing him to marry a woman he loved, who had also worked with the therapist. The couple had gradually built their intimacy in couple's therapy as well as in individual work to reach a solid level of honesty and intimacy in their rapport leading to their decision to get married. The therapist is invited to the wedding and struggles with himself as to whether he should attend or not, given his rigid "countertransference-beware" training. He does finally attend the wedding, and is then invited by the couple to the reception following the wedding. The therapist experiences a heartache at that moment, as he feels torn between his allegiance to the restrictions he was cautioned about in his training and his wish to celebrate with this couple such a happy moment in their lives to which their productive therapeutic work was a significant contributor. The therapist decides not to attend the reception and leaves after the wedding ceremony. However, he experiences a sadness for some time following the wedding regarding his being unable to savor this important moment with two individuals for whom he had a lot of care and admiration. He wonders for quite some time about the authenticity of his decision not to attend the reception, and the restrictions his therapist role places on his spontaneity and humaneness.

The previous examples, culled from the work experiences of different psychotherapists, point to the observation that psychotherapy is no bed of roses for either patients or therapists; giving birth is both a painful and a joyful experience. Although therapist experiences with many patients are positive and moving with uplifting endings, the aforecited incidents illustrate the challenging absurdity inherent to the process of psychotherapy. Psychotherapy is restrictive by definition and it may stunt the therapist's spontaneity. Dr. Atalay Yorukoglu alludes, in his chapter, to the restrictions imposed by "the sacred rules of psychotherapy." The unique nature of the psychotherapist's interpersonal world sometimes dictates that he or she must restrict his or her emotional expressions in certain areas. The chapters by Dr. Thomas Kuhlman and Dr. Allen Surkis address some of the issues confronting therapists working with difficult and/or unappreciative patients. When we add to the preceding stories the sadness of improper terminations and the melancholy of being misinterpreted despite genuinely trying to be of help and showing sound clinical skills, the picture becomes more complete.

However, therapists are admonished in theory to engage in emotional splitting: We need to be extremely sensitive to our patients' feelings yet are simultaneously told by our supervisors during training that we must be analytical regarding our personal feelings, continuously dissecting those feelings instead of expressing them. Such an outlook can exact a heavy toll on the therapist.

If the therapist is a genuinely caring individual, it is difficult to see how he or she could honestly restrict the flow of his or her sensitivity to go only toward the patient's care and not toward his or her own feelings about the patient's behavior. True sensitivity includes the power to be vulnerable. At the same time, being vulnerable requires that a person allow himself or herself to be influenced by his or her own emotional reactions as well as by those of others.

The therapist's vulnerability, when it exists, is useful for patients, but may sometimes be abused by some of them. This vulnerability and sensitivity can have negative consequences for the therapist. The term "therapist burnout" may not be comprehensive enough to account for the therapist's disappointments, the dictates to him or her to swallow emotional reactions, and the high costs of emotional, economic, and legal vulnerability. A more appropriate term describing these issues could be "therapist abuse." The term "abuse" is used here in an inclusive sense to encompass not only the patients' abuses toward the therapist, but also the abuse derived from archaic theories dictating therapist behavior and the abuse perpetrated by solemn societal approaches to living being applied to the process of doing psychotherapy.

If we listen to the professional train passing through the plains of psychotherapy, we can hear numerous recent rumblings expressing concern about the rigid role imposed upon the psychotherapist by earlier models of psychotherapy. The following oversimplified verbal cartoons represent an attempt to illustrate the changing landscape of the therapeutic persona. Some schools of psychotherapy have supported the discarding of nearly all conventions (which sometimes led to "throwing the baby away with the bath water"). Other movements have promulgated an image of the therapist as magician, emerging from the clouds to make patients sleepy while telling them good things about themselves as they revealed their innermost secrets under trance. Some schools propounded the introduction of a guru-like shamanic empathy into the therapeutic process. Yet other therapy movements have attempted to present the therapist as Mr. Goodwrench, a good technician, handy with his tools, who can convey proper techniques to help patients learn new skills and extinguish dysfunctional behavior. Some therapy schools have developed a street cop approach to therapy with the therapist playing snake-charmer to narcissistic and borderline patients, while others have advocated the necessity of the therapist being a confrontive bull, continuously hammering away at patient resistances until the "Walls of Troy" were conquered. Some schools have recommended that the therapist adopt a "secret agent" approach to infiltrate the patient's security system and work on the patient's side while simultaneously being a double agent for change. Other schools have tended to depict the therapist as a movie director, looking for a box-office blockbusting Gestalt on the stage of psychotherapy, while directing the patient to engage in another role-play. Through it all, some schools continue to uphold their vision of the therapist as a high priest who must not soil his sacred cloth by actively interacting with the vox populi patients.

What is exactly taking place in our generation of psychotherapists? Are psychotherapists confronting an identity crisis? Do we suffer from existential malaise? Do all psychotherapists need a global awareness seminar to take care of business? I would propose that a significant problem is the general dissatisfaction within the psychotherapeutic world with the image and role played by psychotherapists. The persona of the guarded, pipe-smoking psychotherapist playing a neutral role is passé. However, no new clearly defined persona has emerged to replace the old image that we were trained to emulate.

I believe that it is the task of this generation of therapists to change the image of the therapist and come up with a more appropriate and healthy image of how a therapist could be-in-the-world with a patient. As the heady chapter by Dr. Julius Heuscher reminds us, we cannot take the Self for granted and must continue to creatively address the challenge of our existence in order to grow. The very nature of psychotherapy teaches us that human beings are continuously evolving, changing creatures. Complacency could well lead to a quagmire of slow emotional decay.

It appears that we don't yet exactly know how we want to be with patients, but we know what we don't want. This generation of psychotherapists has been charged with the task of redefining the therapeutic identity. That is by no means an easy undertaking. Although there has been a gradual erosion of the conventional therapist persona, no sharply defined contemporary picture has emerged to take its place. In addition, the traditional remedies for therapist alienation offered by our psychotherapeutic elders and supervisors don't seem to be sufficient to fulfill our existential yearning for fuller professional/personal identity. Attending professional conferences and workshops, having friends outside of our work, keeping good session records, developing clear office policies, staying pure of inappropriate attachments with patients, and seeking consultation from colleagues when appropriate are all important and constructive undertakings that still fall short of what is needed to be a full, dynamic therapist. These methods don't seem to relieve the need for change in our identity and do not substantially redress our emotional aches.

It is my impression, in summary of many discussions on this subject, that we do not want to be taken for granted. We do not want to let our vulnerability and sensitivity to patients be used against us. We want to bring more of our selves into the therapeutic process. We want to be assertive. We want to express our own feelings about how patients affect us in an honest and compassionate manner. We want to put ourselves on the line when we need to. We want to be more natural in psychotherapy, and to approximate in our psychotherapeutic work more of who we are with our friends and family. We want to take the "sacredness" out of psychotherapy and bring joy into it. We want to be good technicians who can forget about technique. We want to confront our patients as much as we allow them to confront us. We want to let them know that we are not lifeless because we are therapists. Although it is unavoidable that we have power due to the way the therapeutic relationship is structured, we want to give each patient we work with more and more of our power, which is the power of self-transformation. When it is time for our patients to leave therapy, we want to encourage them to do so in whatever ways are realistic and ultimately therapeutic. If patients leave therapy before due time, we want to be able to communicate to them that we do not agree with their decisions.

We need to examine the concept of secrecy vis-à-vis the patient, that is, protecting our patients from truths they are already living. From the perspective of existential authenticity, it is not understandable why any item in the therapist's file cannot be shared with the patient, except in floridly delusional, paranoid, or schizophrenic states. In most cases, the tradition of secrecy appears to be related to control. We know that, in real life, those who keep secrets are both tortured and burdened by them. Our therapy notes, transference interpretation, testing results, and innermost impressions about patients are a fecund soil upon which an authentic and constructive relationship could be built with them. Although confidentiality of patient file contents with regard to being divulged to others is totally in the patients' hands, the development of secret-free relationships with patients is largely in the therapist's hand.

We can share with our patients, in their language, the material developed when we consult about their cases with our colleagues or supervisors. We want to be able to share therapeutic material with patients in a way that is useful to them. We can bring out of the darkness and into the light more of our own thinking regarding our patients. We want to be compassionate without drowning in a sort of pancake syrup.

The corrective emotional experience we often talk about has to be brought home in our lives as therapists; therapy can be a corrective emotional experience for us as well as it is for the patient. Corrective emotional experience, as Franz Alexander might have meant it, did not simply refer to adoption of a constructive and uncondemning therapeutic teaching role. It might have meant more than that for him. It might have meant bringing more human qualities into therapy, helping the patient to be moved out of his or her dysfunctional hibernation by the warmth and vivacity of the therapist's emotional springtime.

It can be tiring to be just a mirror for the patient's behavior. We want to be ourselves. We want to move beyond cliché to challenge. Therapy is a challenge where the patient must be moved beyond complacency through the empowerment that the therapeutic process gives him or her. It is not sufficient to attend a workshop seminar. There has to be more to it to reach inner depths.

Perhaps the deeper issue underlying the foregoing considerations is that the current generation of therapists is questioning exactly what is "therapeutic" for patients. Although we know about some items that are therapeutic, my clinical hunch is that there are many therapeutic change catalysts that we know nothing about. We owe it to ourselves and our patients to find out more about what is therapeutic.

By now, the reader may be wondering what all this has to do with humor in psychotherapy. The answer is that my discussion so far is related to an expansion of the universe of therapeutic possibilities. In the face of so many religionistic, societal, and self-imposed inhibitions, therapeutic work stands out as one place where a sanctuary or reprieve from unnecessary inhibition, anxiety, and fear is provided to patients. There definitely should be freedom in psychotherapy for the patient.

I am also arguing here that therapy should provide some sanctuary and an appropriately free environment for the therapist. The therapist is also a human going through his or her life while he or she shares a moment called "therapy" with another human being. I am arguing for modifying the therapist stance to include a moderate degree of structure coupled with a moderate degree of freedom for us as therapists to maintain our integrity of life no matter what we are doing. Who we are, and can become, is the best we have to offer to anyone.

Humor comes in as an important baseline variable in developing a more complex understanding of the therapist's personality. With humor, a certain therapeutic atmosphere is created that includes both assertiveness and compassion. This atmosphere lets the patient know therapeutic limitations while at the same time allowing him or her to take risks and learn more about who he or she is.

Humor is both a teaching tool and an interactive tool. It catalyzes the move from the remote glacial confines of rigidity and distancing into a more livable and warm human environment where we can meet the patient on the ground of vivacity and freshness. This does not mean that we cannot analyze transference and countertransference reactions, or that we cannot use our previously acquired training. What it means is that we can incorporate our training within a more comprehensive structural framework where humor can help us gain immediate access to the patient while providing relief from our inhibitions and theirs.

Psychoanalysis addresses the therapist's use of self around the concepts of transference and countertransference. What I discuss here is the therapist's use of self in a more comprehensive manner, incorporating the therapist's own energy and gusto. Although it has been acknowledged that "the hardest part of self-analysis is the countertransference," it is also true that the therapist is a pulsating presence who can use himself or herself in a more conducive manner than was traditionally advocated. Transformation of the therapeutic self can occur in ways that transcend the clichés of different therapeutic schools. We need to apply to ourselves the same sound precepts that we proffer to patients. As an ancient Zen master once said: "A cake drawn on paper cannot satisfy hunger." I am advocating that we can significantly reduce existential alienation within the therapeutic context when we liberate ourselves from the unnecessary shackles imposed by cautious predecessors who were so worried about doing the wrong thing that they sometimes missed items of emotional relevance. The combination of increased therapist freedom mixed with moderate therapeutic structure seems to be a reasonable and beneficial way to go.

A crucial element that enters into the formation of the therapist's persona is the educational element. Education contributes to the molding of a professional style and the development of a certain modus operandi. This modus operandi later conditions and influences the way a professional individual relates to his or her world of professional activities, including interactions with patients. If we examine graduate clinical psychology, psychiatry, or mental health training curricula at American universities or other institutions of learning around the world, we notice a gaping disparity between the course contents of graduate clinical mental health programs and the actual work that clinicians carry out on a daily basis. In other words, the basic fund of knowledge needed by therapists in order to survive and flourish in their clinical roles seems to be lacking in many graduate programs. Courses in the various techniques used by different schools of psychotherapy are hard to come by. There are practically no classes on the economic or legal aspects of psychotherapy. Furthermore, and most importantly with respect to the topic of this introduction, there is no instruction about what a healthy therapist persona would be composed of. The education of the graduate student body in the field of mental health regarding what the healthy therapist personality would be, or could be, including various options and therapeutic ways of being that students can consider, is totally nonexistent to this writer's knowledge. The introduction of classes on therapeutic humor, with humor being an important trait in a healthy therapeutic persona, are still the exception rather than the rule. If the graduate student or resident is moderately lucky, he or she may stumble upon some indirect allusions as to what a healthy role model of the therapeutic persona would be. These allusions are gleaned from his or her interactions with veteran supervisors or clinically wise professors. The comments, gestures, and ways of being of such figures are treasured throughout a lifetime and constitute a cherished oral clinical legacy that lives on in the minds of students long after they have graduated from their respective clinical programs. Yet this is not enough. Besides these lucky exceptions, many graduate students are at a loss about how to be psychotherapists. It is clear that a more focused system allowing the burgeoning of healthy therapeutic personae is indicated. Such a system could, in fact, serve as the metaphor for a clinical family within which clinical students are intellectually raised. Following graduation and with the progressive passage of time, the student could gradually incorporate the insights he or she gained from such experiences and classes into his or her creative expression of who he or she is.

This author proposes that specific classes on the therapeutic persona be taught, including the presentation of various options of therapist ways of being. This would allow each clinical student the freedom of considering several healthy role models with the goal of generating a style that works for him or her. Within this context, the student can develop a healthier therapist persona away from rigidity, fear, emotional withholding, or impulsivity. He or she could then experience a sense of personal freedom within an intellectual structure that makes sense to him or her. What is missing in clinical training is the creation of a global, encompassing, and comprehensive framework within which the therapeutic persona can ferment, not indirectly or occasionally, but specifically, intensively, and directly. It is hereby suggested that humor can serve as a potent fertilizer for the development of such a therapeutic persona, and can also inject a component of vivacity and freshness into such a persona. The issue is not so much that the factors that make good therapists are missing, but rather that such factors have not been coalesced into an exciting and facilitative format that promotes the growth of a healthy therapeutic presence. An academic curriculum that can encourage the formation of a therapeutic persona may include courses such as: Role Models in the Field of Psychotherapy (Sigmund Freud, B. F. Skinner, Carl Rogers, Milton Erickson, Albert Ellis, and others), Humor and the Therapist Persona, Appropriate Expressions of

Therapist Affect in Psychotherapy, Models of the Therapist Persona Provided Within Different Theoretical Frameworks, Dos and Don'ts of Therapist Behavior, Psychotherapist's Alternatives in Addressing Negative Developments in Psychotherapy, and other relevant topics that contribute to the Gestalt of a constructive therapeutic persona.   In psychotherapy, as in most everything else, education is the key to liberation.

An important function of humor I have repeatedly experienced both in working with different patients and in my own life is its importance in deflating shame. Many societal precepts have been built on shame. Yet shame ossifies individuals and prevents us from trying again. In the hierarchy of social deterrents, shame may be the least productive and least helpful deterrent for an individual. With shame goes its cousin, blame, which is also emotionally poisonous and unproductive.

Humor helps to liberate us from shame and blame. Its disinhibiting effects allow us to experience a new emotional ambience, relieved of our burdens. The great reformer Martin Luther once said: "If you're not allowed to laugh in heaven, I don't want to go there." Echoing that same view, his Indian counterpart Mahatma Gandhi said: "If I had no sense of humor, I would long ago have committed suicide." Humor is God's antidote to the shame/blame absurdity of mankind, our sanity weapon, our blanket in emotional coldness.

I hope that the chapters of this volume provide you, the reader, with a good flavor of the therapist vitality and liveliness that I have espoused in this introduction. I believe that vivacity and inspiration can be accessed through careful use of therapeutic humor to catalyze therapy and yield higher productivity while bringing out the best in the therapist.

Another goal which I favor being accomplished in reading this volume is the reader's questioning of the therapeutic persona that he or she has thus far developed. Does this persona optimize patient growth while helping the therapist avoid his or her own stagnation? Is this persona simply a safe persona, a defensive persona, or is it a persona that involves more creativity and productive risk-taking? Although I do not have a full delineation of the ideal therapist's persona, I do believe that it is important for the therapeutic community to collectively question its assumptions and continue to review our understanding of what is therapeutic.

Since the publication of our first volume on this subject in 1987, it has become widely recognized that humor is therapeutic. Humor is no longer a questionable intervention modality. This development is evidenced by the widespread attention that therapeutic humor is receiving, as well as by the numerous workshops and conventions throughout the United States and elsewhere regarding the creatively therapeutic values of humor.

At this point, humor has also come to be accepted by most patients as a welcome and positive modality. It is recognized as a sure indication, beyond breathing, that the therapist is a real, sentient human being. It is acknowledged as a powerful tool to be used for constructive change. I predict that humor, following reassessment of what the new therapeutic persona can be, will emerge as one of the more important therapeutic variables in this restructuring.

In keeping with the expansion of therapeutic horizons and of what it means to be "therapeutic," we are presenting here some innovatively creative chapters. We hope that these chapters will stimulate and challenge professionals to broaden their conceptions of what psychotherapy means. Dr. Julius Heuscher takes us to the world of Kierkegaard with his thought-provoking chapter on indirect uses of humor in psychotherapy. Mr. Michael Maher contributes a rather stimulating chapter regarding the use of humor in treating the chemically dependent patient, using the alcoholic's own "drinking stories" as a way of fostering awareness and change. Dr. John McKiernan addresses the dimension of spirituality in psychotherapy as connected with humor, a dimension which has not yet received much attention. It is certainly an important area of exploration, and humor would easily fit with spirituality, as illustrated in the Zen and Sufi spiritual traditions. Dr. Atalay Yorukoglu takes us to the world of children and the use of favorite jokes to help children. It is sometimes difficult for us as therapists to work with children because their emotional and mental processes require a different type of attention than that required by adult patients. Dr. Yorukoglu offers us a compassionate and delightful way of entering into the world of children through their own joke material. Dr. Allen Surkis enters the world of the obsessive-compulsive and comments on the use of humor to interrupt obsessive and ruminative patterns. Dr. Thomas Kuhlman writes about working with patients whom we may not usually think about working with, that is, the severely violent mentally ill and homeless populations whose psychopathologies are clinically multifaceted and highly intricate. He seems to gain an understanding of these patients through the eyes of irony while simultaneously being able to provide solid insight into their treatment. Dr. Gerald Amada invites us to the world of the college student and his or her concerns. College students are psychologically interesting because they go through life transitions that are not usually encountered in other phases of life. They seem to have special needs, interests, and aspirations that are often ignored. Dr. Amada humorously zeros us in on the particular needs and aspirations of college students as well as the needs of the college community around them. Drs. Mosak and Maniacci invite us to humorously examine the therapeutic world from Adler's perspective of paradox, will, and individuality. Dr. John Schimel examines the use of humor with oppositional and adolescent patients - a segment of population with always powerful implications for the future of our society. Chaplain Cy Eberhart explores the applicability of humor and mirth to the field of pastoral counseling. This is again a commonly ignored or misunderstood area of therapeutics which is of widespread importance. Our volume also includes a comprehensive clinical and research bibliography about humor in psychotherapy from 1964 to 1991, including article abstracts, for those readers interested in further research in this field.

As you may have already guessed, we are currently working on Volume III. We are especially eager to obtain chapter contributions from women and minority clinicians regarding new and creative ways of doing psychotherapy that include humor. Other areas of clinical interest that we particularly wish to investigate are the relevance of humor for the treatment of codependency issues, humor with special patient populations, and interfacing humor with other therapeutic techniques and modalities to promote effective patient change.

We would like this series of volumes to continue to be a forum within which many individuals can examine and expand the meanings of the term "therapeutic."

Waleed A. Salameh

ADVANCES IN HUMOR AND PSYCHOTHERAPY

1

An "Alderian" Approach to Humor and Psychotherapy

Harold Mosak and Michael Maniacci

Using an "Alderian" perspective, Drs. Mosak and Maniacci seem to take delight at highlighting refreshingly humorous approaches to psychotherapy. The work of this "pair o' docs" focuses on the use of paradox and reversals to generate a psychological "palace coup" aimed at creating new realities for patients to consider. Their chapter illustrates that humor can be adopted for use within any theoretical orientation as long as the therapist is flexible, open, and creative.

Harold Mosak, PhD, is a well-known Adlerian theoretician, training analyst, and author. His publications include the volume Ha Ha and Aha: The Role of Humor in Psychotherapy *(1987), an investigation of the use of humor in psychotherapy within an Adlerian theoretical framework. Both he and Dr. Michael Maniacci are clinical psychologists in private practice in the greater Chicago area.*

❖   ❖   ❖

If the reader has read accurately, the error in the title ("Alderian" instead of "Adlerian") may have produced a smile, a grin, and a feeling of "oh-oh." As Mosak (1987) has pointed out, there are three broad categories of theories of humor: release-related theories, disparagement-related theories, and incongruity-related theories. Depending upon the theory to which the reader subscribes, the explanation for the emotional response will vary.

In the release-related theories, physiological explanations dominate. Pent-up energy is "released" by the humor, and the physiological act of laughing has a liberating, ventilating effect upon the laughing individual. From this perspective, the reader who laughed is releasing pent-up energy, which, according to Freud (1905/1960), has its basis in sexual and aggressive drives. The reader is sublimating the energy from these drives into socially acceptable channels, thereby reducing the psychic tension. In other words, rather than openly expressing the aggressive, hostile feelings toward others (or at times the sexual erotic feelings toward others), the reader would have repressed them until such time when the affect associated with these pent-up drives can be discharged in a way that will not appear too embarrassing or bring retribution from the superego (internalized parental authority figure).

With the disparagement-related theories, the explanation for the reader's laughter lies in the fact that there is a sense of pleasure in disparaging the authors, the editors, and the typesetters, for having made such a mistake deliberately or accidentally. Freud's opinion of the nature of accidents and slips would have us question just how "accidental" such an accident might be. According to this theory, "wit begins with an intention to injure, which our culture requires us to repress" (Grotjahn, 1966, p. 14). Once again, the reader's laughter is related to repressed aggressive drives. A sense of superiority is gained through the misery or bad fortune of others, and satisfaction is achieved in a proscribed, closely monitored way.

Another approach is the incongruity-related one in which the laughter would be related to the cognitive discrepancy in the title. The reader expected "Adlerian" yet received "Alderian" and the incongruity and subsequent reconciliation occurred. The reader laughed because of a kind of misdirection, similar to that seen when "the teller leads the listener in one direction and then trips him/her up with the punch line because it shifts direction in a way other than the one expected" (Mosak, 1987, p. 24).

Which is it? In order to release tension, clarify the incongruity between expectations, and ward off any potential disparagement the reader may be harboring, an examination of all three and their relation to psychotherapy is in order.

THEORETICAL PERSPECTIVE

Adler (1956) postulated a theory of therapy and personality that can be described as holistic, teleological, social, and field theoretical. Individuals are to be understood within their social environment, as striving toward subjectively perceived goals, and as operating in a unified and self-consistent manner. They are not to be analyzed according to parts; the whole is greater than the sum of its parts, and Adlerians do not divide the personality into such elements as id, ego, and superego. A more detailed description of Adler's theories and treatment strategies can be found in Adler (1956), Manaster and Corsini (1982), and Mosak (1989). Interested readers are referred to these works for more information about Adlerian theory.

Adlerians would generally question the validity of tension-release theories. As Mosak (1987) points out, jokes and humor appear to increase sympathetic nervous system arousal, and the feeling of physical relaxation that follows a good laugh is related to a sense of group fellowship that Adler (1956) called *social interest*. As Adler (1927) noted, emotions are generally of two kinds: conjunctive or disjunctive. Conjunctive emotions bring people together; disjunctive ones create distance. Laughter and joy are conjunctive - they bring people together and facilitate the bonding process. As O'Connell (1975) has emphasized, humor is related to humanistic identification - the ability to feel at home with others and align goals, intentions, and feelings with them in useful, prosocial ways.

Disparagement-related theories of humor have underlying assumptions about human nature that are hostile and negativistic. Although it is true that *some* individuals using humor may manifest this orientation, Adlerians would see these individuals as lacking social interest. Adlerian psychology stresses a psychology-of-use perspective, believing that individuals use certain traits, attitudes, or behaviors in order to move toward goals. In the Adlerian perspective, the issue would be how the humor is used. It is not the humor in itself that is disparaging, but rather how it is applied; what counts is the *purpose* for which the humor is used. As Mosak (1987) points out, the laughter that accompanies the fall of a man into the mud is not necessarily hostile, but one of sympathy with the other person: "That could be us falling" (p. 20). If the humor is used conjunctively, the sympathy for that falling man brings people closer to him and creates a bond of mutual understanding and appreciation of the human condition. If used disjunctively, it may express a flaunting of superiority and hostility, a fact Adler (1956) discussed in detail with regard to neurotic personality development and dynamics.

The incongruity-related theories are more in line with Adlerian conceptualizations. In his paper "Trick and Neurosis"

(1936), Adler discussed the relationship between common sense and private intelligence and jokes. He noted that "In jokes, too, it is a trick that steers away from common sense and presents the 'private intelligence' of a human being" (p. 5). Adler (1956), Ansbacher (1965), and Dreikurs (1973) have discussed the difference between common sense, that is, consensually validated thought, and private intelligence (or logic) that is not bound by the rules of common sense and is an expression of the personal, idiosyncratic meanings individuals attach to experiences not shared by the general group. According to Mosak (1987), every joke has two frames of reference (i.e., "tracks"), and the more successful the joke, "the more likely the frames of reference are equally valid" (p. 25). For Adlerians, humor involves some kind of incongruity, an exaggeration or reversal that taps into a cognitive discrepancy resulting in a change of perspective. In the example of the misspelled title, the incongruity produced a new perspective: Perhaps the "authorities" are not as serious or "authoritative" as typical "experts" seem to be. That may have produced a sense of identification (to use O'Connell's term) with the authors and a bonding between the reader and authors: "They, like me, are not perfect. We're not so dissimilar." The "mistake" tapped into feelings and convictions in the reader about times when he or she made similar mistakes and the feelings or attitudes the reader has about perfection and inferiority.

For Adler (1936, 1956), neurosis, or maladjustment in general, operates in much the same way as a trick or joke. There is an incongruity between the common sense and private intelligence of an individual, but the incongruity is unbalanced in that the private intelligence is given more weight than the common sense. Similarly, a joke is not funny if the two tracks or frames of reference are not (relatively) equally weighted:

How many psychologists does it take to change a light bulb? One, but the light bulb has to want to change.

That joke is funny because the reader has some awareness of both frames of reference, the "psychologist" and the "patient/light bulb." However, to someone unfamiliar with psychotherapeutic theory or terminology (e.g., the foreigner unfamiliar with the language), the joke would not be funny. Adler claimed that neurotic individuals operate as if they were following common sense when in reality they are following their own private intelligence. For example, a patient became terrified every time she left her home. Her husband had to stay with her, and if he was not available, her mother would come stay with her. Her husband was forced to call in and "report" his whereabouts periodically; otherwise, his wife would panic. In this case, there are two frames of reference. The common sense frame of reference is that this patient was terrified of leaving her home and needed her husband's (and mother's) protection. The private frame of reference explained the patient's use of her symptoms: Her husband had been cheating on her, in much the same way as her father had cheated on her mother, which brought considerable pain and hardship to her family during her childhood. Through her symptoms, she kept her husband "in check." In her private intelligence, she reasoned that being helpless and passive would be more "successful" in her goal attainment (i.e., a faithful husband) than to confront him openly or leave him. The neurosis, like the bad joke, becomes understandable once the listener learns to "listen with the third ear" (Reik, 1948) in order to understand both frames of reference.

TECHNIQUES

Kubie (1971) felt that humor has a destructive potential in psychotherapy and warned against its use in psychoanalytic therapy. On the other hand, Adler (1927) noted that:

> I have always considered it a great advantage to keep the level of tension in treatment as low as possible and I have virtually developed it into a method to tell almost every patient that there are jokes like the structure of his particular neurosis, and that therefore one can also take the latter more lightly than he does. (p. 26)

How can the two positions be so different? Briefly, psychoanalytic psychotherapy is based upon an unequal relationship between patient and therapist. The therapist assumes an authoritarian-expert role, and transference is crucial for facilitating insight in psychoanalytic therapy. Humor creates an involvement between patient and therapist that may adversely affect the development of the transference.

Adlerian psychotherapy is based upon different premises. The therapist-patient relationship is based upon equality (Adler, 1956; Manaster & Corsini, 1982; Mosak, 1989). The two parties make a contract to work together as equals in an atmosphere of mutual respect and cooperation. This in turn facilitates the useful reorientation toward common sense and the fostering of social interest. Similarly, but from a different perspective, Marlowe Erickson (1984) makes the point for a "serious case for silliness" in the therapeutic process, based upon an atmosphere of collaboration and mutual enjoyment (p. 49). The use of the techniques outlined in this section are grounded upon the therapeutic perspective espoused by Adler and other Adlerians including the elements of mutual respect, cooperation, and equality. The therapists need to feel comfortable in their work and with themselves in order to aid their patients with the process of collaboration, exploration, and change.

1. *Jokes*. Using jokes to illustrate a point can be quite beneficial. McMullin (1986) uses "multistable figures" (what others have previously referred to as "optical illusions") in order to demonstrate how a change in perspective can bring about new insights and increased awareness. He asks patients to reverse the figure-ground relationship in certain drawings in order to see the previously undiscovered portions in a new light. In much the same way, jokes can bring about new insights and perspectives using verbal, linguistic means rather than visual, perceptual ones. Mosak (1987) provides an extensive list of jokes that can be used for many different therapeutic purposes. Some of the jokes are as follows:

   - For patients who overuse modesty or humility: *Modesty* consists of letting others find out for themselves how great you are.
   - To the chronic worrier: Do you have a contingency plan in case everything goes well?
   - For the hypochondriac: A person who can't leave being well enough alone.
   - For the pessimist: A man had twin sons, an optimist and a pessimist. On Christmas morning, he took them downstairs to see what Santa had left them. As they opened one door, every toy imaginable was spread out across the floor. The pessimistic son looked downhearted. The father asked him why he was not happier, to which the boy replied, "They are only toys, and they'll only break anyway." The father took his optimistic son to the next room.

As he opened the door, to his amazement, horse manure covered the entire floor. His son began to jump for joy. "Why are you so happy?" the father asked, totally bewildered. "Gee, with all this manure around," the optimistic son replied, "there must be a pony here!"

● To emphasize how logic can be used according to the goals and purposes of individuals: A novice psychiatrist was seeing his first patient at a mental hospital. The psychiatrist asked him why he was a patient, to which the patient replied "Because I'm dead." The psychiatrist wanted to clarify the issue, and asked, "But do dead people breathe?" "Yes, they do," replied the patient. Unshaken, the psychiatrist tried again, "Well, do dead people eat?" he asked, having noticed this same patient in the lunchroom previously. "Yes, I guess they do eat," was the determined reply. Somewhat frustrated, the psychiatrist asked, "Well, tell me then, do dead people bleed?" The patient responded with "No, dead people don't bleed." At that point, sensing the opportunity to settle the issue and end the delusion, the psychiatrist took out a needle and pricked the patient's finger and watched as blood trickled out. The psychiatrist sat back and waited for the patient to admit defeat. "Well," proclaimed the patient after scratching his head, "I guess dead people *do* bleed."

Readers interested in therapeutic jokes are encouraged to use their own creativity and listening skills to accumulate their own jokes. Others can be found in Mosak's (1987) work.

2. *Handles.* "Handles" are names that therapists can give to patients which seem to capture the essence of their lifestyles. "Handles" can be used as shorthand reminders of important issues patients need to be aware of or as cues to alter troublesome behaviors or beliefs. For instance, some "handles" might be:

● For the woman who is constantly dwelling upon the past: Lot's Wife (always looking over her shoulder).
● For those who move away from others (Horney, 1945), such as by preferring the company of pets to people: Dr. Doolittle.

- For the person who is always on the attack: Mack the Knife.
- For the mother who always wants to be in control or who is always right: Mrs. God.

The list can go on. Manaster and Corsini (1982) provide several such "handles" covering a wide variety of cases. The point is that "handles" can be a humorous way for patients and therapists to reach a mutual understanding of patients' styles of operating and moving through life.

3. *Images.* Providing images for clients can be a humorous and effective therapeutic tactic. Images become crystallized reminders of issues that patients need to alter or be aware of. Mosak (1989) relates the following story:

> In group therapy, a patient reported difficulty with intercourse. The therapist observed that dogs never seemed to have any difficulty "doing it." The therapist instructed him to think of that image the next time he was attempting intercourse. At that time, the patient was to say to himself "bowwow." Upon his return to group shortly thereafter, the patient reported he had successfully "bowwowed." (p. 92)

A variation of this technique is the use of *concrete images.* Concrete images are so named because they actually exist. They are tangible, concrete reminders patients carry around with them. One of the authors gave a patient a tiny, toy whip to carry around in his pocket to beat himself with when needed. This was in response to the patient's tendency to be what Horney (1950) called self-effacing; he picked on himself very severely. At a psychiatric treatment center, patients who whined or complained too much were given bibs to wear, signifying the "baby" style (Mosak, 1971) they used so well. "Rebels" can be given little Confederate flags, and second-born children who still feel the competitiveness in relationships with the older sibling can be given the "Avis - We try harder" button. Brilliant Enterprises puts out postcards* that can be very funny and highly effective with certain patients. Some of them read:

---

*Those interested in contacting Brilliant Enterprises for a catalog can write to: Brilliant Enterprises, 117 West Valerio Street, Santa Barbara, CA 93101.

- I challenge you to a friendship.
- All I want is a little more than I'll ever get.
- I am unconditionally guaranteed to be full of defects.
- Wait a minute, come back - there's a part of me you haven't stepped on yet.

These can be given to patients to carry around with them.

4. *Breaking the Witches' Circle*. This technique was first described by Wolfe, an early colleague of Adler. In order to encourage his patients to practice involvement with others, Wolfe (1932) would prescribe the following:

> Find a good story and tell it to at least one other person during the day. If the first person you tell the story to does not laugh, continue until you have made someone laugh. If you cannot find anyone to laugh at your stories there is a danger that your sense of humor is perverted. Get someone to tell you a story that he thinks is amusing. Tell this story to someone else until you have established the communal bond of good humor. Continue this prescription until you have experienced the reward of citizenship in the republic of laughter. (pp. 187-188)

Using this tactic, patients will break the "witches' circle" of isolation.

5. *Twisted Adages*. Like images, twisted adages can be useful in prompting patients to stop and think about what they are doing, thereby interrupting their typical transactions and patterns. Here are some twisted adages:

- The best offense is a good pretense.
- If you can't be big, be-little.
- Suffering is the substitution of nobility for no-ability.
- If at first you don't succeed, try lousing it up again.
- He who is impatient remains a patient.
- If you can keep your head while all about you are losing theirs, you don't understand the situation.

Twisted adages can have a refreshing quality to them. In many ways, they sound similar to the types of messages and "shoulds" or "demandments" patients have received from parents and other authority figures in their lives (Ellis, 1973), yet they are different and generally tend to nudge patients to lighten up on the very issues that they have previously taken too seriously.

6. *Parables and Fables*. Parables and fables can be used effectively in psychotherapy (Pancner, 1978). Twisted parables and fables can be used *humorously* and effectively. A twisted parable or fable has an unexpected, humorous edge. Beecher (as cited in Mosak, 1987, p. 123) relates the following:

> A nonconforming song sparrow decided not to fly South for the winter. Weeks passed and the cold drove the bird from his nest. As he flew, ice began to form on his wings and he crashed safely into a barnyard. A cow wandered by and crapped on the dazed bird. The sparrow thought his end had come but instead the cow manure warmed him. His wings defrosted and he even had some lunch. Warm and happy, the little bird began to sing. A cat happened through the barnyard and, hearing the singing, investigated the pile of manure. The cat found the happy sparrow and promptly ate him.

The story has three morals:

a. Everyone who dumps shit on you is not necessarily your enemy.
b. Anyone who takes shit off you is not necessarily your friend.
c. If you are full of shit . . . keep your mouth shut!

7. *The "Crazy" Therapist*. Mosak (1987), O'Connell (1975), Greenwald (1967), Haley (1963), and Rosen (1953) discuss instances in which therapists "out crazy" the patient.

> Told by his patient that she must not relinquish her beliefs "because God would not want me to," [the therapist] looks up to Heaven and inquires, "God is that what you really want her to do or is it possible that. . . ?" (Mosak, 1987, p. 57)

Such a tactic certainly catches the patients' attention. Besides "acting crazy," the act of humorously surprising patients can be highly valuable. A well-timed and sensitive smile or laugh when it is least expected can change the whole tone of a therapeutic session. Such timing and careful use can add the new perspective that many patients have lost when it comes to understanding their situation. The surprise can be as subtle as the aforementioned smile or as "crazy" as pretending to sleep out of boredom with the monotonous patient. One colleague pretended to take out a gun and shoot himself in the head after he heard the same complaints from a patient for the umpteenth time. The patient actually smiled and replied, "You know, you're right. If I have to listen to that again I'll shoot myself. Let's move on."

8. *The "In-Joke."* A private, personal comment that has significance for both patient and therapist can constitute an effective therapeutic tool. A shared insight or awareness can be recaptured with a gesture or a brief yet meaningful phrase. A formerly timid and self-effacing patient smiled every time her therapist mentioned the word "roar." As a result of therapy, she had learned to "roar" and to stand up for herself.

PERTINENT USES

Mosak (1987) cites five specific uses of humor in psychotherapy. Each of these uses will be briefly discussed.

1. *Establishing a Relationship.* Humor can be a very effective means of establishing a relationship between people. As Adler (1927) discussed, joy and similar emotions are generally conjunctive and facilitate bonding among individuals. Patients, for the most part, are preoccupied by their own concerns and their private frames of reference. Humor helps them to open up and interact with others. Adler (1956) characterized the neurotic as someone living in enemy territory, someone who is tense, on guard, vigilant, feeling isolated and without support. Humor can help ease the sense of being in enemy territory, the sense of threatened isolation.

2. *Humor in Diagnosis.* This often overlooked and underappreciated aspect of humor is worthy of attention by clinicians. A basic postulate of Adlerian psychology is the holistic nature of individuals. *Lifestyle* is the phrase used by Adlerians to

characterize and capture the overall patterning and consistent way of moving through life that all individuals display. Every person's lifestyle is unique and made up of idiosyncratic (i.e., private intelligence) ways of thinking about and perceiving the world, others, and self (Shulman & Mosak, 1988). To the trained observer, lifestyle is discernible through many forms of expressive behavior, laughter included. Some lifestyles will not permit laughter (Mosak, 1971, 1987). People whose lifestyles center around convictions such as "To live is to suffer," or "It's a dog-eat-dog world out there, and I'm always the dog that's eaten," usually find little to laugh about. For them, life is difficult and draining.

A patient's relationship to his or her humor can reveal much about his or her general use of emotions. Those who believe that "feelings are dangerous" have a hard time laughing as well. For them, "I think therefore I succeed" is the center of life, and rationality and thought are prized over feelings. These individuals attempt to control life, others, and themselves, and subsequently believe that their own feelings need to be controlled (Mosak, 1971).

Some people revel in laughter, perhaps a bit too much. In contrast to controllers, excitement seekers live for thrills. They can go out of their way to create excitement where none has previously existed (Mosak, 1971). These people may overindulge in their emotions, laughter included, at the expense of planning and forethought.

Another way of using humor diagnostically is to discern how it is used interpersonally by the patient. Some individuals laugh *with* others; some laugh *at* others. What kind of things patients laugh at can be revealing. Do they laugh at cruel jokes? Do they only laugh at their own expense? These types of issues can be indicative of lifestyle dynamics.

3. *Humor and Interpretation.* Confrontation is an important tactic in psychotherapy (Shulman, 1973). Many novice therapists assume that confrontation involves using a "hammer" by being forceful and blunt. Sometimes it does, but not necessarily always. Sometimes confrontation can be done with a "scalpel," gently and with little discomfort. Humor can provide the kind of buffer that facilitates the acceptance of an interpretation. The patient who comes into therapy complaining of how she alone has totally "ruined" her child's life "forever" can be gently, yet decisively, confronted with "Stop

bragging." As Adler (1956) often noted, a person's sense of superiority can frequently be found "hiding" behind self-accusations.

Jokes and humor can be used to point out aspects of life-styles that need to be worked on:

> To the self-centered patient: A noted violinist was being scolded by his manager for his self-adulation. "Every time I see you talking to someone at a cocktail party, you're saying 'I, I, I.' " The violinist, abashed, remarked, "Gee, I didn't know that and I'm sorry. I'll bet I've offended a lot of people that way. I promise I'll never do it again." The following Sunday, both were at a cocktail party and the violinist was "I, I, I-ing" a friend. Suddenly he looked across the room and saw his manager shaking his head in despair. He gave his manager a sign that he remembered the previous week's promise, turned back to his friend, and said, "But enough talking about me. Let's talk about you. How did you like my last concert?" (Mosak, 1987, pp. 94-95)

Moreover, humor can also be used interpretively to facilitate universalization. Patients can begin to realize that their suffering is not unique, that they are not alone, and that others have gone through similar situations. They may begin to realize that they have not been singled out for difficulty.

4. *Turning the Patient Around.* Humor is effective in moving patients in therapeutically productive ways. Adler (1956) and Frankl (1967) have discussed paradoxical intention or anti-suggestion. Humor injected into paradoxical suggestions can make them more palatable and therefore more effective.

Exaggeration of certain problems can place them in proper perspective. McMullin (1986) discusses many ways of doing this from a cognitive perspective, such as by carrying out patients' irrational fears to their logical extreme:

> "Okay, you're afraid no one likes you. Let's assume that you're right - nobody likes you. In fact, no one has *ever* liked you and no one ever will. From the doctors and nurses in the delivery room when you were born to the people who pass you by on the

street . . . they all dislike you!" Adler used to say to paranoid patients who believed that everyone was watching them "Lucky you! When I go out in the street not even my dog pays attention to me." (Mosak, 1987, p. 57)

Psychotherapy is an important process. But as Erickson (1984) astutely points out, *important* does not always equate with *serious*.

5. *Humor as a Criterion for Termination.* Olson (1976) has noted that:

The establishment or return of a positive sense of humor may well be considered a goal, or at least a highly desirable by-product, of psychotherapy, and the degree to which the sense of humor becomes established may be considered one criterion for the success of therapy. (pp. 34-35)

Adlerians use humor, along with dreams (Rosenthal, 1959) and changes in early recollections (Shulman & Mosak, 1988) as a barometer of the conclusion of therapy. Patients who place their problems into perspective and acknowledge their role in creating and maintaining those problems often rediscover their sense of humor. Their private intelligence is realigned with common sense, and each frame of reference becomes balanced.

Humor, like anything else in psychotherapy, needs to be used carefully. If therapists are not comfortable with humor, they ought not use it until they have received further exposure to it together with training in its use. There are many techniques that therapists will never or almost never use, and no therapist can be an expert with all techniques. Similarly, some patients may not appreciate humor, and there are those who will not appreciate it all the time. Patients who experience grief and mourning need not be approached humorously. Introducing it too soon, before the clinician has an accurate assessment of the relevant issues involved in a particular case, can be unwise. As with any technique, sensitivity and mutual respect for the therapeutic partner should be kept in the forefront of the therapist's mind.

CLINICAL VIGNETTES

A patient came into psychotherapy because of repeated episodes of having to "dig" himself out of "jams" in his personal and professional life. The pressure and stress of several years of such living had taken its toll upon him in the form of numerous somatic complaints and increasingly poor physical health. The therapist pinpointed the issue and offered the patient an image:

Patient: So you're implying that I created these minicrises in order to be the hero and. . . .

Therapist: And save the day, yes, it's possible. I keep having this image of you being faced with a crisis, stepping into a phone booth, ripping open your shirt, and there is this huge red "S" on your chest.

Patient: (Laughing) Superman, huh . . . That's hysterical. You know what my nickname was in college?

Therapist: You're kidding (Laughing with him).

Patient: No, really. It was Superman! My friend drew a cartoon of me as Superman, in a cape and everything, carrying a briefcase. God, that must have been 20-plus years ago.

Therapist: I want you to remember that. Let's use that the next time you go about creating another mess for yourself.

This patient grasped onto the image and laughed as he gained a new perspective about himself. Following this interview, he stopped digging himself into holes and found more constructive ways to "save the day."

Another patient, a woman in her late twenties, came into psychotherapy with several complaints. Her lifestyle was that of a "victim" (Mosak, 1971). She had been abused and taken advantage of for years. She reported no joy in her existence since life was, for her, a struggle that she never won. Her therapy took place over a 2-year period with breaks for weeks at a time in between. By her own admission, she was a "sullen, worn-out woman."

Slowly, over the course of weeks, her sense of humor emerged. The therapists* began to gradually nudge her into

---

*Adlerians typically practice and advocate multiple psychotherapy, the use of two therapists with one patient. Interested readers are referred to the text on multiple psychotherapy by Dreikurs, Shulman, and Mosak (1984).

"lightening up" on both herself and others. A turning point in her therapy occurred when one of the therapists looked at her with astonishment and genuine amazement:

Patient: What? What's wrong?
Therapist: What do you mean?
Patient: You looked stunned.
Therapist: I am.
Patient: So, tell me. . . .
Therapist: You're missing the opportunity of a lifetime.
Patient: I don't get it . . . What opportunity?
Therapist: You could be making millions if you wrote this stuff down and published it. This has potential as a soap opera.
Patient: (Laughing) You know, you're going to think I'm crazy . . . but I've always fantasized myself in one of those things. I've thought about writing this down but no one would believe it.

She laughed a deep, sincere laugh. She gained a new outlook on her complaints. She also did write them down - into a book about her life story. At last contact, she was seeking out a publisher, and was also asymptomatic.

Both these brief examples highlight the use of humor in helping to open up patients and giving them a fresh perspective on their lifestyles. Other examples taken from an actual 9-week course of therapy with a patient can be found in Mosak and Maniacci (1989).

SYNTHESIS

Humor is a powerful tool. When used wisely, it can enrich patients' lives and facilitate the psychotherapeutic process. Humor provides a new perspective, an opportunity to surprise ourselves and to tap into our hitherto unformulated expectations. Once we become aware of these different frames of reference and expectations, we can evaluate them in the "light of day."

Finally, and importantly, humor assists in the social bonding between individuals. No matter how far removed some individuals may appear, their connection to the community can always be felt, such as in this parable of the hermit (Pancner, 1978, p. 21):

Once long ago there lived outside a village in a cave an old man, the Hermit. One day the village and its inhabitants were totally destroyed by an erupting volcano. Sadly, the Hermit tied his belongings on his back and set out to find another cave outside another village.

REFERENCES

Adler, A. (1927). *Understanding Human Nature* (W. B. Wolfe, Trans.). New York: Fawcett Premier.

Adler, A. (1936). Trick and neurosis. *International Journal of Individual Psychology, 2,* 3-10.

Adler, A. (1956). *The Individual Psychology of Alfred Adler* (H. L. Ansbacher and R. R. Ansbacher, Eds.). New York: Basic Books.

Ansbacher, H. L. (1965). Sensus privatus versus sensus communis. *Journal of Individual Psychology, 21,* 48-50.

Dreikurs, R. (1973). The private logic. In H. H. Mosak (Ed.), *Alfred Adler: His Influence upon Psychology Today* (pp. 19-32). Park Ridge, NJ: Noyes Press.

Dreikurs, R., Shulman, B. H., & Mosak, H. H. (1984). *Multiple Psychotherapy: The Use of Two Therapists with One Patient.* Chicago: Alfred Adler Institute.

Ellis, A. (1973). *Humanistic Psychotherapy.* New York: McGraw-Hill.

Erickson, M. O. (1984). A serious case for silliness. *Psychotherapy in Private Practice, 2,* 49-55.

Frankl, V. E. (1967). *Psychotherapy and Existentialism.* New York: Touchstone Books.

Freud, S. (1960). *Jokes and Their Relation to the Unconscious* (J. Strachey, Trans.). New York: Norton. (Original work published in 1905)

Greenwald, H. (1967). Play therapy for children over twenty-one. *Psychotherapy, 4,* 44-46.

Grotjahn, M. (1966). *Beyond Laughter: Humor and the Subconscious.* New York: McGraw-Hill.

Haley, J. (1963). *Strategies of Psychotherapy.* New York: Grune & Stratton.

Horney, K. (1945). *Our Inner Conflicts.* New York: Norton.

Horney, K. (1950). *Neurosis and Human Growth.* New York: Norton.

Kubie, L. S. (1971). The destructive potential of humor in psychotherapy. *American Journal of Psychiatry, 127*, 861-866.

Manaster, G. J., & Corsini, R. J. (1982). *Individual Psychology.* Itasca, IL: F. E. Peacock.

McMullin, R. E. (1986). *Handbook of Cognitive Therapy Techniques.* New York: Norton.

Mosak, H. H. (1971). Lifestyle. In A. G. Nikelly (Ed.), *Techniques for Behavior Change* (pp. 77-81). Springfield, IL: Charles C. Thomas.

Mosak, H. H. (1987). *Ha Ha and Aha: The Role of Humor in Psychotherapy.* Muncie, IN: Accelerated Development.

Mosak, H. H. (1989). Adlerian psychotherapy. In R. J. Corsini & D. Wedding (Eds.), *Current Psychotherapies* (4th ed., pp. 65-116). Itasca, IL: F. E. Peacock.

Mosak, H. H., & Maniacci, M. P. (1989). The case of Roger. In D. Wedding & R. J. Corsini (Eds.), *Case Studies in Psychotherapy* (pp. 23-49). Itasca, IL: F. E. Peacock.

O'Connell, W. E. (1975). *Action Therapy and Adlerian Theory.* Chicago: Alfred Adler Institute.

Olson, H. (1976). The use of humor in psychotherapy. *Individual Psychologist, 13*, 34-37.

Pancner, K. (1978). The use of parables and fables in Adlerian psychotherapy. *Individual Psychologist, 15*, 19-29.

Reik, T. (1948). *Listening with the Third Ear.* New York: Farrar, Straus and Company.

Rosen, J. (1953). *Direct Analysis.* New York: Grune & Stratton.

Rosenthal, H. R. (1959). The final dream: A criterion for the termination of therapy. In K. A. Adler & D. Deutsch (Eds.), *Essays in Individual Psychology* (pp. 400-409). New York: Grove Press.

Shulman, B. H. (1973). *Contributions to Individual Psychology.* Chicago: Alfred Adler Institute.

Shulman, B. H., & Mosak, H. H. (1988). *Manual for Life Style Assessment.* Muncie, IN: Accelerated Development.

Wolfe, W. B. (1932). *How to be Happy Though Human.* London: Routledge & Kegan Paul.

2

Humor in
Stressful Milieus*

Thomas L. Kuhlman

Dr. Kuhlman is a profoundly intense, risk-taking, and courageous psychotherapist. Using humor in an ironic yet pure-at-heart mode, Dr. Kuhlman enters into the difficult world of complex psychopathology shown by severely mentally ill and violent individuals. In a sense, his humor use with this patient population is a therapeutically fierce response to the fierce and violent pathology they exhibit. He believes that, within the setting of an inpatient ward for the severely disturbed, humor is not only recommended but necessary for the survival of both patients and staff. He sees humor as having a cohesive value in bonding together the inpatient unit staff as they struggle to develop some meaningfulness out of their work within a seemingly ungratifying and tension-producing context.

Thomas L. Kuhlman, PhD, is currently Senior Clinical Psychologist with Hennepin County Family and Children's Mental Health Center in Minneapolis where his specialty is working with the homeless mentally ill. He is also Adjunct Professor of Psychology at the University of St. Thomas in St. Paul and is in private practice. He is author of the book Humor and Psychotherapy *and his other work on the psychology of humor has been published in the* Journal of Personality and Social Psychology *and* Hospital and Community Psychiatry. *He is a co-founder of the Twin Cities-based* Psychocircus, *a troupe of satirical mental health professionals and comedians who perform for conferences and conventions. He received his doctorate in clinical psychology from Case Western Reserve University and has been on the faculties of Augsburg College, Xavier University, and the University of Cincinnati.*

*The case material in the "Clinical Presentation" section of this chapter first appeared in "Gallows Humor for a Scaffold Setting: Managing Aggressive Patients on a Maximum-Security Forensic Unit" by T. L. Kuhlman, 1988, *Hospital and Community Psychiatry, 39,* pp. 1085-1090. Reprinted by permission of the American Psychiatric Association.

Analogues of the therapeutic humor to be discussed in this chapter are readily available to the reader, who needs only to survey network television programming at the end of the local news tonight. A *M*A*S*H* episode in syndication will appear on one channel, if not two. The reader will be fortunate if the nightly episode is one from the post-Frank Burns era, because it was in the later shows after that one-dimensional foil was gone and "Hot-Lips" Houlihan had become "Margaret," that the humor of *M*A*S*H* shifted from the moralistic satire of "war is wrong" to the more therapeutically leavened gallows humor of "war is crazy." In order to grasp milieu humor, the reader should resist the temptation to focus on the episode's plots and subplots, or on the gags and one-liners and Hawkeye's banter with B. J. Honeycutt. Instead, consider the backdrop to the action; consider the *M*A*S*H* camp as a unified social milieu instead of as a collection of colorful campers.

On another channel at the same time, one would not be surprised to find a syndicated episode of *Hill Street Blues*. This is analogue study #2. To appreciate the therapeutic value of milieu humor in this setting it is important not to miss the first 5 minutes of the show. All *Hill Street* episodes begin with the Roll Call, a 7:00 a.m. shift change report. A calm, even bemused patrol sergeant reads and waxes philosophical from a dreary list of the day's assignments involving carnage, corruption, and other profusions of man's inhumanity to man. The a.m. shift officers endorse their sergeant with wisecracks for each agenda item, no matter how bleak. Again, to appreciate milieu humor one should not focus on which wisecrack is more clever or cynical than the others. The stage is the thing - an overstressed and undermanned inner city police precinct trying to keep its collective head above society's most brackish waters.

This chapter examines the therapeutic importance of milieu humor in stressful clinical settings. Its major concern is humor *among* therapists, that is, humor which functions to help therapists collectively manage stressful working conditions. It addresses the special needs of those who work in psychiatric emergency rooms, maximum security facilities, and other treatment settings that entail chronic stress for therapists. A list of such stressors would include physical dangers inherent to the settings themselves, ongoing involvements with hostile/resistant/untreatable patients, and/or repeated demands upon therapists for high-risk decisions. This chapter is also addressed to consultants who serve police and fire departments, homeless shelters and hospices, or air traffic controllers - any and all work settings in which stress levels are high and unremitting. As outsiders, consultants often fail to appreciate the therapeutic value of humor because their attention is drawn to what they judge to be the inappropriate content or targets of such humor.

Based on my experience in a variety of such settings, I will argue that milieu humor is a therapeutic imperative in stressful work environments. Unfortunately, it may also become a vehicle for patient abuse or, more frequently, a convenient sidetrack for factional conflicts among staff. By chapter's end the reader will hopefully be able to better determine which of these dynamics is operating in a given milieu.

THEORETICAL PERSPECTIVE

Milieu humor of the *M*A*S*H** variety is already prevalent in stressful treatment settings that operate with a team approach. It evolves as a response to stress, yet it has seldom been acknowledged (but see Pogrebin & Poole, 1988). Such humor is usually kept under wraps by the team when administrators, supervisors, site visitors, or representatives of regulatory agencies are present. Obviously it needs to "come out of the closet," but there are two widespread taboos about humor that keep this from occurring.

HUMOR IS UNPROFESSIONAL

Talcott Parsons advanced the most widely accepted definition of what constitutes a profession (Geison, 1983). His three characteristics that distinguish the professions from other occupations are (a) formal, technical training in an institution that certifies quality and competence, (b) demonstrable skills in the pragmatic application of that training, and (c) institutional mechanisms (e.g., licensing) to insure that competencies and skills will be exercised in a socially respectable manner. Clearly, there is nothing in this definition which labels humor or any other kind of social interaction as unprofessional.

Nevertheless, the evolution of modern professionalism has given rise to a humor taboo. Circumscribed codes of professional dress, demeanor, and conduct which are not conducive to humor have emerged. In the beginning these codes served two functions, the first being a need to define the market for newly created services (Larson, 1977). Product-based occupations generate tangible objects with properties that are observed and evaluated by consumers. These properties define the markets for the products. However, the service-based professions generate no such tangible products around which their markets can form. It is to compensate for this market drawback of lacking an identifiable product that service professions have evolved a uniform code of identifiable behaviors.

The second early function of professionalism pertains to the impersonal aspects of a code that maintains social distance between provider and consumer. Such aspects reinforced the ties of the newly established professionals to the preindustrial elite classes; after all, only members of the privileged classes possessed sufficient leisure time, education, and the financial wherewithal to devote to a profession (Larson, 1977). As such, the first professions represented a carryover of the institution of nobility from feudalism to the industrial age. Humor and laughter would serve to undermine such a relational system insofar as they reduce social distance rather than reinforce it (Coser, 1959).

Now that the professions and their roles in the marketplace are well established, have we outlived the validity of professionalism? Not entirely - providers and consumers are thoroughly indoctrinated with the code, and a culture of accouterments, traditions, and expectations has developed around it. A back-slapping psychoanalyst dressed in a tie-dyed shirt and jeans whose favorite word is "ain't" will have trouble establishing a practice no matter how competent and certified he or she is.

On the other hand, there is no empirical basis for inferring that the quality of services rendered is correlated with the degree of professionalism in which such services are packaged. Laughter may not have been considered professional behavior, but it was a powerful therapeutic for Norman Cousins (1979) after professionalized medicine had failed to cure his collagen disease. And is it possible that the codes of professionalism restrict one's range of dress, demeanor, and conduct without also restricting one's range of thought? The treatment settings discussed below entail working with people whose behaviors are dangerous, incorrigible, unpredictable, and sometimes detestable. Those who toil with such patients can ill afford restrictions upon their thought processes. When "working" on these cases fails to yield a desirable solution - as it often does - the treatment staff must be able to shift to a playful frame of mind (humor can be defined most simply as human beings at play). When therapists who work in such settings take liberties with humor, with self-disclosure and/or modes of dress and behavior that alter the professional boundaries as these are normally construed, then they need to be supported for taking novel approaches with difficult patients and not rebuked for having flouted the codes of professionalism.

ACTING-OUT IN HUMOR

The second taboo about humor is rooted in the psychoanalytic view of humor as a thinly veiled expression of unconscious drives and needs, particularly aggression. Psychoanalytic theory proposes that the proper mastery of such forces is to be achieved through introspection, insight, and self-restraint. A therapist should strive never to react personally to a patient's problems. The humorous acting-out of private motives and needs aroused by patients is considered exploitative at best, dangerous at worst.

There is substance to this argument (Kubie, 1971) yet there is also evidence as to the productive psychotherapeutic effects of humor (Fry & Salameh, 1987; Kuhlman, 1984). Of course, the major concern of this chapter is humor among therapists, that is, humor among equals as distinct from the role inequities between therapist and patient in psychotherapy. The difference this makes with respect to joking relationships is considerable, and yet Kubie or others may protest against therapists humorously sharing their common frustrations about a patient's behavior even when the patient is not present to witness this.

Is ventilating frustration through humor "a bad thing?" Does such behavior potentiate aggression or drain it away? Based on her systematic observations of humor among an inpatient psychiatric staff, Coser (1960) endorsed a benign attitude toward such humor: "The release of aggression in a witty manner may do much to prevent the undiagnosed outbreak of hostility or bottling up of frustration" (p. 95).

I have previously reported the case of an intractable borderline patient whose suicidal behavior was managed only after the implementation of a paradoxical strategy involving random reinforcement of behavior according to the roll of a die (Kuhlman, Green, & Sincaban, 1988). Prior to this patient's improvement, the inpatient nursing staff had become so vexed and stressed by the woman that their malignant neglect of her during one of her many suicide attempts seemed possible. As she improved, they improved; their angry mutterings in the staff breakroom gradually turned to gloating amusement with the incongruous predicament that the paradoxical treatment plan posed to her. This "mirth of mastery" was never in evidence out on the ward. Several months after the patient's discharge she wrote an unsolicited letter to the staff in which she acknowledged that she missed everyone. This letter was posted on the bulletin board in the breakroom. The very staff members who had previously laughed at the patient's behavior had, by that time, come around to missing her, too.

Laughter was a safety valve in this instance. It was an outlet for the untoward consequences that occurred after the staff's sympathy, empathy, and commitment to hard work had been exhausted. Laughter is often needed by a psychiatric emergency team manning the graveyard shift on a Saturday night in the inner city. And by the staff of a maximum security ward where patients' rights legislation mandates the release of an assaultive patient from seclusion. And by the child welfare team that must venture into crime-infested neighborhoods to remove an abused child from its parents.

Those who would insist that stoical objectivity and self-restraint be practiced regardless of circumstance can consider the experience of the police profession where restraint-based values have long been emulated. The costs of such a stance have been exorbitant: the American police officer has a life expectancy that is 10 years less than that of the average American. He or she is also far more susceptible to the wide array of physical and psychological maladies associated with prolonged and unremitting stress (Ellison & Genz, 1983). The gastrointestinal and emotional disorders so prevalent among police officers are the result of too much emotional containment and too little emotional expression. It is ironic how police are often criticized by mental health professionals for their insensitive or "macho" style. I submit that such machismo is first cousin to the emotional detachment and self-restraint that many therapists so highly prize in themselves.

Gallows humor offers a promising substitute to machismo as an alternative cognitive set for coping with chronic stress. It takes its name from the genre of jokes concerning the condemned man about to be hanged on the gallows or shot by a firing squad. The hopeless victim, in a seeming no-win situation, finds a way to transcend his existential malaise by reverting to clever or absurd repartee. For example, when the executioner offers him a last cigarette before the blindfold, he responds: "No thanks. I just quit yesterday."

Alford (1982) observed that most humor violates principles of logic (e.g., children's nonsense humor) or principles of conduct (humor content concerned with sex, aggression, intoxication, or scatology). Gallows humor violates principles usually associated with human meanings and values. As such, gallows humor encompasses all content types of humor because it is a broad philosophical attitude (like irony or satire) rather than a thematic category. It is an in-kind response to an absurd dilemma, a way of being sane in an insane place. It is hitting a triple when faced with a double bind, withdrawing an investment after the market has already crashed. It is a coping mechanism.

Freud's (1905/1960) *Jokes and Their Relation to the Unconscious* is his best known work on humor. It emphasizes humor's defensive aspects. Yet Freud often used jokes when conducting treatment (Loewenstein, 1958) and he also offered the following statement as to the therapeutic value of humor:

> It is something fine and elevating. . . . Obviously, what is fine about it is the triumph of narcissism, the ego's victorious assertion of its own invulnerability. It refuses to be hurt by the arrows of reality or to be compelled to suffer. It insists that it is impervious to wounds dealt by the outside world, in fact, that these are merely occasions for affording it pleasure. (Freud, 1928/1957, p. 217)

Gallows humor flourishes when all else fails and there is no reasonable hope for an improvement in conditions. Its stress management functions are greatest in treatment milieus with two characteristics. The first is the presence of ongoing, chronic stressors that cannot be reduced, escaped from, or controlled. This lack of control over stressors may be more crucial for the appearance of gallows humor than the degree of stress *per se*. Dangerous or difficult patients are only one facet of the stress problem. Consider how police, emergency room personnel, and crisis responders of all kinds must endure frequent and unpredictable transitions from boredom to excitement and back again - transitions never of their own making. In time they are rendered "adrenalin junkies," most on edge when they have the least to do. Physiological stability is further disrupted by the requirements of working rotating and/or swing shifts. Nor can the spigots of stress be turned down by scheduling patients on an appointment basis as is done in outpatient work. And there is often an absence of adequate follow-up or support systems. Police wearily bemoan delays and obstacles in the judicial system just as emergency room mental health therapists decry the absence of public sector psychiatric beds for their worst patients. There is no reliable means of mastering all of these stressors. Humor provides playful mastery when no "workful" mastery is possible.

The second condition which gives rise to gallows humor is a prevailing irony, paradox, or cognitive dissonance to the work at hand. This is an existential version of the cognitive incongruity which underlies the simplest forms of humor (Kuhlman, 1985). The reigning paradox for the M*A*S*H* surgeons was to work feverishly to repair and save soldiers so that they could be rushed back to the battlefield to be wounded again. A different incongruity is the clash between one's idealized expectations and the sobering realities of what can be achieved. Child welfare workers start out with a "Save the Children!" fervor but quickly learn that it is a job involving decisions among the lesser of several evils. I knew a psychiatric emergency room therapist who formerly spent his third shifts presiding over suicidal patients who were restrained to stretchers as they waited for state hospital beds to become available the next morning. Because there were never enough beds for all the patients, deciding who would receive one and who would not became a dreary shell game. This therapist offered the following antidote to the dilemma of whom to admit to the hospital: If a restrained patient wanted to be admitted to the hospital, that in itself was an indication that he or she did not need the bed, that is, conditions were so bad at the state hospital that only an institutionalized person would seek such a refuge. Suicide attempts within this framework were thus manipulative in intent and not to be taken seriously. On the other hand, restrained patients who begged and pleaded that they were alright and did not need to go to the hospital surely did need to be hospitalized insofar as their pleadings reflected no insight into the severity of the suicidal act for which they had been restrained in the first place. In short, the therapist's tongue-in-cheek formula was to simply ask a patient if he or she wanted to go to the hospital or not - and then do the opposite of what the patient had requested.

This "treatment plan" was passed around among the team in jest although, like most humor, it contained a kernel of truth. One layer of its humor was the expression of cognitive dissonance among a team of helping professionals who were regularly compelled to make decisions that incurred the wrath of those whom they aspired to help. A second layer was the daily reminder that years of professional training and experience did not make such gut-wrenching decisions any easier. Through humor, a team can honor ideals in play that sometimes cannot be achieved in work.

A frequent source of cognitive dissonance for therapists in stressful settings is being required to help patients whose behaviors are frightening or detestable. This is the paradox of one's professional role being in conflict with one's private sentiments. When I was in charge of a maximum security psychiatric ward (see "Clinical Presentation," pp. 37-42), the state prison railroaded their most difficult inmate to us in order to have a "breather" from him. This man introduced himself to me in a menacing fashion and cited an ominous fact that had already jumped out at me from his accompanying records: "You know, man, they gave me life on account o' my murdering a psychologist like you!" My immediate response was, "I've got no problem with that! I'm sure he deserved it!"

My rejoinder has been variously analyzed as being (a) in the worst of bad taste, or (b) a brilliantly disarming paradoxical intervention. My own self-analysis is this: It was an absurd but health-serving reaction to the no-win dilemma of being forced to "treat" someone who was both terrifying and repulsive. Years later at a drop-in center I observed John, a meek and pious soup kitchen volunteer, receive a vicious, salivated tongue-lashing in Spanish. This verbal assault came from a homeless man to whom John had quietly suggested a wait in line for seconds until everyone else had been served their firsts. A fellow volunteer immediately snapped, "Yeah, he took the words right out of our mouths, John. We all have been trying to tell you that for months!" The slow beam of a smile that crossed John's face was a sign that he was alright again.

And then there are the inherent ironies of the hospice worker who must strive to improve patients' quality of death without follow-up data to say whether it had made a difference or not. And those of the prison psychologist working with an inmate whose earliest release date will be 2031 no matter what is accomplished by treatment.

TECHNIQUE

Many intuitively grasp the role that humor plays in coping with such ongoing dilemmas. The continuing popularity of *M*A*S*H** attests to this. Still, without the ability to create characters and write dialogue, it remains difficult to say how gallows humor comes about. One social engineering project accomplished it in a nursing home (Andrus Volunteers, 1983.) This is the rare case of humor by administrative fiat. More typically, milieu humor represents a spontaneous combustion of therapists and stressors. It is not a simple matter of teaching a technique or writing a program. Rather, it is the cultivation of a playful atmosphere wherein team members take periodic recess periods to reconnect and renew their bonds. Most importantly, their need to do so is respected on site and not driven underground to a nearby tavern after the work shift is over.

To facilitate milieu humor, the workplace could include a room or sequestered area for therapists to retreat to when they are beleaguered and besieged. Here they can decompress alone or be "debriefed" by their fellow therapists. This room can serve as the team's "home territory . . . where regular participants have a relative freedom of behavior and a sense of intimacy and control over the area" (Lyman & Scott, 1967, p. 270). Access to this area by patients and their significant others should be restricted. In fact, both administrators and therapists' significant others should hesitate at its door. In the Pogrebin and Poole (1988) study of Denver police, the precinct briefing room took on this function after the official shift-change responsibilities had been discharged and the officers had gone off-duty. Lunchrooms or lounges in hospitals and clinics can lend themselves for this purpose as long as they shield patients from the goings-on and yet permit therapists easy access back to the "action" if an emergency arises.

Therapists who work in stressful settings must tend to common emotional needs generated by that setting. In the process, they evolve a collective team identity which is not far removed from that of a family or tribe. A subtle yet pervasive resentment is stirred if such a team is denied use of its home territory to tend to itself. If a team is compelled to remain task-oriented and "professional" throughout the work shift, it will tend to create a home territory for self-repair elsewhere, usually adding the disinhibiting effects of alcohol.

Hospitalized patients have been observed to cohere and support one another through humor (Coser, 1959.) Their home territory has been the ward dayroom, traditionally the only part of the hospital milieu that belongs more to the patients than to the staff. Much of the patients' humor targeted doctors and nurses (e.g., "the nurse woke me up to give me a sleeping pill!") who are seldom present to witness it. Coser inferred an underlying positive function of this humor in that complaints were funneled from the solitary angers of individual patients into a communal realm of play. The ward became a more acceptable place to live once the tensions and dissatisfactions had been shared and drained away, a process which Coser labeled "correction for the imperfections" of the doctors and nurses. In her view, the ultimate effect of such humor was to reinforce the structure of the hospital environment rather than undermine it. The same principle applies when the humor is practiced by therapists correcting for the imperfections of patients or administrators.

Milieu humor is also facilitated when status positions within a team are permeable or flexible. This responsibility falls to the team leader who must be able to affirm peer status during recess periods and assert authority and leadership at other times. It may be possible for a leader to benignly endorse humor without taking part (the "Captain Furillo" approach). However, participant leaders who shift in and out of the peer role (the "Colonel Potter" approach) can command as much respect. It is sometimes necessary for the leader to define a situation as grist for the humor mill. Consider the following vignette involving a faculty surgeon and a hated patient of his emergency room:

Most physicians do not like drunks, and Donald is thoroughly detested because he is such an effective drunk. He doesn't just come in drunk, he comes in comatose from ethanol. Some of us will put him on a monitor in Room 17, keep a close eye on him, try to wake him once an hour, and await the moment when he finally will wake up, pull on his trousers, stagger out, protest his unlawful confinement, and demand his civil right to freedom. At which point I get a hospital voucher for cab fare and send him home. On occasion I have admitted him, released him, and then admitted him again within a single 12-hour shift. One night there was an unusually large pool in the betting on his ethanol level; a full crew had mobilized for

a Trauma Red which never materialized and we got 37 en-
tries! By sheer luck I won the pool. . . . The clerk holding
the pool asked me what I was going to do with the money.
"I am going to give it to Donald. You can't buy enough
pizza for $9.25 to feed 37 people, and the ice cream par-
lors don't deliver this time of night. It will save the hospital a cab voucher, and Donald is smart enough to know
the cab fare. Now he can tell the driver 'Stop by the Li-
quor Barn on the way home so I can pick up a fifth of
vodka.' "

None of you in this audience laughed but everyone in
hearing at the time did. . . . He is just too sad a case to cry
over. The only way out is to laugh. And we laughed, and
I am sure it made it a little easier for us to take care of
Donald the next time he came in. (D. Lindsey, personal
communication, 1989)

In addition to posing the "help the despised" paradox, Donald's
never staying "cured" is a recurring mockery of the emergency
room staff's collective effort and expertise. And Donald is the
type of individual who is more likely to offer them a lawsuit than
a handshake of thanks. Without humor, this situation is ripe for
serious acting-out, probably passive-aggressive neglect. However, with humor and the leader's adroit maneuver of the betting
pool, the target also becomes a beneficiary. Of course, the primary beneficiaries are the staff - the leader supports them by his
pizza intentions and then models a gallows humor attitude for
dealing with Donald in the future. It is hard to imagine a better
way to manage the collective resentment of 39 people by one intervention.

Another dimension of milieu humor that underwrites its gallows and therapeutic properties is *target rotation.* Patients and
administrators are fitting targets for a team as long as the team
does not exempt itself or its members from that role. Such
exemptions signal that the team has developed an extreme, inces-
tuous cohesion. The negative consequences include an overprotectiveness among the team about itself, an unduly thick shielding
of the in-group from outside influence, and a tendency to alienate
or vilify out-groups such as patients, administrators, funding
sources, and so on. To be therapeutic, the "nothing is sacred" philosophy of gallows humor needs to apply to all. Thus the team
leader must not simply tolerate humor aimed at his or her own

personal quirks and foibles - such humor is to be welcomed and enjoyed. If such a dynamic does not occur, then the leader is cast as a "sacred cow" which reinforces the team's hierarchy levels at the expense of its communal feeling. Communal feeling is a critical need in settings that cause pervasive wear-and-tear on the emotions. A strong sense of community provides a strong sense of mutual support.

The type of humor that travels exclusively in a downward direction (i.e., from supervisor to subordinate) is endemic to organizations that prize the strict hierarchical structuring of power and decision making. Stressful treatment settings place a premium on communal solidarity over hierarchy. Pogrebin and Poole (1988) frequently observed upward-bound humor in their police department where nonranking patrol officers would openly ridicule the shift sergeants. The authors interpreted this humor as a way of keeping each sergeant "one of the gang" (most had been promoted to sergeant from patrol officer). Even so, upward-bound humor may feel awkward and unnatural to subordinates and supervisors until it is established as part of the in-group culture. A milieu is ripe for the start of this flexibility in the aftermath of a critical incident where a high degree of danger or stress has temporarily leveled the hierarchy, reducing all to equals who must rely upon each other to cope with the serious threat. Once that threat has been mastered, humorous play in the aftermath fuels comradery and cohesion into the future. The following was one police officer's quip when his team reassembled for debriefing at the precinct station after a potential shooting incident had been narrowly averted:

> It's a good thing Wayne didn't have to shoot that scumbag, because we haven't qualified with the shotgun for I don't know how long. He would have shot and probably hit that front window, and that son of a bitch would have opened up on all of us. (Pogrebin & Poole, 1988, p. 198)

This bit of humor reveals group fear about being ill-prepared to manage such a crisis. The attentive leader learns from the content of humor and plans future training accordingly. Note too that this in-group humor targets the in-group itself - this in-group does not spare itself from healthy self-examination. The quintessential court jester was one who mocked himself before all others. This kept his vision insightful and clear.

Visiting Psychiatrist: She called her house-mother names like "bitch," and so on.

Senior Staff Member: (Smiling) Other names, like "other side of tracks?"

Visiting Psychiatrist: No, worse than that. (Senior staff member smiles encouragingly.) Well, to tell you exactly, she called her a God-damned fucking bitch. (The two men laugh very hard and are joined by more subdued laughter from the others.) (Coser, 1960, p. 89)

The preceding excerpt depicts the existential paradox of being torn between the norms of professional dignity (a taboo against such shocking profanity) and the demands of the psychiatric profession (nothing should shock a psychiatrist who must give accurate reports about patients instead of "and so on"). The collaboration of the two men and their shared laughter provides cathartic relief for the whole group.

Milieu humor will also be enhanced by a prop or symbol in the home territory that defines it as a place permissible for play. Such symbols may later acquire a totem status among the ingroup. The maximum security psychiatric ward to which I previously alluded was a milieu that I started "from scratch." Most of the 22 persons initially hired to staff the ward had no mental health training or background, and two professional positions allocated for the ward went unfilled for 2 years due to the nature of the patient population. Consequently, many novice mistakes required correction, but frequent corrections and redirections tend to strengthen a status hierarchy. To dilute this effect, I would facetiously proclaim "that's another pink slip for you" as a preface to correcting someone's error. "Pink slip" traditionally refers to the color of paper used in firing someone; receiving a pink slip for a mistake due only to a lack of training was readily grasped by all as exaggeration humor. It was my way of rendering the tension between superior and subordinates less austere by acting so austerely as to mock my own authority. This sort of cutting up quickly spread among our group in such a way that team members would publicly assign one another pink slips as a way of signaling that some area of team disagreement or conflict had arisen.

Ultimately the pinkest slip of all was delivered up the hierarchy - it was awarded to me by the staff on the occasion of the ward's 1-year anniversary when the hospital administrators had come over to acknowledge our successful first year. It proved to be a real pink slip, woman's undergarment variety, and was presented to me in a gift-wrapped box during a mock ceremony. As will become clear later, it was only natural in that milieu for me to put the slip on over my regular clothes and wear it proudly for the rest of the shift so that all of our patients could have a good look at it.

Again, this echoes the central theme of gallows humor: nothing is sacred, not even one's putative or institutionalized authority. Gallows humor represents a surrender of sacred principles; it is a when-all-else-fails response to insure therapists' survival and replenishment. Those who constantly take the misery and danger of these settings too seriously will not be able to survive them for long.

Death is entitled to no more sacred treatment than any other topic. In the emergency room, a patient's impending demise prompts calls for a "carpentry consult" (pine box by bedside) or doctor's orders to "give her a Bible and tell her to study for the finals" (Lindsey & Benjamin, 1981.) Nor is such treatment reserved only for the "common patient":

> One day I was called and told that a friend of mine, a fellow surgeon, would be brought in DOA - Dead On Arrival, self-inflicted gunshot wound of the head. I knew that he was facing a crisis, but I had not known it was that bad. He left a note stating that he was a failure as a husband and a father.
>
> All I could do was turn to the nurse and express my grief. He shouldn't have done it. He shouldn't have shot himself. He should have *hung* himself. Why? Because he was a plastic surgeon. (Lindsey & Benjamin, 1981, p. 76)

Meanwhile, down at the precinct station . . .

> . . . the suspect requested to see his "good friend" on the force, Lieutenant Williams. . . . When the lieutenant arrived, he briefly talked with the suspect, explaining the procedures to be followed in Driving Under the Influence

cases, then drove the suspect home. A few hours later the suspect committed suicide.

When the graveyard shift came off the street at 8 a.m., Lieutenant Williams was in the briefing room and the discussion focused immediately on the suicide. It was soon learned that the suspect was not the lieutenant's close friend; rather, at best he was a casual acquaintance whom the lieutenant saw infrequently at a local stable where they both kept their horses. Once the relationship had been clarified, the patrol officers saw the opportunity to diffuse the tragic elements of the case for the lieutenant:

"I saw the guy in here when he was waiting to blow in the machine (breathalyzer). He didn't look too depressed. What the hell did you say to him to depress him to the point he blew himself away? You didn't bore him to death with all those horse stories you always tell?" (Pogrebin & Poole, 1988, pp. 199-200)

PERTINENT USES

Humor brings both short-term and long-term benefits to the stress-laden milieu. The short-term benefits issue from the stress management properties of humor. The autonomic arousal pattern associated with laughter is similar to the patterns aroused by fear, anger, profound sadness, or other unpleasant emotions. Each of these emotional states lends itself to a laughter conversion provided that the subject's cognitive perspective can be appropriately shifted. As Schachter demonstrated in his classic experiment involving epinephrine-injected subjects, the positive or negative valence of an emotional state is a function of the subject's ongoing evaluation of the environment (Schachter & Singer, 1962). The stresses of a treatment milieu induce autonomic arousal, but the therapists who staff it can make the cognitive adjustments that will minimize the toll on them.

Furthermore, the nature of the settings described previously is such that other methods of stress management are not feasible. One must often make split-second decisions that do not allow the luxury of time to seek counsel from colleagues or supervisors who are removed from the fray. Nor is there time to find a comfortable easy chair in which one can engage in transcendental meditation, progressive relaxation, or self-hypnosis. There is no biofeedback machine to hook up to, no time to run 3 miles in some quiet woodland. Medicating oneself is now out of vogue, and screaming out the window is less professional than humor is. What stress management tactics remain?!

And yet it is beyond these incident-to-incident, "comic relief" aspects that humor's greater value lies. For humor nourishes the social network, the in-group, the support system. As Coser (1959) summarized:

> Humor allows the participants, in a brief span of time and with a minimum of effort, mutually to reinterpret their experiences, to entertain, reassure, and communicate; to convey their interest in one another, to pull the group together by transforming what is individual into collective experience, and to strengthen the social structure within which the group functions. (p. 180)

In short, humor builds and maintains teamwork.

Often in dealing with difficult patients, the support and acknowledgment of one's teammates is the only reward for a job well done. What makes many settings stressful is the unresponsiveness of patients to available treatment methods, or the fact that no matter how good the treatments are, the social environment to which the patients return will erode or undermine those treatments. In the long run, hope for significant change lies in political, social, administrative, and research initiatives. But those who must cope in the day-to-day run must rely on humor and other team processes to help them resist burnout and pathological cynicism. Thus the betting pool over Donald's blood alcohol level was a collective empathic decision that it was alright not to fake "professional" concern with a type of patient who makes those laboring under the Hippocratic oath feel hypocritical. In a similar vein, who but fellow police officers are in a position to desensitize their lieutenant (note upward-bound humor) to his second-guessing and doubts following the alcoholic's suicide? About 50 years ago Obrdlik (1942) wrote that a national outbreak of gallows humor played a role in maintaining the collective morale of the Czechoslovakian people during that country's World War II occupation by the Nazis.

It is unfortunate that such instances of therapeutic humor among in-groups have been overshadowed by studies of the demoralizing and alienating effects of humor upon targeted outgroups, that is, minority and ethnic humor. Gallows humor in "scaffold" settings seeks neither to alienate nor to demoralize any out-groups. Its targeting rotates from in-group to out-group and back again without becoming fixed upon any single target. When such fixations occur, milieu humor has exchanged its therapeutic role for a weaponry role. I was once part of such a transformation among a psychiatric emergency room team. First there was a change in administrations and philosophies that took place at great expense to members of my mental health discipline. Bitter negotiations failed to reduce this expense: resignations, increased sick-time usage, and other signs of organizational strife soon ensued. In-group humor that had previously been both plentiful and rotational in its targeting came to focus exclusively upon the new administrators. It lost its whimsy and acquired a palpable hostility. Ultimately, patient care suffered. Such outcomes become considerably worse when certain types of patients become the fixated targets of a team's hostility.

Barring such developments, humor is a language of healthy cohesion. It reduces the social distance among participants and opposes tendencies toward rigidity of social structures within which the participants coexist. Humor is a vehicle for momentary emotional involvements among comrades; it underlines their mutual dependence for insuring one another's safety and well-being under trying circumstances.

Some would argue that humor is an indirect form of communication - why not strive for something more direct and forthright? A stressful workplace entails a peculiar mixture of intimacy and distance. Intimacy resides in the fact that others must be relied upon to meet one's security needs that are chronically threatened by psychological and/or physical threats. On the other hand, it is unlikely that there will be close bonds between therapists aside from this focal emotional dependency. Only rarely are therapists married to one another or related by family or tribe. Outside the workplace, in-group members may have little in common. Furthermore, the emotional interdependence of team members lasts for 8-hour shifts. Between shifts are 16 hours during which in-group cohesion and bonding are irrelevant. In short, stressful milieus incubate their own strange mix of intimacy and distance among the in-group, and humor is a language that expresses both sides of this mix. Stressful settings thus promote "joking relationships," a term first coined by Radcliffe-Brown (1940, 1949) to describe similar conditions and bonds underlying in-law relationships in various African cultures.

CLINICAL PRESENTATION*

The milieu to be described is a 14-bed maximum security psychiatric ward of a state forensic hospital. This ward was specifically designed for managing chronic, assaultive male patients. When the ward opened it received all of its initial patients from a solitary confinement unit that had been staffed by prison guards. These guards were not shy about acknowledging that they would gang up and use corporal punishment to keep patients in line. The new ward, called the Management Unit (MU), was conceived as a humane alternative. Yet it was also to serve as both a "back ward" and a "hole" by housing a potpourri of the most intractable and dangerous patients from the state's mental hospitals and prisons.

It is my belief that MU represents the first preconceived induction of a humorous atmosphere into the day-to-day operation of a psychiatric unit. This was grounded in the "no-win" assumption that all MU patients were hopeless cases. Gallows humor sprang readily from this assumption because the two milieu conditions requisite for its appearance were abundant. The ongoing, inescapable stressors were the patients themselves. During its first year the unit averaged almost two assaults per day. Many of the patients attacked unpredictably or in accord with some psychotic source that we did not understand. Nor could we escape such patients by discharging or transferring them. Most mental health settings have a place to refer (dump) the inappropriate (scary) patients in the patients' best interests (to be rid of them). MU, however, was "the dump." The more frequently a patient displayed assaultive behavior, the more justification there was for keeping the patient on MU.

One of the most fearsome of the original patients was *Big Mac,* a withdrawn, reclusive sort who nevertheless maintained his king-of-the-hill status by sucker-punching new patients during their first few days on the ward. Big Mac proved able to break the noses of several patients even after he had been outfitted with a set of ambulatory restraints. He thus created a thriving business for the local emergency room and nothing but headaches and heartaches for the staff, because we could not protect the patients or ourselves from his unprovoked attacks. Eventually we grew

---

*Names and other identifying characteristics in this clinical presentation have been altered sufficiently to protect the confidentiality of the individuals.

accustomed to this powerlessness and learned to shrug it off. His assaults came to be known as "Big Mac attacks." On one particularly ludicrous day, the evening shift decided to go to McDonald's for dinner solely because a Big Mac attack had occurred during the morning shift that day. The moral of the story: When a stressor cannot be removed or escaped it must be celebrated.

On another evening I was returning *Alice Cooper,* one of the most regressed patients, to his room after having played on the same team with him in a basketball game on the ward's courtyard. He had already slapped my derriere twice during the game, which was marginally acceptable in a teammate context. As I was unlocking the door to his room I saw from over my shoulder that another slap was coming. But this slap proved to be different: the knuckle of his middle finger was bent at a right angle, forming as nasty a projectile as I had ever seen. It landed and penetrated with unusual force into my anus. I was left with a lingering physical impression that I had just been raped.

Alice was secluded with minimal assistance. As the physical aspects of my pain diminished the emotional ones increased, and I had no appetite at all for finishing my shift that night or coming back to work on the next day or month or year. However, my staff took care of me as we went about our work. They teased me wordlessly about my walking somewhat on tiptoes from the waning pain, and soon most of them were also walking around on tiptoes in mockery of me. One very psychotic patient began mimicking them as well, and by the end of the shift we were all laughing and I was feeling much better and walking around on tiptoes better than any of them.

After all the patients had been locked in for the night, the staff suddenly turned sympathetic to my plight, something they could not have afforded to do earlier when the patients were still out and about. But by this time I didn't need their sympathy anymore; they had already "cured" me. So when the group offered to take me out and buy me a drink, I politely declined, explaining that I felt a strange compulsion to go touring the gay bars by myself. We laughed together at that so long and hard that the security guards monitoring the building from the medium security side thought something was wrong and came over to investigate.

Something was wrong, of course. I would have to see Alice Cooper the next day, and the next 100 days after that. This man had virtually raped me but I had to "treat" him the next day. How can one cope with such a situation except with humor?

The second milieu condition for gallows humor, existential incongruity, was present on MU in multiple layers. First, the staff had no valid deterrents for aggressive behavior. The original patients came to us on high doses of medication, and a 4-hour seclusion is meaningless to someone who had previously been in solitary confinement 23-1/2 hours a day. Pressing criminal charges was a useless exercise, and there were no more restrictive units to which a patient could be sent for punishment. Finally, the typical positive incentives for inhibiting aggressive behavior were absent. Our original patients never had visitors. They had been confined in maximum security for so long that they had lost meaningful relations with their support systems. There was no one on the outside to encourage or wait for them.

Ironically, some patients did have incentives to maintain the perception that they were dangerous tough guys who needed maximum security. It is from such reputations that they drew what little self-esteem they possessed. This reasoning best explains the behavior of Big Mac described previously, and also that of *Blowhard,* a patient who threatened to fight the entire unit to the death if we dared move him to one of the less secure wards "with all them wimps." In short, MU staff faced serious aggression with few means to deter patients from aggressive behaviors. This dilemma was acknowledged in the name "Management Unit" with its implication that effective treatment was not to be expected.

A profound paradox of the ward was the fact that the more aggressive the patient was, the more he belonged there. MU was the incongruous social unit where aggression served to bind the group and to keep individuals part of the milieu. This gross absurdity runs counter to all Darwinian survival principles. To cope with such a paradox demands a sense of humor.

One of the younger male staff members once received a bloody nose and a puffy eye in a struggle to seclude a patient whom I had thought ready for transfer to a less restrictive ward. Even as someone held an ice pack to his face, this staff member needled me: "You almost made a big mistake there, Doc, and it's a good thing he did that here today or we'd never have known what a bad idea of yours it was to try and move him."

Recognizing and embracing the absurdities of the ward not only gave the team a means of coping with specific incidents but also became a way of life on the job. Shortly after the ward opened, my whimsical response to a first challenge from Blowhard helped set a tone of gallows humor.

Blowhard was the oldest patient on the ward. He maintained his tough-guy reputation with a loud, blustery voice and well-placed, well-timed sucker-punches. He was chronically psychotic and did not want psychiatric treatment. He wanted to live out his days on the ward and die there as a tough guy.

One day Blowhard approached me in the dayroom, knowing full well that I was in charge of the ward and that my official title was "unit chief." Nevertheless, he strode up to me in front of other patients and staff and said challengingly in his surliest, most sarcastic voice: "So you're the unit chief, huh?" My response was, "Sorry, that's not technically correct. On this ward we have a king, not a mere unit chief. And I've been debating whether patients and staff should have to kiss my ring when they approach me like you're doing just now. What do you think?"

Blowhard was incredulous for a few moments - and that made two of us! Finally, he broke out into raucous laughter and pointed at me derisively. "He thinks he's a king!" he bellowed to the other patients who, like Blowhard, were equal parts amused and confused. Henceforth Blowhard would facetiously address me as "your majesty" - yet whenever he was close to becoming violent I was able to manage him better than anyone else. Ultimately we were able to persuade him to retire as a tough guy and move to a less restrictive unit. He is now living in stable condition in a community-based facility.

The initial intervention would have been fine if it had ended there, but it did not. At our next staff meeting I was presented with a cardboard crown from Burger King, a scepter fashioned from aluminum foil, and a "regal" terry cloth robe. The staff proclaimed me King Thomas I. Our head nurse was later presented with an army helmet; the staff changed his job title to "Lieutenant" and put small plastic soldiers on his desk to represent each of the staff who worked under him.

Shenanigans like these shaped MU into an unusual milieu. In most maximum-security settings, machismo prevails among staff, based on the premise that "We're tougher than them and we'll show 'em!" On MU, humor supplanted machismo. It provided a light, carefree atmosphere with enhanced security for all in a dreary and dangerous environment. Our goals were to manage aggressive behavior and prevent people from being hurt. We did not try to show the patients that we were tougher than they were, nor did we adopt the health care equivalent of this attitude by acting as though "We know what's best for you if you'll only comply." The king routine signaled to patients and staff early on that the normal channels and underpinnings of authority, power, and coercion could be abandoned at any time.

The evolution of MU's emotional tone is reflected in the logos of two MU staff T-shirts which were designed by front-line staff. The first shirt was issued 6 months after the ward opened. It depicted Popeye (with an "MU" across his shirt) saying "I'm strong to da finich 'cause I eats me spinach." Elements of machismo are present in Popeye's veiled threat, but the threat is expressed conditionally and Popeye is, of course, a friendly and likable character when the Brutuses of the world are not bothering him. The shirt's yellow color suggested the staff's early fears. The overall portrait is of a group that is not yet comfortable with the stress and insanity of its mission.

The second staff T-shirt was issued during MU's second year after many of its birthing dilemmas had been solved. The yellow color was changed to white. It depicted a cow saying "MU" (in place of "Moo"). Instead of playing on the tendentious theme of aggression, a different humor technique - a simple, homophonic pun on "MU" - was used. The macho image of Popeye the fighter was replaced by the nurturant symbol of a cow.

Such T-shirts of course reflect staff solidarity. *Esprit de corps* is a crucial therapeutic resource whenever the stress level of a venture increases and the likelihood of achieving objective success decreases. On MU several built-in features promoted team spirit and the in-group humor that nourished it. All management staff spent one 8-hour shift each week in the shoes of the front-line nursing staff. We called this practice "floorwalking." It was done during the 3:00 p.m. to 11:00 p.m. shift to help keep the night workers in touch with what the day staff were doing. When management staff floorwalked, they may have had to help wrestle patients into seclusion or clean up feces flung onto the walls. In return, the front-line staff handled a share of the managers' routine paperwork.

Ward business was conducted each day in the mid-afternoon, when the morning and evening shifts overlapped for an hour. The patients were locked in their rooms during this extended cross-shift period (a defensible practice in a maximum security setting) so that staff could mingle, heal each other, laugh together, and re-affirm their bonds without having to constantly look over their shoulders. These meetings took place in the smaller of the two dayrooms, a home territory from which sound would not travel down the hall to the patients' rooms. Through these meetings and the attendant humor which punctuated them, we developed our own definitions of a job well done among incorrigible patients. For example, a physically huge paranoid schizophrenic patient, who had once literally broken a staff member's face, was gradually "tamed" by the food we gave him as reinforcement for not being aggressive. He became sluggish and meek after gaining 80 pounds, and we congratulated ourselves for having "cured" him through our invention of "carbohydrate therapy."

The word "cure" was regularly abused to call attention to work well done that would either go unnoticed by an outsider or be considered an insignificant achievement anywhere else. When Alice Cooper was finally persuaded to mop up his floor after months of hoarding food under his bed, the staff member who had persuaded him to do it came to a cross-shift meeting and asked to be credited with a cure. We promptly applied our prevailing objective standards for that cure: We took a vote on it.

SYNTHESIS

This chapter has sought to legitimize the therapy of humor for those who work in stressful settings. Prevailing taboos that humor is unprofessional and that it signifies inappropriate acting-out must be more thoughtfully evaluated in the context of what is known about the excesses of unrelieved stoicism and self-restraint. Amidst a stressful environment complicated by reigning paradoxes and cognitive dissonance, a therapeutic team generates humor for short-term stress management and for long-term cohesiveness. This in turn helps to shape and maintain a collection of individuals as an in-group. Among such a team, "insider" humor can strengthen morale, satisfy security needs, and serve as both a language of emotional support and as a reinforcer amidst chronically difficult working conditions. Humor targeted "up" toward administrators or "down" toward patients can be part of a therapeutic milieu if practiced privately on the team's home territory where no motive to antagonize these out-groups can be inferred. Milieu humor is healthy when there is frequent rotation of targets to include the in-group itself and all of its members regardless of status position. Nicknaming patients "Big Mac" and "Blowhard" is balanced by nicknaming staff "Your Majesty" and "Lieutenant." Humor thus serves as a prophylactic and antidote for the phenomenon of burnout. However, if target rotation decreases or "sacred cows" are elevated, such humor loses its therapeutic value and may actually detract from the overall health of the milieu.

One might argue that this is all well and good, except that it is much ado about therapists when we should be concentrating on treating patients. I submit that such humor has *everything* to do with treating patients. Milieu humor fosters a humane environment for therapists which is passed on to the patients. Six years after its opening, MU shows many signs of success. The frequency and intensity of aggression has declined significantly over the years, and it has not yet become necessary to lock the ward down for a cooling-off period. All of MU's original "Dirty Dozen" patients (except for two with brain damage) have improved despite original dire predictions to the contrary. They now live in less restrictive environments where periods between their aggressive episodes are measured in months rather than hours. Interestingly, although all of them are now "tamed," their chronic mental illnesses persist. Thus MU appears to be effective in curtailing aggressive behavior but not in curing chronic mental illness - except in the staff's aforecited private sense of "cure." Moreover, the staff turnover rate on MU has been less than or equal to the turnover rates of three other less dangerous wards that were opened at the same time.

There are other signs of success. MU has attracted site visitors from several states and has spawned a number of training programs and publications. One site visitor representing the American Psychiatric Association nominated the ward for an APA Gold Medal Award. And it is worth noting that MU thrived as a therapeutic milieu despite the significant administrative travails that go along with being part of a state institution.

This is not to suggest that humor alone accomplished all of these things (see Kuhlman, 1988). However, it was humor that initially shaped a stressful ward into a unique social milieu, and it was also humor that cemented the cohesiveness of the ward in the face of chronic aggression.

REFERENCES

Alford, F. (1982, August). *The Evolutionary Significance of the Human Humor Response.* Paper presentation to the Third International Conference on Humor, Washington, DC.

Andrus Volunteers. (1983). *Humor: The Tonic You Can Afford.* Los Angeles: University of Southern California Press.

Coser, R. L. (1959). Some social functions of laughter. *Human Relations, 12,* 171-182.

Coser, R. L. (1960). Laughter among colleagues. *Psychiatry, 23,* 81-95.

Cousins, N. (1979). *The Anatomy of an Illness.* New York: W. W. Norton.

Ellison, K. W., & Genz, J. L. (1983). *Stress and the Police Officer.* Springfield, IL: Charles C. Thomas.

Freud, S. (1957). Humour. In J. Strachey (Ed. and Trans.), *Collected Papers* (Volume V). New York: Basic Books. (Originally, *International Journal of Psychoanalysis, 1928, 9,* 1-6)

Freud, S. (1960). *Jokes and Their Relation to the Unconscious* (J. Strachey, Trans.). New York: W. W. Norton. (Originally *Der Witz und Seine Beziehung zum Uhewussten.* [1905]. Leipzig & Vienna: Deuticke.)

Fry, W. F., Jr., & Salameh, W. A. (Eds.). (1987). *Handbook of Humor and Psychotherapy: Advances in the Clinical Use of Humor.* Sarasota, FL: Professional Resource Exchange.

Geison, G. (1983). Introduction. In G. Geison (Ed.), *Professions and Professional Ideologies in America* (pp. 1-5). Chapel Hill, NC: University of North Carolina Press.

Kubie, L. (1971). The destructive potential of humor in psychotherapy. *American Journal of Psychiatry, 127,* 861-866.

Kuhlman, T. L. (1984). *Humor and Psychotherapy.* Homewood, IL: Dow Jones-Irwin.

Kuhlman, T. L. (1985). A study of salience and motivational theories of humor. *Journal of Personality and Social Psychology, 49,* 281-286.

Kuhlman, T. L. (1988). Gallows humor for a scaffold setting: Managing aggressive patients on a maximum-security forensic unit. *Hospital and Community Psychiatry, 39,* 1085-1090.

Kuhlman, T. L., Green, J. R, & Sincaban, V. A. (1988). Dice therapy: Deterring the suicidal behavior of a borderline patient. *Hospital and Community Psychiatry, 39,* 992-994.

Larson, M. S. (1977). *The Rise of Professionalism.* Berkeley: University of California Press.

Lindsey, D., & Benjamin, J. (1981). Humor in the emergency room. In H. Mindess & J. Turek (Eds.), *The Study of Humor* (pp. 73-76). Los Angeles: Antioch University Press.

Loewenstein, R. (1958). Variations in classical technique: Concluding remarks. *International Journal of Psychoanalysis, 39,* 240-242.

Lyman, S. M., & Scott, M. B. (1967). Territoriality: A neglected sociological dimension. *Social Problems, 15,* 236-249.

Obrdlik, A. J. (1942). Gallows humor: A sociological phenomenon. *American Journal of Sociology, 47,* 709-716.

Pogrebin, M. R., & Poole, E. D. (1988). Humor in the briefing room: A study of the strategic uses of humor among the police. *Journal of Contemporary Ethnography, 17,* 183-210.

Radcliffe-Brown, A. R. (1940). On joking relationships. *Africa, 13,* 195-210.

Radcliffe-Brown, A. R. (1949). A further note on joking relationships. *Africa, 19,* 133-140.

Schachter, S., & Singer, J. E. (1962). Cognitive, social, and physiological determinants of emotional state. *Psychological Review, 69,* 379-399.

3

Reflections on the Function of Humor in Psychotherapy, Especially with Adolescents

John L. Schimel

Dr. Schimel addresses the issue of oppositional patients, with special focus on the oppositional adolescent, who come into therapy not so much to obtain treatment but to test the therapist's limits and challenge his or her transferential cloak of authority. Dr. Schimel does respond to the challenge, while administering some healthy doses of "Victor's disease" to his patients in such a way that, in the end, the victory is the learning gained from the therapeutic process.

John L. Schimel, MD, is Associate Director of the William Alanson White Psychoanalytic Institute and maintains a private psychiatric practice in New York City. He is a past president of both the American Academy of Psychoanalysis and the American Society of Adolescent Psychiatry, and has authored over 150 publications including four books on the subject of adolescent clinical concerns.

❖　　　　❖　　　　❖

THEORETICAL PERSPECTIVE

Erich Fromm has pointed out that if the average psychotherapeutic session were filmed, the viewer might conclude that something momentous was going on, no matter how trivial the subject under discussion. It is this author's viewpoint that the use of humor can be the leaven of life, causing the recipient's spirits to lighten. In psychotherapeutic practice it may open the patient to a different view of his or her life situation, one that may seem less worrisome and hence facilitative of insight. Psychotherapy may then evolve into something less grim and threatening than it often is. Indeed, so-called insight accompanied by bitterness or rage may be seen to contain significant resistances. The use of humor and subsequent laughter can provide an opportunity for a guilt-free expression of aggressive and sexual impulses. It can serve self-esteem on a cognitive perceptual level in which "getting the joke" produces a sense of mastery over the symbolism and multi-leveled meanings. "Making the joke" provides a similar opportunity. There can be a creative dimension in humor because the synthesis of disparate levels of symbolism and meaning resulting in laughter parallels other creative acts. An example:

Patient: (Complaining) You always point out the positive aspects of everything.
Psychoanalyst: That isn't true.
Patient: Then what is true?
Psychoanalyst: I simply point out the areas you habitually neglect.

The result was laughter. Indeed the exchange highlighted for patient and psychoanalyst the patient's dour and unremittingly morose view of his life events.

The dialogue provided previously is an example of the use of wit. Wit is sharp, intellectual, clever, subtle, and not particularly kind, although not necessarily unkind. There is a linkage of ideas that gets through to the patient and results in laughter. It highlights the patient's depressive and obsessional preoccupation with the possibly negative aspects of his or her living. It links the patient's complaint about the analyst with his or her consistently complaining attitude in general. The consequence is laughter and a subsequent reduction in anxiety. The result is not necessarily insight but an opportunity for insight. We cannot teach; we provide an opportunity for learning. The working through, consensual validation, and repetition necessary for functional insight is still required.

The insight alluded to in the humorous remark and confirmed by the laughter must subsequently be clarified in everyday terms. Therapist and patient can then agree on the actual meaning of the insight, a process referred to as the "working through." Repetition of the material is usually required because with patients of all ages some insights tend to be forgotten. One often hears a patient remark something like, "I see what you mean. We really have discussed this before but I seem to have forgotten it." The agreement and subsequent applications of the insight by the patient results in a state referred to as "consensual validation."

Humor, as contrasted to wit, implies broader human sympathy than does wit. It is more kindly and may even be combined with pathos. It conveys an appreciation of the patient's thorough humanity. Webster's dictionary defines humor as "the mental facility of discovering, expressing, or appreciating ludicrous or absurdly incongruous elements in ideas, situations or acts."

Ogden Nash wrote:

What is life? Life is stepping down a stair
Sitting in a chair
And it isn't there.

TECHNIQUE

My use of humor, I believe, is inherent in my makeup and my capacity to recognize the absurdity in many of life's contretemps. My awareness of my use of humor became sharpened by an encounter with an esteemed psychoanalytic supervisor, Frieda Fromm-Reichmann, author of *Principles of Intensive Psychotherapy* (1950). One day she timidly asked me if I were Jewish. I readily confessed, wondering what would come next. She went on, "I've observed a kind of wry humor in your remarks to your patients that I associate with Jewishness." That statement worried me. I decided not to give up being Jewish, but rather to become more aware of such usage and its effects on my patients. Over the years, I attempted to become adept in using humor in an ameliorative and nonthreatening manner.

The foregoing is a personal illustration of how the therapist's persona - his or her appearance, dress, accent or lack of accent, office decor, and, most importantly, level of discourse - affects the patient. From this perspective, all the patient's productions can be viewed as artifacts, as ways of relating to his or her (often unconscious) perceptions of the therapist's persona. The use of traditional wry Jewish humor on my part has had a perceptible effect on many of my patients.

PERTINENT USES

Lawrence Kubie (1971) warned against the possible destructive use of humor. It was only after many years of practice, he believed, that a therapist could use humor in a nondestructive manner. I do not believe the therapist must grow old or even wait until well into the psychotherapeutic process to be able to use humor constructively.

As with all therapeutic modalities, a process of trial and error, with perhaps some mishaps along the way, is required. One can learn, with experience, to become more adept at this strategy.

CLINICAL PRESENTATIONS

CASE 1

A middle-aged white female social worker, in her initial psychotherapeutic interview, was nervously asking her therapist a series of questions about his beliefs and practices, presumably following some approved instruction for finding out about the qualifications of the therapist. She knew perfectly well who and what he was from her referral source. The following encounter took place:

Patient: Do you do brief psychotherapy?
Psychoanalyst: All the time.
Patient: But you are a psychoanalyst.
Psychoanalyst: Sometimes it takes a little longer.

The patient was taken aback. She laughed. The interchange became a leitmotif of her subsequent therapy. She referred to it often. It had spotlighted her worrisome approach to life situations. It also alerted her to the fact that there was another person in the room to whom she had better attend. She had previously worked with therapists whose contributions she had quite devalued and ignored.

The patient had come to realize that there was someone else in the consulting room besides herself. Psychotherapy is not a soliloquy. It is a process that should actively involve two people, actively searching out the whys and wherefores of living.

The patient subsequently requested postponing payment for her therapy sessions because her only resources were sequestered in an interest-bearing account. She did not want to interrupt her financial plan or lose any interest. She assured her therapist that she was a responsible person and would certainly take care of her obligation to him in time. She demanded:

Patient:	Isn't that fair?
Psychoanalyst:	No, it isn't fair.
Patient:	Well, why not (Belligerently)?
Psychoanalyst:	You will be earning interest that I will be losing.
Patient:	(Laughing) I hadn't thought of that. But isn't it reasonable?
Psychoanalyst:	No.
Patient:	(Laughing) I think I see what you mean.

The course of treatment was frequently stormy for this patient. However, we shared frequent subsequent references to the aforecited encounters and how they had highlighted her difficulties with spouse, in-laws, and children. She came to some appreciation of her aggressive and demanding manner with the significant others in her life and the ultimate absurdity of her belligerence.

CASE 2

Humor, as well as other psychotherapeutic interventions, must be tailored to the patient's age, intelligence, and life situation.

The following encounter took place with a female adolescent who was breathlessly recounting a series of painful encounters with other girls in her dormitory. She had reported how selfish, inconsiderate, and rude they were to her. It all sounded very familiar. The therapist interrupted:

Therapist:	(Bored) So what else is new?
Patient:	You mean I've done this bit before.
Therapist:	Many times.
Patient:	But it undermines me. How can I be sure of myself with all this going on? I have to feel certain before I can do anything.
Therapist:	No you don't.
Patient:	But it's true. Some people do feel *absolutely* certain. They have confidence in themselves.

Therapist: When we find people who are *absolutely* certain we lock them up.

Patient: You mean that's crazy. But some people are more sure of themselves. Mary always seems sure of herself.

Therapist: Maybe you don't know her very well. Everyone is uncertain at times.

Patient: Many of my friends are like me, scared of their own shadows. Maybe I should try new friends.

Therapist: It might be a good idea. Anyway, if you really need someone you can always count on, you can try God.

Patient: I've been trying to get a date with Him, but He's all booked up. But, really it's hard to do things you're afraid of or that you don't like doing.

Therapist: People do it all the time.

CASE 3

A very competitive prowess-oriented adolescent who happened to be both a great athlete and an intelligent youngster started the hour in a gloomy mood and recounted a number of personal defeats.

Patient: And not only that, but I'm feeling lousy. I had to go to the doctor.

Therapist: What's wrong?

Patient: I have Victor's Disease.

Therapist: Congratulations. What did you win this time?

Patient: I didn't win anything. I have sore gums, ulcers, the doctor said. He was surprised. He said only poor people, who are malnourished, get it.

Therapist: Oh, that's Vincent's Disease.

Patient: I can't believe it. You've been telling me I'm too busy with who's on top. Victor's Disease. So that's my problem.

In my experience, few adolescents are so damaged that they cannot appreciate humor or cannot laugh, even at themselves. Humor can facilitate the process of acquiring insight. Most importantly, it makes the patient feel good rather than sad, troubled, or lugubrious.

The foregoing vignettes can be examined from a number of other viewpoints. They demonstrate interventions that change the character of the therapeutic encounter toward a more thoughtful climate. They permit a broader perspective from which to view the patient's concerns. They facilitate access to introspection and insight. Such interventions tend to push the inquiry away from the gloomy, overly serious, and dark outlook on life that characterizes many adolescents and some therapists.

It is well to wonder when listening to an encounter being reported by an adolescent how he or she might relate the same material to a peer. Many adolescents have a stereotyped mode of relating to adults that may markedly contrast with their conduct toward peers. An incident related to an adult may bear little resemblance to the same matter related to a peer and lead to inaccurate psychodynamic formulations. An adolescent girl, apparently grief-stricken, and filled with feelings of guilt and fear about the possibility that she had become pregnant, began to laugh through her tears when asked if she had told any of her girlfriends. Yes, she said, she had bragged to several because she was the first in her peer group to have had sexual intercourse. She had long discussions with them about her wish to raise the baby, if she were indeed pregnant.

SYNTHESIS

The use of wit and humor requires close attention to the use of language, a shrewd anticipation of the effect of humor on the patient, and a constant monitoring of his or her anxiety level. The successful use of wit and humor requires that simple, direct, pithy, earthy, and colloquial speech be employed. Above all, therapists must be themselves and avoid stilted or pompous language. They must also not stoop to gutter-level language that certain patients may find entirely inappropriate for a professional to use, therefore turning the therapist off in the encounter.

Perhaps the greatest benefit of the use of wit and humor in the treatment of adolescents and other patients is that it offers an opportunity to acquire a sense of mastery. Patients who have learned to laugh at behaviors that once troubled, angered, or embittered them or filled them with guilt or shame are no longer the same after the laughter experience. They have had new experiences in sharing and have learned something about new and nonthreatening behavior in human encounters. A shared laugh can communicate a feeling of liking and regard for each other.

The preceding should not be construed as magic or a new school of psychotherapy. Without careful monitoring of the psychotherapeutic situation, the use of humor may be counterproductive. Properly employed, however, wit and humor may tap into the patient's liveliness and even exuberance in exploring human motivation and behavior. A good laugh helps.

In discussing the uses of humor in psychotherapy before audiences in various parts of the country, a number of interesting observations were made by members of the audience, which are summarized herein.

A number allowed that they were humorous in the treatment situation but did not report it to teachers or colleagues. One therapist said he thought that the use of humor in psychotherapy was frowned on by the "establishment." There were references to Kubie's (1971) article condemning the use of humor in the practice of psychotherapy. A surprising number reported that they utilized humor but were afraid to mention it to fellow professionals. One may conclude that the use of humor in the practice of psychotherapy is fairly widespread, more than one might surmise from verbal and published reports of the process of psychotherapy. One esteemed colleague wrote me that she wished she had been more forthright in her recently published book. She had advised her readers to be "light" in their handling of the psychotherapeutic encounter but had not dared to pursue the subject further.

It is true that some patients may resent even the most innocuous use of humor. It may have to be worked through. One adolescent patient, the veteran of several previous psychotherapeutic encounters, admonished me when he first heard me laugh during a session. "You guys aren't supposed to do that."

It can be important for the therapist, as well as the patients, to enjoy the work. Several of my supervisees have stated that what they had learned from me was how to enjoy the practice of psychotherapy.

In this communication, I have tried to indicate something of the process involved in the use of humor in psychotherapy with patients, particularly adolescents. The uses and caveats have been indicated as well as the need for attention to the ambiance of the psychotherapeutic encounter, including timing, manner of presentation, and, above all, language.

REFERENCES

Bateson, G. (1969). The position of humor in human communication. In J. Levine (Ed.), *Motivation in Humor*. New York: Atherton Press.

Bruch, H. (1988). *Conversations with Anorexics*. New York: Basic Books.

Cousins, N. (1976). Anatomy of an illness (as perceived by the patient). *New England Journal of Medicine, 295,* 1458-1463.

Fromm-Reichmann, F. (1950). *Principles of Intensive Psychotherapy*. Chicago: The University of Chicago Press.

Fry, W. F., Jr., & Salameh, W. A. (Eds.). (1987). *Handbook of Humor and Psychotherapy: Advances in the Clinical Use of Humor.* Sarasota, FL: Professional Resource Exchange.

Grotjahn, M. (1957). *Beyond Laughter.* New York: McGraw-Hill.

Kubie, L. (1971). The destructive potential of humor in psychotherapy. *American Journal of Psychiatry, 127,* 861-866.

Levine, J. (1969). *Motivation in Humor.* New York: Atherton Press.

Schimel, J. (1978, July). The function of wit and humor in psychoanalysis. *Journal of the American Academy of Psychoanalysis, 6,* 369-379.

Schimel, J. (1986). Psychotherapy with adolescents: The act of interpretation. In S. Feinstein (Ed.), *Adolescent Psychiatry.* Chicago: University of Chicago Press.

4

Favorite Jokes and
Their Use in Psychotherapy
with Children and Parents*

Atalay Yorukoglu

A little bit of the child must come out in therapists if they are to relate to children who come to them for treatment. In discussing the use of humor in his psychotherapeutic work with children, Dr. Yorukoglu's own warm, accepting, and gentle child emerges - a smiling and wise child who can protect as well as enlighten the younger children coming to play with him. Through the tool of humor, Dr. Yorukoglu is able to help children open up and speak about their fears and family heartaches. By asking the children what their favorite jokes are, he starts at the ground floor, exactly where the children are, understanding their concerns and quickly delineating their conflicts. He then includes the parents in the therapeutic process by offering them their children's jokes as a symbolic vehicle for heightening parental awareness of the childrens' dilemmas. Given the nonthreatening and humorous way in which family conflicts are presented, the parents seem to respond positively toward the resolution of the family problems at hand.

Atalay Yorukoglu, MD, is currently Chief of the Child and Adolescent Psychiatry division at Hacettepe University Medical School in Ankara, Turkey; maintains a private psychiatric practice in Ankara; and has previously served as an expert adviser to the World Pediatric Association. Dr. Yorukoglu is considered the "Dr. Spock" of Turkey. His first book, Child Mental Health *(1979), won the First Award of the Institute of Turkish Language and has been reprinted 15 times thus far. He has also written* Child and Family in a Changing Society *(1983) and* Emotional Problems of Adolescence *(1985), and is co-author of a textbook entitled* Mental Health and Mental Illness *(1981). He is currently working on a book dealing with his favorite subject:* Sense of Humor and Mental Health.

*I wish to express my appreciation to Dr. Waleed A. Salameh for his valuable comments and editorial help as I was developing my manuscript.

THEORETICAL PERSPECTIVE

I view humor, like love, as a favorite catalyst for molding human relationships. Humor enables us to communicate better with others and with ourselves. Through wit and humor, we express an endless variety of thoughts and feelings in a socially acceptable manner. Humor helps us to discharge our tensions, reduce our anxiety, and overcome our frustrations. It gives us freedom from our inner restraints and rigid moral judgments. By releasing us from our conventional logic, it makes us more tolerant of human flaws in others and in ourselves. Humor affords us a victory over reality. This victory may be temporary, but it renews our inner strength and kindness. Humor and wit, by removing our masks of pretense, dare us to look into the human heart as it is. Humor is not a form of escaping reality; rather, it is a playful way of perceiving and evaluating reality. Needless to say, life without humor would be unbearably dull.

Goethe has stated that: "A mature man is someone who can laugh at himself," implying that the ability to laugh at one's own weaknesses is a sign of mental health. As a reflection of a flexible ego, a sense of humor sometimes becomes a mind-saving adaptation to the stresses of life. Therefore, I believe that humor is essential to our mental health, and that we can effectively use it to ameliorate our patients' suffering. Psychotherapists have long dealt with emotions like fear, worry, anger, and sadness, but they often have neglected such an essential emotion as humor. Only recently have we begun to realize the potential of humor as a psychotherapeutic tool.

Back in the 1960s, during my psychiatric training in the United States, I was exposed to and fascinated by dynamically oriented psychotherapy. While avidly reading Freud, I tried to identify with my supervisors by assuming a neutral, empathic, and pondering attitude toward my patients. Whenever my patients made humorous remarks, I restrained myself from laughing or responding to them. I focused my attention on my patients' symptoms and negative emotions. At that time, I thought that psychotherapy was not a laughing matter, so I temporarily adhered to the sacred rules of psychotherapy and remained a good and understanding listener. I later noticed that, during my supervisory hours, I had been omitting the humorous exchanges that occurred between my patients and myself. Perhaps as a reaction to the grim and mirthless atmosphere of the psychiatric wards where I worked, I decided to study the humor appreciation of in-patients by using a battery of cartoons and jokes (Yorukoglu & Silverman, 1963).

When I entered my training in child psychiatry, I discovered that it was more fun working with children because they seemed to have a better sense of humor. During play therapy sessions, they told me jokes and funny stories, drew funny pictures, challenged me with riddles, and invited me to tell my own jokes. Subsequently, I felt that I had to take these humorous activities seriously, observe them carefully, and make use of them. Gradually, I became a more active participant in the children's humorous activities. Since 1964, I have collected hundreds of favorite jokes from children.

As pointed out by Freud (1905/1938, 1927/1950), humor is an important key for understanding dynamic forces within the human psyche. From a psychoanalytic point of view, all forms of humor provide us with a release of energy no longer needed for repressive purposes. The infantile pleasure enacted in playing with words serves to remove repression and suppression. Laughter occurs when energy used for repression is suddenly released.

Jokes disguise unconscious tendencies, expressing them in masked form through mechanisms such as distortion, condensation, and displacement. In jokes, as in dreams, the original tendency undergoes disguise and symbolization before it can break through into consciousness. Yet, unlike a dream, a joke is a social process. Moreover, it creates a bridge between unconscious and conscious processes. When a joke is successful, the aggressive impulse remains intelligible despite the disguise and can be perceived by the listener within a socially acceptable form. This element was stressed long ago by La Rochefoucauld, who noted that "Wit enables us to act rudely with impunity."

Through humor, we can master anxiety and relieve painful affects. Although a joke's source of pleasure may be in the release of aggression, the saving of emotion in humor also becomes pleasurable. In humorous attitudes, the superego treats the ego as a tolerant and understanding parent does his or her child, thereby permitting the ego to regress temporarily. Thus, humor signifies the triumph not only of the ego but also of the pleasure principle. In humor the ego turns away from harsh realities and enjoys a partial return to a guilt-free narcissistic stage. This triumph over reality, coupled with a momentary escape from the control of the superego, gives the individual a feeling of strength. Hence, humor can be conceived as the "loftiest" of all defense mechanisms. It may serve to ward off anxiety, or it may function as a mechanism of denial, regression, or sublimation.

The appreciation of humor is as varied as the different personalities of the individuals responding to it. As a personality trait, it is specific to every individual. Humorless individuals are usually thought of as rigid and inhibited persons with a cruel superego that forbids them the enjoyment afforded by humorous attitudes. Humorists or habitual jokers, on the other hand, are individuals who use humor exclusively as a defense mechanism.

Redlich, Levine, and Sohler (1951), using a "Mirth Response Test," investigated the humor responses of both neurotic and psychotic patients. They concluded that disturbances in humor behavior are associated with disturbances in other emotional areas. The degree of disturbance seemed to correspond to the patient's level of regression and to his or her capacity for reality testing. The humor behavior of neurotics seemed less disturbed than that of psychotics. In general, there was a close dynamic relationship between the patient's pathology and his or her humor preferences as well as his or her misunderstanding of cartoons and jokes. Yorukoglu and Silverman (1963), using a battery of cartoons and jokes, studied the humor appreciation of psychiatric patients and obtained similar findings.

Levine and Redlich (1955) showed how, in some instances, the failure to elicit a joke may represent a patient's attempt to protect himself or herself against awareness of unconscious strivings. For a person to avoid understanding a simple joke or cartoon, some denial-based intellectual or perceptual blocking must occur. Occasionally, disgust or open revulsion to humor suggests that the humor has touched off a strong emotional conflict. Grotjahn (1951) drew attention to the fact that jokes, like dreams, are easily forgotten:

> On hearing a joke, unconscious impulses in the listener are activated, but censorship requires their repression. The momentary release is a factor of enjoyment. Listening to a joke is a passive experience. Retelling it is an act of will and may require stricter censorship. The eruption of the repressed occurs at the moment of laughter; forgetting prevents the crime of retelling. By forgetting the joke we avoid the guilt of participation in an aggression, no matter how well disguised. (p. 193)

On the other hand, certain anxiety-provoking themes may become the subject of some preferred jokes. Zwerling (1955) noted: "The very themes most provocative of anxiety are precisely the subject of the jokes" (p. 112).

Coriat (1939), Brill (1940), and Grotjahn (1957) seem to have been among the first therapists to observe that some patients under analysis tell jokes, make witty remarks, or exhibit humorous attitudes. The jokes that spontaneously appear during the flow of free associations may contain the key to understanding what the patient wants to express. They may be closely linked to the patient's conflicts or related to transference reactions.

CHILDREN'S HUMOR

Children under age 6 usually cannot enjoy jokes. They prefer to tell funny stories that they personally invent. They are fascinated with rhymes and like playing with words. They also have a keen sense of the comic. They seldom miss anything funny or unusual about people around them. Different shapes, appearances, movements, or character traits will strike them as funny. They are very amused when they see people fall or objects break. They frequently tease each other, kid around, giggle, and laugh.

Jokes call for abstract thinking and a peculiar logic that is acquired following the onset of latency. In fact, at the latency stage, children suddenly develop a great interest in hearing and telling jokes. During latency, children enjoy riddles because of their double meaning and verbal play aspects. By constantly repeating riddles, they test the intelligence of their peers as well as that of grownups. When the answer is not right, they laugh victoriously and feel superior. At this age, children are especially interested in joking riddles concerning the behavior of a "dumb guy" or "little moron" because they are preoccupied with the question of who is smart and who is dumb. Jokes are initially appealing to them because they find jokes cognitively challenging. Also, at this age children begin to realize that humor is a socially acceptable form of discharging aggression, tension, and frustration. Certain jokes that correspond to their emotional conflicts are enjoyed most and become repeatable. As Wolfenstein (1953) noted: "The child who has found in joking a particularly valuable device for solving emotional difficulties is apt to gain a quicker mastery of the joke technique" (p. 170). From an early age, children try to ease their anxiety through joking. They thus transform the painful into the enjoyable, and turn impossible wishes as well as the envied "big-ness" and power of adults into something ridiculous. They seek relief through mockery. Wolfenstein (1954) pointed out that "They seize with delight on the opportunities to show that the grown-ups are not infallibly good" (p. 45).

Despite an abundance of published literature dealing with humor appreciation in children, there are few studies concerning the humorous behavior of children during the psychotherapeutic session. Wolfenstein (1954) gives an interesting example of joke inventing during therapy by a 10-year-old boy who had a learning difficulty:

> Alfred felt humiliated that he had to work with me be-cause of learning difficulties and was worried that I might consider him defective. One day he came in with his jacket and cap on backwards and remarked nonchalantly: "Some people think I'm backward. Isn't that ridicu-lous?" . . . Through the double meaning of "backward" he has discovered a way of transforming his present difficul-ty into a more childish one which need not be taken seri-ously. (p. 50)

Wolfenstein does not say whether she made use of this joke as a tool of interpretation.

Tolor (1966) noted that, in therapy, "Joke-telling implies an ability of the child to assert himself and to display his growing mastery over affect-laden material" (p. 296). Aichhorn (1935) reported that he told jokes to delinquents by way of making an in-troduction, which afforded him an opportunity to size up the sit-uation and establish a good contact with the youths being inter-viewed. Harms (1941) used children's drawings as a diagnostic aid during clinical interviews. By having children draw comical or funny pictures, he encouraged them to verbalize their fears and thoughts in a relaxed atmosphere. Shaw (1961) stressed the im-portance of a humorous attitude on the therapist's part in conduct-ing diagnostic and therapeutic interviews with children:

> In the course of a humor-oriented interview, the child will often discuss subjects or express thoughts that he would never approach in a more direct or sober type of inter-view. He seems to feel that he is on a safer ground, that

there is a kind of pact between him and the examiner, that there is a person who can meet him on his own level. (p. 378)

TECHNIQUE

At an appropriate moment in the first few interviews, during a discussion of the children's various interests, I ask them what kinds of things make them laugh, and whether they like funny stories or jokes. The answer is usually in the affirmative. Then I inquire about their family's attitude toward joking; what they laugh about, how often they share laughter, and who is funny in the family. After such an introduction, I encourage them to tell me the "favorite," "best," or "funniest" joke they have heard or read. If the joke turns out to be their last or "most recently heard" joke, I ask them to remember their favorite one. I write down the child's favorite joke exactly as he or she narrates it. After sharing the laughter I say to the child: "That was a good joke. I enjoyed it very much. Now tell me what strikes you as funny about this joke?" Then I may tell him or her what part I myself enjoyed most. If the child is hesitant about reporting his or her favorite joke, I may "break the ice" by telling a joke or asking a joking riddle such as: "Which president wears the biggest hat?" The majority of Turkish children come up with the same answer: "Ataturk" to which I reply "No, the one with the biggest head!" Encouraged by my humorous approach, children either remember their favorite jokes later in the hour or eagerly bring them up in the next session. If the dynamic meaning of the favorite joke is obvious to me, I may point this out to the child right away and discuss the joke with him or her: Why do you like this joke best? Does this joke remind you of someone or something that happened to you? Then I ask the child's permission to mention it in my interview with his or her parents.

PERTINENT USES

The exposure to humor as well as the age and intelligence of the child are important determining factors in a child's acquisition of a favorite joke. Therefore I ask only primary school-aged and older children with an age range of 7 to 16 to tell me their favorite jokes. As previously discussed, preschoolers usually cannot enjoy jokes; instead, they talk about funny things or tell funny stories they make up. It must be noted that not all children report a favorite joke. Of all the children I have worked with, one-fourth were usually able to tell a favorite joke. The ratio was somewhat higher in children I was seeing in long-term psychotherapy. The number of boys who told jokes was about double that of girls. Even when we consider the high ratio of girls over boys in an outpatient clinic population, the difference is still disproportionately in favor of boys. This finding lends credence to the common belief that women generally tell fewer jokes than men.

Asking a child whether he or she is interested in jokes or funny stories is the safest way of achieving rapport, provided that the right moment is chosen. With children who have recently undergone a trauma or suffered a loss in the family, the favorite joke approach should be used at a later and more appropriate time. Needless to say, the favorite joke approach may not be productive with distrustful or mute children. Overall, in my experience, this approach cannot possibly have any destructive effect on the therapeutic relationship, even if the therapist fails to elicit a favorable response from the child. However, the therapist should always be in tune with the child's mood as to the timing for introducing humor. If the child does not report a favorite joke in the first few sessions, the same approach can be attempted at a later time once a firm therapeutic rapport has been established.

CLINICAL PRESENTATIONS

CASE 1

Kaan, an 11-year-old boy, was referred to the Child Psychiatry Clinic because of daydreaming and sadness. The family history revealed that Kaan had suffered from chorea minor a few months ago, which was successfully treated. When he initially contracted the illness, his symptoms were so severe that he could not hold a spoon or walk straight. His entire family was understandably very worried about him, thinking that Kaan would remain paralyzed for the rest of his life. The mother stated that her son's symptoms subsided rapidly, but that his moodiness and irritability persisted. He lost interest in all the activities he had previously enjoyed and was reported to be daydreaming frequently in the classroom. Prior to his illness, he had been a cheerful and well-adjusted boy.

During the first interview with me, Kaan looked tired and sad. I remarked that he looked unhappy so he must be worrying about something. Without denying it he said: "Yes I worry about dying all the time." When asked why, he proceeded to tell me how the family's neighbor, a healthy young man, had suddenly died. I replied: "Since you yourself had been ill for a few months, you must have been afraid of dying?" Kaan stated: "Yes, I was scared to death! My mom cried a lot and stayed by my bed every night. Besides, nobody, not even the doctors, told me anything about my illness." I reassured him that, although very distressing, his illness was not a dangerous one and that his recovery was complete: "It's all over, you can cheer up now! Now I will ask you a riddle and you will tell me your favorite joke. Which president wears the biggest hat?" "I give up." "The one with the biggest head!" Kaan then told me the following joke:

One day Nasreddin Hodja* died. They put him in a coffin. Then his relatives and friends began to argue about which side of the coffin people should stand next to. At that moment, Hodja stuck his head out of the coffin and said: "It doesn't matter where you stand as long as you're not in it!"

We both laughed loudly. Then I remarked: "Kaan, I thought the subject of death was over. Now you bring it up again, this time in the form of a joke. Now I realize how really scared you had been. But I am happy to see you laugh about it!" I subsequently invited Kaan's parents in. I summarized to the parents what Kaan and I had discussed. I asked Kaan to repeat his favorite joke, which he did. We all laughed again!

Another child, a 10-year-old girl with many worries and a fear of death, reported the following Nasreddin Hodja joke as her favorite:

Someone asked Hodja: "Hodja, tell me when will people stop dying?" Hodja replied: "When Heaven becomes full!"

As I have indicated in a previous publication (Yorukoglu, 1974), the favorite joke in such cases seems to serve primarily as

---

*Nasreddin Hodja is a beloved Turkish folkloric figure and "wise fool" to whom innumerable jokes are attributed.

a counterphobic device and a denial mechanism to ward off the child's anxiety.

CASE 2

Turgut, a boy of 11 and the oldest of two children, was brought in because of lying, stealing, and poor school performance. His father described him as a smart but mischievous boy who had been spoiled by his grandmother for the past 8 years. When the grandmother left the family to live elsewhere with her daughter, Turgut's behavior started to change dramatically. He started to take money from his mother's purse and harass his 5-year-old sister, thus provoking his mother until he got a spanking from her. The mother was a high-strung woman who openly favored her daughter, stating that raising girls is much easier. The mother-in-law's presence at the family's home was a constant source of tension and quarrels between Turgut's parents. Turgut's mother would frequently argue with his grandmother over the grandmother's overprotectiveness of Turgut. Following the grandmother's departure, the marital conflicts diminished, but Turgut's behavior worsened. As a result of losing his best ally, the youngster became more demanding and unmanageable. The mother accused her husband of encouraging the boy's misbehavior by taking a passive approach. The mother would get so furious with Turgut at times that she would first spank him and then insult her husband for not doing anything about his son's misbehavior. Around this time, Turgut wrote a letter to his grandmother and his aunt begging them to adopt him as their son.

During the first interview, when asked to draw a man, he drew a picture of a person without arms. He stated that this man was raised by his aunt after his mother died. It was obvious that Turgut felt he had been rejected by both his grandmother and his mother. His misbehavior, which was motivated by his awareness of this rejection, invited further rejection from his mother. His anger at his mother was clearly manifested by his stealing from her purse. Turgut's favorite joke was the following:

> Nasreddin Hodja was lying in his bed and was about to die. He whispered in his wife's ear: "Please put on your wedding gown and come here." His wife, astonished, asked: "Why on earth do you want to see me in my wedding gown at such a time?" Hodja replied: "When the

Death Angel comes to take me, He (or She?) may like you in it and take you away instead of me!"

At first glance, this joke pointed to the deadly hostility the husband harbored for his wife. But it also reflected Turgut's intensely negative feelings toward his mother whom he perceived as an unloving and rejecting individual. He identified himself with the armless man who was raised by his aunt rather than by his mother. Bringing up Turgut's joke in the initial interviews with the family members would not have helped to improve family relationships, so its use was postponed.

CASE 3

Hakan, a 9-year-old boy, was referred because of facial tics of 2 years' duration. According to his parents, these tics appeared shortly after Hakan fell into a dry well. He was described as a restless and naughty boy. The mother, who had been previously treated for anxiety attacks, was a nervous woman who resented her role as a housewife. She repeatedly complained that Hakan never listened to her. On the other hand, Hakan constantly tried to get his mother's attention by teasing and clowning. She would lose her control and spank him, then cry out of desperation. When the father came home, Hakan became very docile and quiet. The father, a stern-looking school teacher, was a disciplinarian feared by everyone at home, including the mother. He spoke very little and rarely laughed. Interestingly, the father was also Hakan's teacher at school. In order to set an example for the rest of the class, he treated his son harshly and forced him to study harder. Furthermore, Hakan's classmates made fun of him, stating that his father gave him special treatment! In the first interview, I asked Hakan if he had a favorite joke. He related the following joke to me:

One day, an army officer took his soldiers to visit the house of Nasreddin Hodja. The house had only one wall yet the entry door had a big lock! So the officer told his soldiers: "If any of you can come out of the house without laughing, I will grant him a 2-month leave of absence." One soldier came out without laughing. But that night the same soldier woke up laughing loudly. He laughed so long and so hard that his fellow soldiers could not stop him. Finally, when asked what made him laugh so much, he replied: "I had a dream about Nasreddin Hodja sitting backwards on his donkey." Then he started to laugh again. The officer then told the soldier that he lost the reward.

In the joke, the authority figure, namely the officer, asks his soldiers to suppress a most natural emotional reaction, expecting the impossible from them. This joke was certainly an excellent caricature of Hakan's rigid and harsh father. Following a shared laugh, I asked Hakan if the officer in the joke reminded him of someone else. He said "my father!" We both laughed again. I remarked: "Like the soldier in the joke, it seems like you cannot please your daddy no matter how hard you try." During the interview with the parents, I brought up Hakan's joke. The father laughed for the first time in my presence, expressing his surprise; "Hakan told you that joke?" "Of course he told me the joke. He would not dare tell jokes in your presence!" The three of us laughed again. The mother was very happy about the relaxed atmosphere and took the opportunity to complain about her husband. My first suggestion was to change Hakan's class, stating that an authoritarian father and a disciplinarian teacher were too much for a 9-year-old boy to deal with. I also encouraged the father to increase his dialogue with his son.

CASE 4

Erol, an 11-year-old boy and the youngest of two children, was referred because of bellyaches, nervousness, and mischievous behavior. Erol's bellyaches dated back to his mother's abdominal surgery 3 years ago. Whenever he was upset or worried, he would start to complain of bellyaches. Erol was described as a very intelligent boy with many talents. Both at school and at home, he constantly tried to be the center of attention. For example, when he lost the election for class president, he was so upset that he did not go school for 2 days. When his wishes were denied he would scream, kick, and threaten his parents with running away from home. He cuddled up to his mother and wanted to sleep with her. The mother was a depressed woman with numerous psychosomatic complaints who had been previously followed in psychotherapeutic treatment. She stated that she had been unable to take care of herself, let alone give her boy the extra attention he sought. The older sister, with whom Erol was competing and clashing all the time, had also received psychiatric care due to excessive crying and lack of interest in school work. The father, a passive and tolerant man, reacted to Erol's temper tantrums by assuming a sarcastic attitude: "Good for you! Keep on kicking, throw some more things!" Both parents had been rather ineffective and inconsistent in their handling of their children. The mother tried to appease Erol by bribing him, while simultaneously undermining his striving for independence by always keeping him at home. During the first interview, Erol struck me as a bright and talkative boy. When asked to tell his favorite joke, he readily responded:

> Once there were four crazy fellows. One of them thought he was a bull, and the other three thought they were matadors. One day the guy who thought he was a bull saw a high tower and climbed up to the top of it. The three fellows below stretched a red blanket and started shouting "Jump, jump!" The bull jumped. Right at that moment, the three matadors shouted "Olé!" and pulled aside the blanket.

Erol apparently identified himself with the bull in the story. Being a restless boy, like the crazy "bull," he could not control himself. Yet when he expected to be controlled and helped to set limits, he could not find anyone to count on. Those who are theoretically in a position to help him turn out to be as "crazy" as he is. In a family where the other three members were in need of psychotherapeutic help, he did not know whom to turn to. With the help of this favorite joke, the parents were easily convinced that psychotherapeutic follow-up was needed for all family members.

CASE 5

Nilgun, a 9-year-old girl and an only child, was referred to the Child Psychiatry Clinic because of insomnia. Nilgun was described as an anxious and moody child who worried a lot and cried easily. She had always been stubborn and hard to please. In the past 2 months, she had difficulty falling asleep, frequently calling her mother to sleep with her. The parents noticed that she had also become reluctant to go to school, clinging to her mother.

Her parents had been arguing and quarreling since the beginning of their marriage. There had been frequent physical fights between them. The mother had fainted on numerous occasions during these quarrels, especially when physically abused by her jealous husband. In the past, the mother had left home many times, only to return in a few days. After a terrible fight 4 months prior to the current intervention, Nilgun's mother had left home and did not return for 2 months; no one knew where she was during this time period. Nilgun's insomnia dated back to her mother's returning home.

During the first interview with me, Nilgun looked depressed and unwilling to talk. With some encouragement on my part, she agreed to tell a story about a picture she drew. A girl with her arms stretched forward was running to meet her parents whom she had never seen before. When I remarked that "This girl must be the happiest child in the world," Nilgun said: "But she is not sure they will stay with her for long." At that juncture, I realized that I was dealing with an intelligent and sensitive girl. So I decided to be more careful about my remarks. Halfway into the interview, she opened up and started to talk about the fights at home. Nilgun said that both of her parents were sick! "They should go to see a doctor. Instead they brought me here." I remarked: "Maybe you are right. I am trying to get to know you and your parents. When there is so much going on at home, you can't possibly feel all right. In fact, you don't look very happy. You can't sleep well and you lost interest in school. You are a smart girl, and you know what is going on in the family. If you agree to come to the clinic regularly, we can try to find out what's going on inside you."

In the next therapy hour, Nilgun appeared relaxed and almost cheerful. When I asked her if she was interested in jokes, she said yes and reported the following:

> A child was running around his bed at night. His mother asked him why he was running like that. The child replied: "I lost my sleep and I am trying to catch it."

Nilgun obviously identified herself with the child in the joke. When I pointed out this similarity to her, she agreed with me. But when I remarked that she lost her sleep because her mother left home, she objected: "But my mom came back!" to which I replied "I think like the girl you drew you are also afraid that she might leave you again." With the help of this favorite joke, I explained to her parents the dilemma Nilgun was in and the reasons underlying her depression. They then accepted a psychotherapeutic plan for all family members.

CASE 6

Kaya, a boy of 14, was referred on account of lying and stealing. He was reported to be taking money from his mother's purse for the past few years. If he could not steal anything from home he would borrow some money from family friends, which he would spend on trivial items or to buy presents for his playmates. He mostly enjoyed playing with boys younger than himself. His school performance was poor, yet he did not seem too worried about it. The mother was a meticulous woman who shouted at Kaya constantly yet still could not get him to obey her. She fainted whenever she got very angry. The father was a passive and quiet man, unable to be firm with either of his sons. He saw Kaya's behavior as childish, yet did not think of Kaya as a bad boy. He stated that Kaya had slept in his parents' bedroom until the age of 5. During these early years, Kaya had been spoiled by his grandfather who was generous with pocket money.

Kaya's responses to the Thematic Apperception Test consisted of stories about robberies and stealing. In one of them he talked about "A fatherless boy who lived alone with his mother." Moreover, he drew a picture of a boy who, despite many hardships, managed to become a man of importance. Kaya, who did not seem to be a bright boy, was having difficulty controlling his impulses. His passive father and his narcissistic mother were not of much help to him in this regard. He appeared to vacillate between becoming a good boy and giving free rein to his infantile impulses. His favorite joke was this one:

A boy says to his father: "You know, Dad, today I stepped on a guy's foot and said 'I am sorry.'" His father says: "Very good, my boy, now suppose he gave you a dime when you said you are sorry, what would you do?" The boy replied: "I would step on the other foot and say I am sorry again!"

In this joke, the father is pictured as a man who gives conflicting messages to his son. And the boy's reply reflects his ambivalence concerning goodness and badness. As the joke concludes, the child's antisocial tendencies outweigh his desire to be good. With the help of this joke, the parents were advised to be more firm and consistent with Kaya. They favorably responded to therapeutic suggestions and cooperated with the therapist throughout the course of a brief therapy intervention lasting only six sessions.

CASE 7

Another boy of 13 was brought in because of behavior problems and school failure. His father was an episodic heavy drinker. In the first interview, the boy reported the following favorite joke:

> One day a man went to see a doctor about his drinking problem. The doctor advised him to limit his drinking to one shot per day. The man agreed and left the doctor's office only to enter a bar next door. The doctor passed by some time later and saw the man drinking. He asked him: "Didn't I tell you to drink no more than one shot per day?" The man replied "Yes you did. That is exactly what I am doing. I am drinking today all the shots you have prescribed for me for the next 30 days!"

When I took this joke up with the parents, the father went into an uncontrollable laughing fit. Encouraged by her husband's mirth, the mother started to complain about his excessive drinking. She stated that, like the man in the joke, he had promised to quit drinking several times yet never kept his word. The father said: "This time, Doc, I swear I will keep my word and accept your treatment plan." As the family never returned to the clinic, I still don't know whether the father kept his promise or visited the closest bar to celebrate the treatment plan!

CASE 8

Levent, a boy of 15, was referred to the Child Psychiatry Clinic because of slow learning and lack of self-confidence. When he was a baby, he had developed encephalitis following a smallpox vaccination. Subsequently his mental development was slow. At the time I saw him he was functioning at about dull normal intelligence. Nevertheless, he studied hard to keep up with his class-mates. He was described as a good-natured youngster who got along well with everybody. The mother's only complaint about him was that he lacked self-confidence and that he sometimes lost his personal belongings. The mother, who held herself responsi-ble for her son's slow development, had overprotected him to the extreme. In order to take better care of him, she did not want to have more children. She always helped him with his lessons, spending at least 2 hours with him daily. She felt that boys sometimes made fun of Levent's naïveté, which led her to restrict his social activities. She stated that she had also tried to protect him from bad company he may see around him. Although he played drums and basketball rather well, his mother also limited these activities so that they would not interfere with his studies. Levent rarely complained about his mother's restrictions.

During the first interview, Levent presented as a tall and childish-looking youngster who was eager to please the therapist. He boasted about how well he played basketball and stated that he planned to become a professional basketball player. He also said that he had many good friends and had no problems. When asked if he had a favorite joke, he said he knew a good one about "a dumb guy."

A dumb guy was walking down a street. All of a sudden he stumbled on a bottle. Smoke went up from the bottle and a genie appeared saying: "What is your wish, my master?" Surprised, the dumb guy replied "I only wish your pardon!"

This favorite joke hardly requires any interpretation. Being aware of his limited capacity, this youngster does not hope to achieve much. Moreover, like the man in the joke, he does not expect miracles, so he does not dare wish anything for himself. The good genie seems to represent his devoted mother who hovers over him and provides the best of everything for him.

For obvious reasons, the interpretation of the joke was omitted. My only remark was: "This guy must be a happy fel-low. He is content with what he already has!" Right after this in-terview, I invited the mother in and took up Levent's joke with her toward the end of the session. The mother reacted to it with a smile and tears in her eyes. She was then supported in her efforts to help her son. The youngster's need for acceptance by his peers was emphasized, and his mother agreed to let Levent play more basketball.

CASE 9

Aydin, an 8-year-old boy and the youngest of two children, was brought to the Child Psychiatric Clinic because of alopecia. Aydin was described as a very bright boy who was usually first in his class. Although he was not very active socially, he was well-adjusted and well-behaved at school. In contrast to his school behavior, he acted childishly at home. He was a picky eater, and demanded to sleep with his mother. He bit his fingernails and got along poorly with his older sister. When he was about 4 years old his sister started taking piano lessons. While his sister was practicing piano, he would watch her closely and insist on playing the piano as well, thus distracting the sister. Each time his parents pushed him away and told him not to bother his sister, Aydin would react by throwing a temper tantrum. About 6 months later, the parents noticed that Aydin could play the piano by ear. So they took him to a music teacher to test his talent and were told that the boy was exceptionally gifted. He was then placed on a rigorous piano training program. Aydin was reluctant to practice classical music, and enjoyed playing popular music instead. This triggered an ongoing battle between him and his parents. He would anger his parents by reverting to popular music in the midst of playing a classical piece. Around this time, his parents noticed that he had developed alopecia; he lost most of his crown hair within a period of 3 months.

During the first interview Aydin almost looked like a professional pianist with his bow tie and balding head. He was very polite and formal. He denied having any problems either in school or at home. His only complaint was that his parents did not allow him to play his favorite piano pieces. In order to soften his defensive attitude, I told him a few joking riddles, to which he responded with his own riddles. For him the exchange of riddles was a clash of wits rather than a sharing of humor. When asked if he had a favorite joke, he reported the following joke to me:

One day Nasreddin Hodja went to the market where he spotted a parrot for sale. He asked the man the price of the parrot, then ran home and came back with a turkey. The salesman asked him: "How much do you want for this turkey?" Hodja replied: "Two hundred liras!" "It is twice as expensive as my parrot. Mine talks like a man, what does yours do?" Hodja retorted: "Mine gobbles like a man!"

As this joke indicates, Aydin is rebelling against being trained like a parrot. He would rather be a freely gobbling turkey than a show animal. In other words, he is fighting for his freedom of choice. Let me note that Aydin has changed the joke's punch line. In the original version, the punch line is: "Mine thinks like a man!" Aydin's identification with the turkey is further illustrated by the fact that, in the Turkish language, the term "turkey" is also used to describe a "bald girl."

Once I was able to control my laughter, I told Aydin that I really enjoyed his joke. I further added: "I myself would prefer to be like a freely gobbling turkey than a parrot." I then tied his joke in with his resistance to playing classical music. He smiled and seemed relieved that he had finally met someone who understood his situation. When I took this up with his parents, who both happened to be well-educated people, they laughed heartily and got the message right away. Then we proceeded to discuss how to relieve Aydin from pressure without wasting his talent.

The following joke was recently reported by a 10-year-old severely obsessive-compulsive boy with numerous doubts and rituals who is currently in psychotherapy with one of my junior associates. I am sure the reader would not need to know more than this child's diagnosis to appreciate his well-fitting joke:

A boy went to see his doctor who prescribed him two kinds of pills in two different bottles. In one bottle there were red pills, in the other green ones. The red pills have to be taken before meals and the green ones after meals. The boy went home but forgot which pills to take before meals. So he called his doctor to ask. The doctor said: "Red pills before meals and green ones after meals!" The boy thanked him and hung up. But soon he was unsure of himself so he called his doctor again and again. After the fifth telephone call, the doctor was so furious that he shouted: "If you call me once again, I will come over and punch you in the nose!" After a while, the boy called his doctor up once more and asked: "Doc, when you punch me in the nose, will you do it before meals or after meals?"

I believe that the preceding favorite joke, if used properly, could be a most effective therapeutic tool. The joke may be used over and over again during the course of therapy, to show this boy the absurdity of his rituals and his resistance to change. Obsessive-compulsive children are besieged by their rigid Super-ego that dictates to them in black and white (or red and green!). Consequently, they think and act as if they are under a bad spell. They lack spontaneity and flexibility, and that is exactly why they need humor most. Through humor, we may be able to alter their grim outlook on life and free them from their crippling inhibitions. As Greenwald (1987) pointed out:

> The obsessive-compulsive outlook leads to a very un-humorous, grim way of looking at life. Although these patients are suffering from the grimness, from their compulsions, from their obsessiveness, it often helps for them to see the absurdity of that obsession. As they become aware of the absurdity of their undertakings, their obsessiveness appears to diminish. (p. 44)

I would like to add some explanatory clinical comments regarding the previous cases:

1. The favorite joke technique, as it is demonstrated in the cases presented above, can be very useful in elucidating child psychodynamics. In most instances, the favorite joke supports or verifies the dynamic formulation that the clinician has arrived at by other means of clinical evaluation. The joke also seems to emphasize the most important conflict that the patient is actually struggling with. In the majority of cases, the dynamic relationship between the favorite joke and the patient's emotional conflict can be clearly established. In some cases this relationship is amazingly striking. Additionally, in a few instances the favorite joke proves to be the only means of attaining a direct insight into an otherwise obscure conflict area. For example, a boy of 13, having reported two jokes in the first hour, said he knew another one that was really his favorite. He hesitated to tell it since it was not "a clean joke." Finally, he decided to tell his joke, which dealt with

the subject of masturbation. Before any interpretation was made, he confided to the therapist that he was preoccupied with masturbation and curious about sexual matters.

2. In general, the favorite jokes of neurotic children seem to differ in kind from those of children with behavioral problems. Many children with behavioral problems relate jokes that clearly indicate their antisocial tendencies. However, some neurotic children also tell jokes that reveal their conflicts about their aggressive impulses.

3. Children who come from families with acute or chronic marital discord generally tell jokes directly touching upon this area (Yorukoglu, 1977). This is best seen in the favorite joke told by Turgut (Case 2). An additional example will illustrate this proposition: I was interviewing a boy of 11 whose father had left home a few moths ago to live with a young woman. The boy reacted so strongly to his father's leaving that he developed behavior problems and his school performance went down precipitously. He even wrote letters begging his father to come back. But at home and in the interview he openly expressed his hatred and anger and claimed that he didn't want to see his father again, because his father preferred to live with a "whore." His favorite joke was about a flirting man who, while traveling, offers $10 to the lady sitting next to him if she would lift her skirt to show him her legs.

4. Children who have experienced a death in the family and those who have been preoccupied with the fear of death invariably tell jokes reflecting their anxiety in this area. In these cases, the favorite joke seems to serve as a counterphobic tool and denial mechanism to relieve the child's death anxiety. This finding confirms my previous observations (Yorukoglu, 1971) in working with children who have suffered a recent trauma or loss in the family. These children appear unaffected by the death of a loved one, and may even act gay and silly as if no one was missing at home. They may avoid asking questions or talking about the traumatic event. They try to master the anxiety generated by an overwhelming trauma by taking refuge in the mechanism of denial.

5. Another interesting observation is how some children distort well-known jokes (Case 9). These distortions, which are generally fueled by the children's unconscious needs, can al-

ter a joke's content to the extent that the joke is no longer funny.

6. Occasionally, after telling their favorite joke, some children volunteer to tell another joke they like. These "second-best jokes," curiously enough, are frequently complementary to the favorite one in indicating the unconscious conflicts. Some children ask me to tell them my favorite joke after they relate theirs, thus attempting to build rapport. Other children in treatment keep bringing in new jokes and riddles to their sessions. These children try to turn the therapeutic hour into an occasion for intellectual competition at sharing jokes.

7. Some favorite jokes deal with the anxiety secondary to the patient's symptom rather than with an underlying conflict. For example, a boy who stuttered told a joke that revealed his anxiety about his difficulty in uttering words: "A teacher asks a child to tell him the longest word. The student answers: 'rubber.' 'Why rubber?' asks the teacher. The child replies: 'Because you can stretch it as long as you want!' "

8. In a few instances, different children with similar conflicts report the same jokes to be their favorite ones. This observation further supports the theory that the selection of a favorite joke is not a random process, but is determined by similar unconscious needs. In a favorite joke the latent contents or forbidden impulses are sufficiently disguised to enable a particular child to repeat it without feeling guilty. The economy of expression makes a favorite joke a highly effective vehicle for discharging the inner tension. Because the selection of a favorite joke is a dynamic process, the favorite joke may, in time, be replaced by new and different jokes whenever different kinds of conflicts come to the foreground. Moreover, various types of preferred jokes may correspond to different conflicts experienced by a particular child.

9. With some children, the favorite joke technique gave immediate therapeutic results. A striking example of this is the case of Kaan (Case 1). Another good illustration is the case of a 12-year-old boy who, following a minor traffic accident, developed an acute fear of dying. His grandfather had previously died 30 days after a serious traffic accident. Instead of bringing in a joke, he read me a story he had written. This story concerned a boy who had lost his father in a war. The discussion of this story made it clear that the patient had a fear of dying in the same way that his grandfather had died.

Once this theme was interpreted, the boy's fears rapidly subsided.

10. The favorite joke can be utilized effectively as an interpretive tool with both children and parents. In fact, some children spontaneously volunteered the hidden connection between their favorite joke and their conflict. Moreover, they seldom resisted the therapist's comments about the close connection between the favorite joke and their problem. An interpretation in the form of humor has a distinct advantage over an intellectual one: It bypasses the resistance and the patient's censorship mechanism, thus leading him or her to laughingly accept the interpretation. Greenwald (1987) expressed this pointedly: "If humor is used properly the patient will laugh appreciatively because a chord of truth has been activated" (p. 45). Thus the insight gained through humor becomes a corrective emotional experience for the patient.

11. The discussion of the children's favorite jokes with their parents also proved to be most fruitful. All of them expressed their surprise and pride when the child's favorite joke was mentioned to them. They saw it as a sign of their child's cleverness. The joke, as concrete evidence of the child's conflict, enabled the parents to bridge to the child's level and achieve better empathy with him or her. In most instances, the parents quickly grasped the truth behind the joke, thus gaining better awareness of their own issues in a nonthreatening manner. They responded with smiles and laughter, and sometimes with tears in their eyes, yet rarely needed any lengthy interpretation. Consequently, their resistance to the therapist's suggestions was minimized and the way was cleared for further communication and cooperation. In other words, the favorite joke is not only a diagnostic tool but is also a spear used to pierce through the family's defensive armor and penetrate to the level of insight while pointing out constructive solutions to which the parents may be more receptive.

12. Adams (1982) has discussed the use of the favorite joke technique with children in psychotherapy:

> When it comes to the child's *favorite jokes*, the evidence is mounting that a device of great utility is at hand. Atalay Yorukoglu has found that the child's favorite joke furnishes the sensitive observer with a

> convenient index to the child's basic life setting,
> wrapping up his major conflicts in a neat package for
> us to open, helping the child. (p. 160)

Adams (1982) reports the favorite joke of a 10-year-old girl with an Oedipal attachment to her father. Her joke clearly recapitulated her central problems and cravings.

A child therapist cannot be neutral with children. He or she must be, first of all, a warm, congenial, concerned, and interested person. He or she should be an active participant in the therapeutic process, not a passive, pondering observer. A humorous attitude on the child therapist's part is a valuable asset that paves the road toward a good therapeutic alliance. A smiling, joking therapist is usually perceived by children as a warm and friendly person who is on their side.

The therapist who utilizes humor properly helps his or her patients gain a new outlook, a healthy coping device that makes them more resilient to the stresses of life. Salameh (1987) has concisely emphasized this point: "The therapist who uses humor and encourages a healthy humorous perspective on the patient's part is indirectly inculcating a mechanism of attitudinal healing, a back-up (or back-off) system that can be expected to kick in during periods of distress to provide perspective, self-nurturance, and courage" (p. 201).

SYNTHESIS

My mother, who told me so many Nasreddin Hodja jokes during my childhood, once asked me to explain to her the meaning of psychotherapy. I tried to explain to her in nontechnical terms what I understood psychotherapy to be and what I was trying to achieve with my patients. She interrupted me and said: "I see what you mean, man takes away his fellow man's poison. You are trying to detoxify or purify your patients' souls." Since then, I have adhered to this poignant definition of psychotherapy as a detoxification process. And what better purifying agent than humor can one find in the service of therapy? We cannot cry or suffer with our patients, but we can certainly share laughter and enjoy humor with them. This makes us more human. Psychotherapy does not have to be a dull experience. Humor can add a fruitful dimension and vitality to the therapeutic interaction. Humor liberates us from the tyranny of pure logic and from our self-imposed inhibitions. It may help us to perceive life and our fellow human beings from a different angle, playfully but realistically. By refining our own sense of humor as psychotherapists, we can contribute a great deal to our patients' development of a healthy humorous outlook regarding themselves and life in general.

In psychotherapy, humor can be an invaluable tool to generate insight and improvement. If dreams are the royal road to the unconscious, then humor is a more enjoyable path, a shortcut to the human psyche. The voice of humor is gentle, yet it is penetrating and insight giving.

Nasreddin Hodja jokes are frequently reported by Turkish children as their favorite ones. This is because Turkish children are exposed to Nasreddin Hodja jokes from an early age. They learn to appreciate humor by hearing these jokes at home, at school, and everywhere else. For more than 5 centuries, Turks young and old have enjoyed the earthy humor of Hodja who was a teacher-priest and a folk philosopher. His jokes, witty remarks, and anecdotes have been repeated so often that they have become part of Turkish folklore. Because some of the best jokes were attributed to him, Hodja seems to symbolically embody Turkish humor itself. As a beloved figure, even the mention of his name is enough to make Turkish faces break into a grin of anticipation. He was unique in pointing out the ridiculousness in the "wise doings" of others as contrasted with the wisdom in his own "foolish doings." I would like to conclude with one of the best Hodja jokes, which is also one of my favorites:

> Hodja's mother-in-law fell into the water while crossing a river. Although the villagers went downstream in search of the body, Hodja insisted on going upstream. When asked why he was going in the wrong direction, Hodja replied: "If you knew her as well as I did, you would know what a contrary woman she was!"

REFERENCES

Adams, P. L. (1982). *A Primer of Child Psychotherapy*. Boston: Little, Brown and Company.

Aichhorn, A. (1935). *Wayward Youth*. New York: Viking.

Brill, A. A. (1940). The mechanism of wit and humor in normal and psychopathic states. *Psychiatric Quarterly, 14,* 731-749.

Coriat, I. H. (1939). Humor and hypomania. *Psychiatric Quarterly, 13,* 631-688.

Freud, S. (1938). Wit and its relation to the unconscious. In A. A. Brill (Ed. and Trans.), *The Basic Writings of Sigmund Freud* (pp. 633-805). New York: Modern Library. (Original work published 1905)

Freud, S. (1950). Humour. In J. Strachey (Ed. and Trans.), *Collected Papers* (Vol. 5, pp. 215-221). London: Hogarth Press. (Original work published 1928)

Greenwald, H. (1987). The humorous decision. In W. F. Fry, Jr. & W. A. Salameh (Eds.), *Handbook of Humor and Psychotherapy: Advances in the Clinical Use of Humor* (pp. 41-54). Sarasota, FL: Professional Resource Exchange.

Grotjahn, M. (1951). The inability to remember dreams and jokes. *Psychoanalytic Quarterly, 20,* 284-286.

Grotjahn, M. (1957). *Beyond Laughter.* New York: McGraw-Hill.

Harms, E. (1941). The child's art as an aid in diagnosis of juvenile neurosis. *American Journal of Orthopsychiatry, 11,* 191-209.

Levine, J., & Redlich, F. C. (1955). Failure to understand humor. *Psychoanalytic Quarterly, 24,* 560-572.

Redlich, F. C., Levine, J., & Sohler, T. P. (1951). A mirth response test. *American Journal of Orthopsychiatry, 21,* 717-733.

Salameh, W. A. (1987). Humor in integrative short-term psychotherapy. In W. F. Fry, Jr. & W. A. Salameh (Eds.), *Handbook of Humor and Psychotherapy: Advances in the Clinical Use of Humor* (pp. 195-240). Sarasota, FL: Professional Resource Exchange.

Shaw, C. R. (1961). The use of humor in child psychiatry. *American Journal of Psychotherapy, 15,* 368-381.

Tolor, A. (1966). Observations on joke-telling by children in therapy. *Mental Hygiene, 50,* 295-296.

Wolfenstein, M. (1953). Children's understanding of jokes. *The Psychoanalytic Study of the Child, 9,* 162-173.

Wolfenstein, M. (1954). *Children's Humor.* Glencoe, IL: The Free Press.

Yorukoglu, A. (1971). Children's immediate reaction to death in the family. *Turkish Journal of Pediatrics, 13,* 72-84.

Yorukoglu, A. (1974). Children's favorite jokes and their relation to emotional conflicts. *Journal of American Academy of Child Psychiatry, 13,* 677-690.

Yorukoglu, A. (1977). Favorite jokes of children and their dynamic relation to intra-familial conflicts. In A. J. Chapman & H. C. Foot (Eds.), *It's a Funny Thing, Humour* (pp. 407-411). New York: Pergamon.

Yorukoglu, A., & Silverman, J. S. (1963). Responses of psychiatric patients to a battery of cartoons and jokes. *Psychiatric Communications, 6,* 9-16.

Zwerling, I. (1955). The favorite joke technique in diagnostic and therapeutic interviewing. *Psychoanalytic Quarterly, 24,* 104-115.

5

Humor in Substance Abuse Treatment

Michael Maher

Michael Maher is no strange duck. He is a committed professional who happens to enjoy duck jokes while being fully dedicated to the chemical dependency rehabilitation field. His use of the alcoholic's "drunk stories" illustrates a cogent viewpoint about the potency of humor for transforming apparently negative events into positive experiences. While the alcoholic's tragic stories are evidently saddening at one level, the fact that such stories are being reported within a recovery context and with the eye of at least partial hindsight allows for their constructive humorous utilization. The message is that it is preferable to laugh and gain perspective than to be immersed in tragedy and continue one's dysfunction.

Michael Maher is a certified addictions counselor and the founder and executive director of ACT NOW!, an outpatient alcohol and drug education program in San Diego, California. He also currently serves as a consultant to the chemical dependency treatment programs at Alvarado Parkway Institute (API) in La Mesa, California. After getting help for his own obsessive-compulsive behaviors, he began to work with others who were chemically dependent. Since 1983, he has been involved in the administration and development of new chemical dependency programs, primarily in hospital settings. He has also gained recognition for his ability to work with the impaired professional in the medical, legal, and ecclesiastic communities.

❖   ❖   ❖

THEORETICAL PERSPECTIVE

A Drunk Walks into a Bar and . . .

Since the beginning of time, or perhaps even before, and at least since the discovery of what could be done with the grape -

not including the California Raisin - humankind has enjoyed making fun of the drunk. Much laughter has been elicited by the humorous aspects of what drunks do, and how their drunkenness manifests itself. Moreover, the stressful situations drunks find themselves in, and the tragic aftermaths of episodic bouts of intoxication, have long been fodder for authors, playwrights, and pundits.

In starting my work with the chemically dependent over 15 years ago, I was immediately fascinated with this population's endless stories regarding their own foibles. I initially thought that many of these anecdotes were hilarious but could serve no positive therapeutic purpose in the patient's recovery plan. I reasoned that, although the stories were certainly entertaining, they were simultaneously very depressing and could hold no real benefit.

However, I later came to realize that the key to recovery from any of life's problems has to do with acknowledging the truth - the very existence - of the problematic situation. I then began to understand that alcoholics had already initiated their own therapy by telling their "funny drunk" stories.

At that juncture in my career as a therapist, I further thought that the bittersweet aspect of the drunks' daily bottle battles could be woven into the overall therapeutic plan to help them gain insight into their own denial systems as well as to better see the negative consequences associated with continued use.

However, there were certain dangers in the drunks' retelling of their "funny drunk" stories. As they shared the tragi-comic events that had unfolded in their life, the laughter that erupted around them fed their narcissistic tendencies and almost gave a certain measure of acceptance to their unacceptable behavior. Moreover, the humor became a defense mechanism that helped them cope with realities they could not consciously absorb while giving a boost to their self-esteem. Thus, while their problem worsened on the one hand, they were getting an almost equal positive response on the other. Perhaps this is what has helped typical alcoholics to somehow hang in there at all costs, until either death or recovery came along.

Today, with the rise of illegal drug use and the synergistic effect of polydrug abuse, addicts present themselves for some form of treatment sooner than was customary in the past decades. Yet they still seem to have been out there long enough to develop a vast repertoire of humorous stories. I theorized that if there was a way to utilize the historic comical data in a group setting, the overall effect could speed up the recovery process for all concerned, cut short the debilitating relapse dynamics for some, and certainly make the group more fun. After all, if synergism worked to speed up the addict's disease process, shouldn't the synergistic effect of one drunk's pratfalls affect others in the group in much the same way?

To test this theory, I first attended a number of both Alcoholics Anonymous (AA) and Narcotics Anonymous (NA) meetings. I would strongly recommend these meetings for anyone intending to do even the most casual work with addicts of any kind or their families.

One of the recurring themes in these meetings was the members' sharing of their own experiences in the context of what they used to be like, what happened to evoke change, and what they are like now. In the course of this verbal autobiography, the flirtation with near total self-destruction is apparent, but also, in nearly every case, the room usually erupts with laughter as the drunks or the dopers weave their tales.

TECHNIQUE

To be used therapeutically, humor needs to maintain a certain lightness (heavy humor cannot be carried without strain except by the most muscular therapists), exhibit function, and be executed with precise timing and style. I came to this realization slowly and in response to my own entrance into a treatment facility many years ago. My first day there I was told to go to a classroom in the treatment center to listen to a lecture on powerlessness and unmanageability in the alcoholic. As I listened to the therapist talk of the loss of control over the alcohol and the growing list of negative consequences in the drinker's life, I was more intent on trying to figure out how to correct a mistake that I saw in the room. Behind the podium there were two massive oak tablets affixed to the wall with the "Twelve Steps" of Alcoholics Anonymous carefully and artistically wood-burned into the oak. The First Step had, however, a word spelled incorrectly. As the speaker continued his discourse on powerlessness and unmanageability I kept rereading the First Step - "We admitted we were powerless over alcohol - that our lives had become *unmanagable* [*sic*]" (Alcoholics Anonymous, 1976).

After the hour had passed and the speaker, as well as all of the patients, had departed, I found a piece of chalk and went up to those mighty oaks and with an arrow and a circle added the "e" where it belonged. I felt better - as if I had regained some control over my life.

The following day, I shared the event with my therapist since I felt certain he would want to have those oak tablets fixed as soon as possible. He showed little interest in what I had said, except to make some comment about how powerless I must be if I had to spend that whole hour obsessing on a rather inconsequential object. He laughed and said my own unmanageability was probably spelled with too many "i's." My own recovery became more meaningful at that point.

Today, I often use humor as a contradiction in terms or to double-bind a patient or family member. For example, family members rarely want to do much to change their own situation. They will generally expect that if the addict does what he or she is supposed to do, the family will once again be whole and content. To elicit their support and encourage them to attend family activities as well as self-help groups such as Alanon or Naranon, I will often playfully tell them that they do not need to attend anything. When they look at me with some skepticism, I will add ". . . unless you want to feel better."

Family members often use humor pertaining to the addict but in a rather counterproductive manner. They may take a humorous event or episode and make fun of the addict rather than using it to a positive end. At times they also use humor to minimize the addict or alcoholic's behavior, thus sending a message to the person in question that the behavior was acceptable.

Humor can be applied to assist an addict in making a decision to remain in therapy as opposed to leaving treatment prematurely. I will often tell the patient that he or she cannot leave yet because he or she is too well and needs to remain to help the others.

The use of humor is also beneficial in building alliances with patients. When a particular patient was looking for a good reason to remain in treatment I reminded her that her referring therapist was in a different league than she and I and that she needed to continue to play ball with me until being recalled to the majors. She later remarked to her therapist that this reference to "our" uniqueness had helped her to align with me for the duration of her care.

On another occasion, a patient wanted a special pass to leave the hospital to attend a heavy metals convention. We informed him that it would not be possible because then all of the other patients would want to attend the Lite beer convention.

PERTINENT USES

. . . Sees a Lady Sitting with a Duck

If chemically dependent people are able to see the humor in their former situation and use it as a therapeutic device in their recovery, then the clinician should also be able to utilize the same device with the newly recovering client. My own experience suggests that even the most troubled patients in the greatest denial can somehow see the folly of their ways and will respond in a positive manner when their sense of humor is provoked.

Initially, it works well to listen to the stories told by the alcoholics or their spouses as to the episodic nature of the problem. No drunk ever had more than one too many, more than one "driving under the influence" charge, or more than one problem at home as a result of the intoxication. It generally works well to later repeat to the patient the story he or she told in the initial interview, but repeating it as if it pertains to yet another party.

The humor of their situation never escapes drunks when it is played back to them in a palatable way. Their need to be the center of attention assures their complete cooperation and understanding. Many humorous occurrences are reported in a group setting, and the therapist's challenge becomes to productively utilize each of these situations as they arise and look for therapeutic opportunities to process the humor in a constructive manner. Again, it can be helpful to rephrase the anecdote using an empty chair to represent an outside calling third party, and asking the group to acknowledge the metaphorical aspect of the humor in their own lives.

Usually, it works well to ask individual members how a particular anecdote presented by a group member pertains to their own situations. This will often result in a "snowball" effect with group members now vying to recount the best and/or funniest episode of their drinking and using days.

When viewed in proper perspective, the stories garner much power in helping the addict see the helplessness and hopelessness of each situation. Each vignette then has its own part to play in breaking through the denial that has kept the addict from initiating positive life changes.

He Says to the Bartender,
"Buy Them a Drink on Me"

In general, humor can be used to effect synergy in the chemically dependent person and affected family members. Rather than allowing the alcoholic or addictive patterns to continue for many more months or years waiting to hit "bottom," humor can be utilized as an intervention to speed up the recovery process. For example, a spouse can point out some particularly humorous but embarrassing episodes which occurred during a drinking spree and then discuss with the inflicted party whether or not the behavior would be considered appropriate in normal circumstances. Helping the addict to see the truth of a given situation, while perhaps funny in its own way, is an important part of the intervention process.

Humor is often more effective with the sophisticated client or the person who intellectualizes to extremes. Patients with greater ego strengths will respond more favorably than those who have few defenses left. I would not recommend the use of humor with the overly fragile person or the person with very low self-esteem.

It can also be helpful to match the humor to the personality type. For example, a straightforward individual may respond better to direct humor, while the more reticent might perhaps appreciate a more subtle wit. Because the reverse can also be true, it is helpful to explore different types of humor with the patient during early assessment before utilizing a particular humorous approach.

In addition to using the addicts' own anecdotes we can certainly utilize our own to strengthen the case or as an aid in breaking through the denial. Although humor can be used with the client who is still toxic, it is not generally recommended, because most of the effect will escape the person, and others may perhaps see it as a bit cruel.

Showing a certain sensitivity to the suffering alcoholic or addict can be very important in establishing a therapeutic bond. Humor, when used callously or at the expense of someone else, will have no useful value and will only serve to create a nearly impenetrable wall between therapist and client. The humor used with alcoholics or addicts must be compassionate, uncritical, non-sarcastic, caring, and helpful.

Then He Looks Over and Says,
"Where'd You Get That Pig?"

CASE 1*

Tom, age 36, an active, practicing alcoholic since his late teens, presented himself in a treatment setting for his alcoholism. He had been a very successful salesman and came to treatment only to please his wife. In a group setting he was showing substantial denial and was having difficulty relating to the other patients. He didn't feel like he belonged with these other "losers."

As the group progressed I could sense that Tom wanted to get involved in some way. He started to speak on several occasions, but would back off. Other patients were relating incidents that had occurred while they were under the influence of mind-altering chemicals of one kind or another.

It seemed to me that Tom wanted to let the group know in some way that he was as good as they were, while, at the same time, assuring them that he wasn't like them and didn't belong. With some prodding from me and encouragement from the group, Tom began to relate an episode from his own drinking experience. . . . "I don't really have a problem," he said, "except with my wife. She doesn't like to socialize much so I don't have anyone to have a few beers with. I figured that if I could find some people similar to me at a nice bar where I could stop after work now and then, I could keep my wife off my back.

"Well, one night she asked me to go to the store to get some milk for the kids. We hadn't lived in this area very long and I didn't know my way around too well, but I found this Safeway about 2 miles from the house. Right next to it was a nice-looking Polynesian-type lounge. So before getting the milk, I just stopped into the lounge for a couple of drinks to see what the place was like. I got all engrossed in a conversation with some folks and didn't leave the place until 2:00 a.m.

"The Safeway was closed, so I just got into my car and headed home. As I left the parking lot I noticed a police car sitting off to the side. I waved to them just to be friendly, hoping they wouldn't think I'd had too much to drink. Then I ran a red light right outside the parking lot and of course, they pulled me over.

---

*Names and other identifying characteristics in this and the following case presentations have been altered sufficiently to protect the confidentiality of the individuals.

"I got out of the car and walked back toward the cops so they could see that I was sober. They didn't think I was, but they were nice and told me to lock the car and they would give me a ride home. No ticket! And a ride home to boot, so I was real nice, small-talking with them. When we got to my place, I thanked them. They insisted on coming up to the house with me and I got a little irritated but didn't say anything. I fumbled with my keys and couldn't get the door unlocked so I rang the doorbell several times. When my wife came to the door she was pretty upset - late, no milk, police.

"Well, anyway, they told her I wasn't to go back that night to get the car; that if I did they would arrest me because I had had too much to drink. I really got angry and started calling them names and told them to get off my property. They just shook their heads and asked my wife if I always could be so nice and then flip over to being so mean. 'When he drinks,' she said.

"So . . . about a month later, my wife asks me to go to the store to get some milk for the kids . . . I go to this Safeway near the house, but first I go into this little Polynesian place next door. As you can probably guess, I didn't get the milk.

"When I left at closing time, I had made a couple of friends and I thought this would be the place I could stop in once in a while and my wife wouldn't bug me anymore. I was feeling pretty good, happy but not drunk.

"As I head out to the parking lot, I see another police car and I think 'it couldn't possibly happen again' so I wave to them and pull out of the lot not paying too much attention as I run a red light. Well, their lights go on and I pull right over. I get out of the car and I see that it's the same guys who got me before. So I say, 'I'm glad it's you, cuz I never got to thank you for what you did for me before and I didn't have your names or badge numbers or anything.' Well, you know, these guys were real nice and said they'd take me home again if I promised not to make a scene like the last time.

"I said, 'I don't know what got into me; I'm not that way.' They know me by my first name by now and take me straight home. I get the door open okay this time. I thank them and go in and lock the door. Then, for some reason, I open the window and start calling them names and getting real mad. They tell me that if they ever catch me again for even a minor violation I'll go to jail for a long time.

"Fortunately, we lived right on the edge of the city, so for the next year until we moved I just drove around the city to get home, never through it."

The group thought Tom's story was the funniest thing they had heard. Initially, Tom didn't think so, but when he saw the acceptance he got from the rest of the members he began to feel more at home in the group. I asked him to look at his powerlessness in those situations and he started to see that his actions certainly weren't normal. This was a real breakthrough for Tom. The rest of his treatment was uneventful, but he has been sober for over 5 years now.

The Lady Looks Indignant and Says . . .

CASE 2

Harry, a minister, age 42, entered the treatment facility rather despondent. He had lost his church due to his periodic unexplained absences, as well as attempting to preach on several occasions in a rather obvious state of intoxication. His wife and children were on the verge of moving out of the state and returning to live with his wife's family.

Harry, feeling that his life would never again be productive, had expressed his sense of despair to the staff and suggested that there was really no reason to go on living. He did not verbalize any plan of action to harm himself, but was making very little progress in the treatment program until one day during a lecture on feelings he volunteered to take some action to change his feelings. He stated that he was presently feeling sad and depressed. He was asked what he would be willing to do to change those feelings and he responded, "Anything!"

I asked him to come before "the gathered faithful," to turn around 3 times, and pretend that he was a helicopter. He initially balked, but then complied after some urging from the group. Everyone laughed including Harry. He seemed to enjoy the light-heartedness of the event and stated that although he had felt somewhat silly, he certainly felt less sad and depressed.

Harry began to participate in group actively and within a short time became a patient leader. Upon completion of his treatment he was active in his aftercare group and went on to become a volunteer co-facilitator. He continues to be an active volunteer after several years, and also provides pastoral counseling to new patients on a regular basis. His family is intact and he was recently given a new church by his denomination.

"I'll Have You Know
That This Is a Prize Duck"

CASE 3

AnnMarie had been a rather successful musician for the past 10 years. She had never married, due, she said, to too much travel and not enough time to develop an intimate relationship.

In her college days she had developed a dependency on diet pills. This quickly escalated into illegal methamphetamines and some occasional cocaine. She presented herself at the treatment center subsequent to an arrest for attempting to defraud.

Now in her early thirties, AnnMarie was a vibrant, buoyant, and articulate patient who really could not understand her need for treatment. Her very first day in group therapy she proceeded to share with the group that she had really been "railroaded" into this by some friends and her attorney who stated that she would have a better chance with her legal case if she entered some kind of rehabilitation program.

She was honest with the group in acknowledging that she had been arrested for felony fraud, but that, of course, it was all really a misunderstanding. She said that she had just been trying to have a good time and had perhaps gotten a little carried away. She related that she had been on tour in the Midwest when she got caught in a snowstorm in Minneapolis, Minnesota. During the layover she evidently started partying, initially with other members of her musical group, but after some time she either got cut off from them or left them and continued to party with another group of people.

By her own recollection, her next memory was that of being on a Greyhound Supercruiser. There were 20 or so other individuals on the bus with a bar set up in the rear and a small combo playing soft music near the center.

She felt disoriented, so she went up to the bus driver and asked where the bus was going. He said, "You chartered this for Winnipeg; we'll be there in about an hour." AnnMarie inquired further as to who had hired the bus and the driver again told her that she had, as well as the band and the bar.

She insisted that there must be some mistake and ordered the driver to turn the bus around and take her back to Minneapolis, several hundred miles away. The driver promptly complied, informing her that she had also paid for the return trip. She asked him how she had paid and was informed that it had been by personal check.

When she returned to the Twin Cities she contacted her bank and stopped payment on the check. All of this had happened in a blackout and she was arrested several weeks later after she had returned to the West Coast.

She thought her story was quite cute and figured that everyone could understand that she must have been slipped something in a drink, that soon the truth would come out, and that she would be vindicated.

For the next several days the group worked with her, reminding her of the funnier aspects of her story. The more she resisted, the more they reminded her. After more than a week of daily group work she began to buckle somewhat and started to tell more stories of odd things that had happened during her days on the road including the things she would do to make sure that she had a steady supply of her favorite drugs.

AnnMarie is now an active member of Narcotics Anonymous and tells me that she relates her "Winnipeg" story to many NA newcomers. She reports that it is no longer painful for her to relate this episode, and that she enjoys the laughter and attention she gets when she shares her story. She also states that she is at times approached by young women after NA meetings who share with her that until they heard her story they were unable to relate to the other addicts.

SYNTHESIS

The Drunk Says, Somewhat Arrogantly,
"Lady, I Was Talking to the Duck!"

Humor, when used in a chemical dependency setting, can be an effective therapeutic device. Presented with due caution and sensitivity, it can aid in speeding up the healing process and can ultimately assist alcoholics or addicts to find a more palatable method of self-acceptance for the ironies that befell them during their active using days.

This chapter has focused on the interventions conducted with the primary chemically dependent person, but the data is similar when working with the addict's family. In fact, although more bittersweet, their stories are often even more humorous because they present a less clouded perspective. However, the family members' stories are also usually laced with more obvious pain.

The newly recovering addict or alcoholic has often been blessed with only enough recall to fill the needs of the moment. It would most likely make recovery rather difficult if all of the anecdotes and their negative consequences had to be recounted and reckoned with all at once. It is therefore important to utilize the humorous episodes with care, making sure that the addict is not stripped of all defenses too soon.

In my experience, in almost every instance where the humor was allowed to brew and simmer, the synergy mentioned earlier brought about a festive dinner.

Did You Hear the One About . . .

REFERENCES

Alcoholics Anonymous (3rd ed.). (1976). New York: A. A. World Services.

As Bill Sees It. (1967). New York: A. A. World Services.

Chapman, A. J., & Foot, H. C. (Eds.). (1977). *It's a Funny Thing, Humour.* Oxford: Pergamon.

Ellenbogen, G. (Ed.). (1986). Oral sadism and the vegetarian personality. *Readings from the Journal of Polymorphous Perversity.* New York: Wry-Bred.

Ellenbogen, G. (Ed.). (1989). The primal whimper. *More Readings from the Journal of Polymorphous Perversity.* New York: Guilford.

Hall, L., & Cohn, L. (Eds.). (1987). *Recoveries. True Stories by People Who Conquered Addictions and Compulsions.* Los Angeles: Gurze Books.

6

Humor as a
Religious Experience

Chaplain Elvin (Cy) Eberhart

Chaplain Elvin "Cy" Eberhart is concerned with the applications of humor in the arena of pastoral counseling. He appears to favor humor as a path leading to both spiritual awareness and psychological health. Accordingly, Eberhart sensitively utilizes humor within the pastoral counseling context to provide some meaningful insights about God's cosmic humor while addressing the pastorate's ongoing struggles to find emotional and spiritual peace. The work of Chaplain Eberhart is an indication of the widening range of the applicability of humor to various counseling and therapeutic settings.

Elvin "Cy" Eberhart, ThM, is a practicing minister and program developer with special interest in the synthesis of humor, play, and spirituality. His published works in humor and play include In the Presence of Humor: A Guide to the Humorous Life *(1984) and* Playlife: Rediscovering the Secrets of Childhood *(1988).*

❖   ❖   ❖

Two Jews were sitting in a coffee house discussing the fate of their people. "How miserable is our lot," one said. "Plagues, quotas, discrimination, Hitler, the Ku Klux Klan. Sometimes I think we'd be better off if we'd never been born."

"Of course," said the other, "but who has that much luck? Not one in 50,000!"

It was in the chance reading of this anecdote that I first recognized that the *experiencing* of humor could have a religious function. At the same time it challenged me to develop methods people could use to actively and deliberately realize humor's sublime values. The tie between humor and religion became readily apparent, but the formulating of an applied system was quite another matter.

THEORETICAL PERSPECTIVE

The religious quality is clear when this anecdote is compared to the same thought expressed by the Preacher in the Book of Ecclesiastes:

I thought the dead who are already dead more fortunate than the living who are still alive; but better than both is he who has not yet been, and has not seen the evil deeds that are done under the sun. (4:2, 3)

The biblical treatment doesn't do much for one's spirit. Indeed, if you happened to be depressed and turned to the Bible for solace, the words of the Preacher would only deepen your discouragement.

Yet the preceding anecdote has quite a different effect. In the twinkling of an eye the humor integrates, resolves, refreshes, and motivates one to get on with the business at hand. The anecdote makes this connection without minimizing or denying the untenable dimensions of the situation faced. It provides no escape, and neither does it offer a solution or remedy. In fact, the anecdote doesn't even have the courtesy to sympathize. It says, "Yes, it is true, every single bit of it" (Eberhart, 1984, p. 36).

It is this particular characteristic of humor, its reinterpretation of life's demoralizing aspects in ways that strengthen one's morale for living, that elevates it to the level of a religious experience.

The morale-building aspect of the humor experience is consistent with William H. Bernhardt's view of the function of religion as a form of "behavior whereby persons are prepared intellectually and emotionally to meet the non-manipulable aspects of existence positively by means of a reinterpretation of the total situation" (Bernhardt, 1964, p. 157).

The Jewish anecdote illustrates another important aspect of humor: Humor is an experience, not a body of knowledge. The experiencing of humor instantly affects the reinterpretation of the situation at hand. Any intellectual insights and readjustments that may have taken place followed the humor. In humor we experience the oneness that philosophy and theology talk about.

The anecdote further illustrates that humor is not intimidated by the "hard" profound issues of life. This makes it a viable experience in dealing with the ultimate nonmanipulable aspects of existence - the limitations inherent in the human condition. And of course, living successfully with these limitations is the central focus of the religious enterprise.

Erich Fromm (1966) described the human condition as follows:

> Man is beset by the existential dichotomy of being within nature and yet transcending it by the fact of having self-awareness and choice; he can solve this dichotomy only by going forward. Man has to experience himself as a stranger in the world, estranged from himself and from nature, in order to be able to become one again with himself, with his fellow man, and with nature, on a higher level. He has to experience the split between himself as subject and the world as object as the condition for overcoming this very split. (p. 71)

Happily, the proper experiencing of humor brings about a welcome oneness between subject and object or between other seemingly opposed dimensions.

One of the dominant ways that the human dichotomy plays itself out is in humans denying their limitations and trying instead to be God just like the comedian, George Burns, in the movie *"O God!"* In the words of humor writer George Mikes (1971):

> One of the curses of humanity is man's God-complex. . . . Most people see themselves as Gods or god-like creatures. All little children want to be God when they grow up and many, by the time they have grown up, think they have achieved their ambitions. (p. 54)

A comic viewpoint can reveal the humor in the fruitless desire for godhood. The existential dilemma is reinterpreted, changing the conflict and tension into liberating acceptance.

In the laughter of accepting our limitations, "we are restored to our rightful nature, becoming again as human and not as God. In the laughter . . . we hear God saying, 'Leave the godding to me. You can't do it, it's too much for you. It will wear you out, you'll only fail. That's my job. Yours is to be human' " (Eberhart, 1984,

p. 44). Accepting one's self incomplete or imperfect with joy, appreciation, and enthusiasm is humor's sublime gift to the human spirit.

However, a rationale for humor's sublime relevance is not the same as a working system. An Old Testament professor at my seminary, Lindsay Longacre, was fond of saying, "That sounds good if you say it fast enough."

An applied experiential process that can actively engage humor at its sublime level has to be able to:

1. *Intercede in life's most difficult moments.* To be a functioning religious resource the sense of humor must be more than a fair-weather friend. It is in our difficulties that humor's ministry is most needed. As was said long ago, we have need of the physician when we are ill, not when we are well.
2. *Be active in those times when we just don't feel like being funny.* Our hurts, pains, stresses, and despairs are all too real. The emotions are so strong and powerful that the humorous spirit in us must not retreat.
3. *Be active when we are willingly seduced by our own egos.* We become so enthralled with our godlike pursuits and posturing that our pride will not admit the needed humor.
4. *Engage the comic viewpoint in a very personal and intimate way.* Experiences of pain, stress, and ego involve primary issues in our lives. Some issues are so uniquely subjective that they could not be wholly shared even if we wanted to share them. As far as humor is concerned, the only entrance to this inner world is through our own comic viewpoint, not that of another.
5. *Make one's self the object of humor.* Self-targeted humor is a necessary component of humor's spiritual force. The religious life is the art of accepting oneself as one is without complaints or conditions. This involves laughing more at ourselves than at others.

The above entails acquiring what Dudley Zuver (Zuver, 1935, p. 6) called a "humorous attitude . . . a kind of mental equipment with which one meets any and every possible experience, rather than a quality of single experiences no matter how numerous or varied they be."

Because I initially lacked the necessary tools for any process-related psychological experiencing, I pursued training several years ago in "Human Social Functioning" (Heimler, 1975), a counseling method developed by Eugene Heimler based upon his survival experiences in the World War II Nazi concentration camps. The Human Social Functioning system gave me some experiential tools to advance my own psychological awareness. Briefly put, the system gives individuals a nonthreatening structure to reflect on their felt satisfactions and frustrations. The process enables them to direct frustrated energies into more creative channels that increase their level of satisfaction. The increased satisfaction is the result of making decisions and initiating actions that are more consistent with their own basic or core values, giving them a sense of meaning and purpose for both their present and their future.

I also became interested in the experience of play. An autobiographical account by Carl Jung caught my imagination (Jung, 1963). He described in detail the time when, as a 36-year-old man, he returned to a play activity he had enjoyed as a child, describing the event as the turning point of his fate. Using gathered stones and mud as mortar, he built cottages, a castle, a whole village. He went at his task with great passion:

> I went on with my building game after the noon meal every day, whenever the weather permitted. As soon as I was through eating, I began playing, and continued to do so until the patients arrived; and if I was finished with my work early enough in the evening, I went back to building. In the course of this activity my thoughts clarified, and I was able to grasp the fantasies whose presence in myself I dimly felt. (p. 174)

What struck me in Jung's account is that it might be possible for others to have similar experiences as well. After all isn't there a Huck Finn, Tom Sawyer, or Becky Thatcher in each of us? Why not bring it to life and get the same benefits Jung found for himself in his journey into childhood?

I turned my attention to play experiences, and quite naturally turned to Social Functioning methodologies because I had successfully experimented with these in hospital staff development programs (contemplation of death and dying, and confronting change and transitions). The methods are easier to implement than they are to describe. Their simplicity in execution belies their effectiveness. Any method designed to engage the dynamics found in Social Functioning must include these three features:

1. The subjective: a nonthreatening structure that stimulates individuals to freely reflect upon given personal experiences.
2. The objective: a means by which individuals can detach themselves from the subjective and give it an interpretation that has meaning for them.
3. The synthesis: integrating all the energies generated by the aforecited process and directing these toward the goals and challenges relevant to the individual's present life situation.

In the contemplation of death program, for example, I used the "ambiguous question," a standard Social Functioning structure. There are 30 such questions in this small-group program:

Do you give adequate thought
to your own death and dying?   YES   PERHAPS   NO

Of those close to you is there
one death that would be more
traumatic for you than that
of the others?   YES   PERHAPS   NO

In giving an answer to such questions the participants must assign their own meanings to various word symbols. The subjectivity is continued as they then reflect in conversation or within their imagination about the feelings, thoughts, and experiences that prompted their particular answers to a given question.

Next comes the objective feature. Participants "stand outside" the subjective experience by reflecting on what they have been saying, thinking, and feeling about the question under consideration. Then they make a personalized written statement that summarizes for them the essence of their own reflections.

While such written summaries are an early part of the synthesis process, it comes into full play when the participants examine their written summaries. Here they determine the key thought or message these summaries hold as it relates to their current life situation.

It is important to notice that these methodologies make each participant both the examiner and the interpreter of his or her own experiences. The therapist's or leader's viewpoint remains outside the process. In the instance of play I centered my approach on our enjoyment of and interest in nostalgia (Eberhart, 1985). The initial objective was to harness the energy that nostalgia generates. Most of us are willing to go to class reunions, look up childhood friends when we travel on vacations, and spend hours reminiscing. We will watch rerun movies on TV and listen to recorded music that dates back to our childhood. We will display artifacts in our homes that remind us of a time that is no more. We get good feelings from the days gone by. Why?

Through nostalgia we are permitted to return to a time when our hope had a future. Nostalgia recalls, in feeling at least, the hope that once was ours. What does this have to do with the activity of play? First consider the naturalness of hope. It is an intrinsic part of our nature. As Erich Fromm put it, "We start out with hope . . . (it is an) unconscious 'no-thought' quality of the sperm and the egg, of their union, of the growth of the fetus and its birth" (Fromm, 1968, p. 19).

How else can the hoping person respond to life except in playfulness and celebration? Fears, risks, or the unknown do not inhibit the spirit of the person who has hope. So we play in the form of specific activities, many of our own creation. Our attitude of hope is an unconscious but significant ingredient in making the specific play activity pleasant and joyful.

In this mode, we find heightened sensitivity to our hidden potentials. We are free of the restrictive demands of instincts or organic drives. We exude seemingly unbounded energy. Novelty, spontaneity, imagination, enthusiasm, and creativity are now the characteristics that fill the moment. Dreams we could never articulate burst forth with this new-found energy.

It is my thesis that specific youthful play activities we engaged in as children are psychological doors for us today. We can open such doors and once again bring forth hidden energy and hope into our here and now. Our reborn hope then becomes far more than just a nostalgic feeling or an incidental event.

TECHNIQUE

I would like to fit the technical aspects of my work within the framework of ministry because ministry is the basis for all my work.

A word must be said, therefore, about a unique feature of the clergy in terms of counseling. It is true that in recent years much pastoral counseling has been influenced by the medical model, that is, the person *initiates* the visit and *goes to* the professional. The era of specialization and the time constraints on both laity and clergy have helped encourage this pattern. In this model, parishioners go to the pastor's office to talk about problems, and staff counselors see parishioners by appointment. In many cases separate church counseling centers are created, and are run in much the same way as any other counseling center.

This medical model ignores the uniqueness of the clergy's role. Among the helping professions, the clergy is the only group privileged to initiate the contact. In the pastoral model the routine visit provides the pastor the opportunity to discover parishioners' needs and provide the necessary ministry. This is as true for chaplains in hospitals as well. Traditionally, when one is under the care of a physician, it is because the person first sought the physician. The physician then "orders" others to attend the patient for specific reasons that are clear to everyone.

However, in terms of pastoral care the chaplain is free to initiate the visit without need for a referral, order, or specific reason. In pastoral care terms the purpose of the visit is to "be with" the patient. In this being-with, the chaplain relies on his or her skills to be sensitive to whatever needs the patient may evidence.

Faddism is incompatible with good pastoral care. In the use of fads something is *done to* the person. In ministry one is not trying to *do anything to* anyone.

Another factor that can influence the responsiveness of the patient or parishioner is the state of the chaplain's own humor. For example, I returned to my hospital duties the day following an international humor conference. Emotionally I was still buoyant with the high spirits the conference gave me. I was struck by the fact that every patient I visited that morning seemed upbeat, and the focus was on very positive events in their lives. Two visits were actually punctuated by humorous stories and events in the patients' lives. I did not initiate any humorous comments, nor did I even hint that I'd been to a humor conference.

The nature of those visits stood in contrast to the time I was having severe back pain. On my visits I made no reference to my pain, nor did I show outwardly that I was in pain. Yet in each and every visit, the patient's concern was about his or her pain.

Such a subjective matter may be beyond conscious control, but it does raise an interesting question concerning "techniques."

While certain techniques of humor may be more useful or appropriate than others, I wonder if the reasons for their degree of appropriateness reside with the patient or with me?

To summarize, techniques compatible with the humor-religion theory I am proposing would accomplish one or more of the following:

1. provide an experience that will generate hope and confidence
2. be accessible in vital life situations
3. be accessible when one's mood may not be "humorous"
4. engage the comic viewpoint in personal and intimate ways
5. make one's self the object of the humor

I will now discuss several techniques I have used to further the humor-religion process.

TECHNIQUES IN PLAYFULNESS

The objective of these techniques is to make the emotional energy that accompanies pleasant childhood memories a creative factor in the individual's current life. This effort consists of two parts. The sequence of the first part is as follows:

1. In dyads participants engage in rapid free association of childhood memories in relation to each of the five senses. For example, the "sights of childhood" could bring forth images of "icicles hanging from the roof, a red wagon, Mother in the kitchen."
2. Then they recall several pleasant childhood play activities and make written note of these: "I enjoyed watching the clouds drift overhead on a summer day."
3. They identify further those written activities that garner enough emotional appeal that the individual would want to do them again, much as Jung wanted to do his activity again. They also consider the features that made these experiences so pleasant or satisfying, for example, adventure, companionship, using one's hands, and learning skills. These activities are then compared to the participants' present adult play experiences to determine if they incorporate the underlying features of the childhood play. If they do not - and most often they don't - they decide what they can do to bring these

features into their current living. A simple example is that of the man who realized that a satisfying part of his childhood play was the companionship it offered. As an adult his leisure had turned into solitary experiences. With this awareness he began inviting others to participate with him, recapturing the companionship he enjoyed in childhood.

The sequence of the second part is as follows:

1. Through the eyes of their "rediscovered child," participants examine the world around them, letting the environment stimulate playfulness. For example, walking along the street, what would this child be inclined to do at the sight of a tree, or a mud puddle?
2. Similarly what in the environment would stimulate this child's imagination, causing him or her to wonder? The purpose of this activity is to practice seeing the familiar in new ways. For example, on seeing two shrubs, one with green leaves and one with red, a child might wonder, "How do bushes get red leaves?" And then an answer follows: not a scientific explanation, but the kind of answer an imaginative child might fashion.
3. Finally, participants determine fantasies or playful approaches they might use to keep their unique qualities of playfulness alive in their individual life setting. Here is a personal example from my days as a hospital chaplain. Since adventure is an important feature in my playfulness, I asked myself the question: "What would my child do in a place like this?"

    The answer came almost immediately. The child saw the hospital as a place controlled by some sinister force, keeping patients there against their will. In this setting I became an undercover agent walking the halls setting up secret talks with the patients, helping them find ways to escape. There was nothing in this fantasy to interfere with my required responsibilities or with the effectiveness of my work. In fact, when my spirit of adventure was present, I did my best work.

In the context of patient visits, the first part of this technique, when appropriate, is easily initiated by simply inquiring about the patient's childhood play experiences. The underlying purpose is to bring the dynamics of hope into the patient's present situation.

TECHNIQUES FOR INCREASING
AWARENESS OF HUMOR AS AN
EVER-PRESENT RESOURCE (GROUP ACTIVITY)

The Embarrassing Moment. Sharing embarrassing moments helps people become aware of the fact that the elements of humor are always around, even in difficult times. I ask the patient (or the group, if it is a group program) to remember embarrassing moments they previously experienced. This sharing is usually done with much laughter. The point is easily grasped that the essence of this humor was equally present at the time the embarrassing event happened. The only difference is the necessary emotional distance from the event that is created by the time lag between then and now. The point can then be expanded into the perspective that humor *is* available as an ever-present resource.

The "Norman Rockwell" Method. Another technique accomplishes this by what I call the "Norman Rockwell" method. The participants imagine a scene of their own choosing where there is some tension or conflict. I usually suggest a domestic scene, and ask them to "feel" the tension. I then ask them to visualize in their mind's eye how Norman Rockwell might illustrate the scene. Reactions vary from smiles to guffaws as the participants experience the shift in their emotions. This technique also demonstrates the way that a comical viewpoint can alter one's perception of a situation.

TECHNIQUES THAT ACTIVATE THE INDIVIDUAL'S
COMIC VIEWPOINT IN A SELF-DIRECTED WAY

The Humorist Method. The patient is asked to name his or her favorite humorist. More often than not the patient interprets "humorist" to mean a comic, for instance Johnny Carson, or a particular character in a comedy role, such as "Murphy Brown" in the *Murphy Brown* show or "Hawkeye Pierce" in *M*A*S*H**. This chosen character becomes a symbol of the patient's own comic viewpoint. The patient is then asked to imagine the selected humorist in the same situation as the patient, and to describe what the humorist might say or do.

This technique introduces the comical perspective into the patients' life situations, allowing them to see themselves from a personalized comical point of view.

The Clown Method. I have discovered that one of humor's universal symbols, the clown, is an excellent vehicle for stimulating the humor-religion process. The clown figure became a major part of humor elicitation in my work and connected well with the Social Functioning methodologies. It provided the needed objective framework to interpret any personal experience from a comic viewpoint.

There is an image of a clown within each person's imagination that is representative of the person's comic viewpoint. Incorporating this image into a technique requires the individual to spend time "getting acquainted" with that inner clown: To picture the clown in action and "watch" his or her behavior in numerous situations and circumstances.

Once one is familiar with the clown, it is "called upon" to interact with specific circumstances or situations within one's life. The clown's behavior is then observed within one's imagination for a period of time, and the individual interprets the *meaning* of this behavior. This interpretation becomes the "message" of one's comical viewpoint.

For this method to be effective the individual must be emotionally involved in his or her selected situations. A previous work, *In the Presence of Humor: A Guide to the Humorous Life* (Eberhart, 1984), uses written essays to help the reader associate significant personal experiences with the essay's theme. The worksheet on pages 117 and 118 (from Eberhart, 1984, p. 72) illustrates the clowning process in connection with an essay on the theme of rebirth.

Variation on the Clown Method. A workable variation on the clown method was developed by Carol Peterson, of Clackamas Community College in Oregon City, Oregon. Her method is to allow one's sense of humor to take its own form instead of making it into a clown. One then feels its presence, letting it materialize into its own particular animated form. In this imagery exercise, the eyes may be closed or open as the individual participant wishes. The sense of humor takes different forms for different people. It has been depicted as a butterfly, a young seal, a Raggedy Ann doll, and a dog. It can be anything that feels right. In fact, the shape of one man's sense of humor was a big, black glob.

After the sense of humor has taken its shape, one asks, "Where does it live," taking the time to determine where the sense of humor has its home: Does it reside in one's head, one's heart, on the shoulder, behind the ear, or in the stomach? By discovering where the sense of humor lives, the individual knows where to find it when needed.

The interaction with specific situations is carried on as with the clown method described previously.

TECHNIQUES WHEN THE EGO OR
MOOD BLUNTS THE HUMOROUS EXPERIENCE

The If-You-Can't-Laugh Method. One takes the "non-laughable" thought, event, or situation as the theme of a song. Then one writes the words to a simple tune, such as "Row, Row, Row Your Boat."

The demand for rhyme and meter reveals the absurdity of the "unlaughable" characteristics. Then there's nothing to do but smile . . . maybe even laugh.   ·

WORKSHOP TECHNIQUES

Social Functioning methodologies are designed for one-on-one counseling situations. However, they can be effectively applied to groups when the integrity of the process is maintained. The key elements are the private reflections that go on in an individual's mind and the individual's written statements and summaries of these reflections.

The function of any group discussions, interactions, or activities with respect to these methods is to expand the individual's awareness of his or her own experiences and to do so in a non-threatening way. The objective is for the individual to make "use of already learned experiences, attempting to unify these into a kind of synthesis. . . . Access to these experiences is possible only if (one) can create a framework or a container into which such synthesized experiences can be drawn" (Heimler, 1975, p. 79).

To interpret another's remarks or to confront or challenge another does not create an effective framework within this particular process. For group work I have coined the phrase, "guided conversation" or "guided activities." The general subject matter directs the participants' focus toward certain experiences, in the same way that a play workshop focuses on play. Given a particular focus, the participants explore their experiences within the structure of the particular technique being used.

For example, in the dyad portion of the play workshop, participants are "guided" into recalling certain experiences related to the five senses, and the recollections of one participant triggers the forgotten experiences of another participant. Later on in the workshop, when the written part of the process begins, participants become cognizant that they have gained a better awareness of their own past than when they began the exercise.

Similarly, in the humor workshop, the participants open each session with a discussion that is "guided" by the essay theme for a given session, such as hope, joy, self-acceptance, love, and so forth. The discussion is in terms of their experiences that relate to the theme. During the interchange each considers within his or her own imagination the perspectives and thoughts offered by the others. When it is time to write each is more sensitive to his or her own experiences than before the discussion began.

In the reflections, writings, and summaries the participants are in complete charge of their own processes.

PERTINENT USES

SITUATIONAL HUMOR

Individual situations often offer special opportunities for using humor.

During a visit the patient or parishioner may say something that presents a perfect opening for humor. This happened when one woman went on and on about what a terrible wife and mother she was. She dramatically made her point when she said, "I've been so terrible, even God couldn't forgive me."

I said, "Oh, I think God can get over it."

At first she looked as though I'd slapped her. Then she broke into a hearty laugh. The comic viewpoint altered her perception of her situation.

Humor can also play a positive role in times of extreme tension, anxiety, or stress, such as when a family sits helpless in a hospital waiting room. It is a situation clergy are well acquainted with. Although I am not comfortable in intentionally introducing humor into these situations, I have observed that humor often arises spontaneously. As family members keep vigil, humor is present, waiting to be invited in. Someone will break the emotional tension by remembering a humorous incident or remark that involved the ill patient.

It is appropriate to encourage and support the continuation of such remarks for as long as the family chooses to do so. Such lighthearted moments alleviate the emotional burden for at least a time, allowing some spiritual reconstitution to occur.

Bereavement is another situational occasion where humor has a place.

"What do you remember about him or her?" has been one of my standard questions for years when meeting with a family in preparation for a funeral. Almost without exception important memories with twists of humor and laughter flow into the conversation. The heaviness of grief is lightened as the person's significance is crystallized in the presence of humor. Then I, the officiating clergyman, have everything I need for a relevant funeral meditation. Even when families are total strangers to the clergy, the process works well this way.

Getting information in this manner keeps the funeral from being like the one where the clergyman was extolling the virtues of the departed grandfather. After awhile the mourning father asked his son to look in the casket to make sure they were at the right funeral.

INTERRUPTING THE
PREOCCUPATION OF SELF-CONCERN

Humor can be used to interrupt the focusing on self that often accompanies pain, depression, or anxiety. One example from the favorite-humorist technique:

> A male patient in his mid-60s had been in the hospital for over a week. On one visit his chronic pain occupied most of his thoughts. In the course of our conversation I asked, "Who's your favorite humorist?"
>
> "Archie Bunker," he said.
>
> "Okay! If Archie Bunker were here in your place, what do you think he would say or do?"
>
> He looked up at the ceiling and thought for a moment. A smile inched across his face. "He'd say, 'Can't you see I'm hurtin'? Now leave me alone so I can enjoy it.' "

His comic viewpoint, for a moment at least, had interrupted his spiral of self-pity as he saw himself from a different perspective, and from the laugh this brought him, his morale lifted, at least for awhile.

The versatile play technique can be used in similar situations. Here are two examples I've recounted elsewhere (Eberhart, 1985).

A physician asked me to call on a depressed 68-year-old widow. He had reluctantly scheduled her discharge for that afternoon. I think he hoped I would wave my magic wand, sending the depression to the far winds. I did not. Instead, in the course of our visit I asked what kind of play she enjoyed as a child. She answered immediately. "I enjoyed painting faces on china dolls."

There was no mistaking the truth of her statement. The thoughts of her childhood activity transformed her expression. Her face turned radiant. Her eyes sparkled with new life. I encouraged her to tell me about this interest. She did so, and with enthusiasm.

Her recalling the memory tapped some hidden or forgotten energy source. So the obvious next step was to suggest that she pick up the activity once again. Unfortunately, the idea didn't interest her, and there was little time to give her the necessary support and encouragement to try and revive her interest in the play activity. It was unfortunate, for it seemed that her hope to reclaim her life was within her grasp. She left that afternoon, taking her depression with her.

Another hospital incident also involved a depressed widow of similar age. She had called for me, wanting to talk about the unpleasant prospects of going back to her lonely home. She had been widowed for over a year. In caring for her husband through his extended illness, she had gradually given up all of her outside activities. She found her past year lonely, boring, and without purpose or meaning. She wanted some way to bring change into her life.

In exploring her situation she brought out the fact that her most enjoyable interest before her husband became ill was entertaining in her home. It was relatively easy to point her toward entertaining once again. What startled me was the near immediate emotional change that came over her as we clarified her course of action. Enthusiasm quickly replaced depression.

As our conversation continued it came out that as a child one of her favorite pastimes was the make-believe tea party, complete with gourmet mud pies. In the hospital room, making plans for her immediate future, she had unwittingly tapped a hidden energy supply by extending her childhood play experiences into her adult world.

Integrating humorous experiences into one's philosophy of life is another pertinent use of humor that lies at the core of my professional interest.

For this I rely heavily on the clowning method as illustrated in connection with the sample worksheet described on pages 117 and 118. In the summarizing process of the different worksheets, individuals isolate underlying attitudes or themes present in their recorded responses. From these they can extrapolate values that inhabit their own comical viewpoints. It is in being faithful to these values that individuals can achieve the humorous attitude.

Here's the way one woman described the effects of this integrative process in her life:

> I am not personally tossed about by my desires any more. By doing the clowning "continuum of desires," my clown showed me that even after a desire is fulfilled, there will be a new desire. I've learned to live with this ongoing parade. Once in a while I satisfy a desire, but without getting caught up in the disappointment that its fulfillment wasn't the cure-all that I had anticipated. As a matter of fact, now I can realistically forecast exactly what the next desire will probably be: there's an ongoing fountain of the little buggers.

CLINICAL PRESENTATIONS

Once one's clown is fully personalized, it can be successfully used for individual situations where strong emotions are at play as in the following situations:

1. A parish pastor felt that his time in a particular church had run out. Relationships with some parishioners were quite

strained. He had about decided to look for a new parish but had not yet set the machinery in motion. Following a Sunday service while collecting his material from the pulpit, he decided to see what his clown might do with the thought that he was leaving the church. The moment he visualized the clown in the sanctuary, the clown did back flips up and down the aisle. The pastor decided it was indeed time to move on.

2. A man was about to move to a new community. A few weeks earlier he had a misunderstanding with an acquaintance. The acquaintance became so angry that he refused to even talk to the man. The man wanted a reconciliation before he left town but was unsure how to go about it or if any approach would be fruitful.

    Driving home one evening he came to the street where the acquaintance lived. He stopped his car to consider whether to have one last try. He could not make up his mind as to what to do. Then he put his clown into the situation. Immediately the clown opened the car door, got out, walked to the side of the road, slumped down in the gutter, and fell asleep. The man started his car and drove home.

For me the group workshop has been the best method to pursue this humor-religion process. The workshop gives an adequate time frame to employ the several methods and techniques for personalizing and integrating the comical viewpoint into one's philosophy of life. This format is especially suitable for staff development. It gives the staff a support group while they are practicing using their own comic viewpoints on the job.

3. During an extended workshop, the home assignment was to physically do something that would be consistent with one's own spirit of play. A nurse decided, that for her, flying a kite would do it. She procrastinated because she felt silly in doing it. Finally swallowing her pride, she went to a vacant spot with kite in hand. Shortly after she began her kiting three other people had joined her with their kites.

4. In exploring her childhood play, a mother became aware that one of her great child-pleasures was reading alone in her room. At the same time she realized she was unjustly critical of her daughter for doing the same thing. As a result, she acquired a new understanding of her daughter.

The when-you-can't-laugh method can be modified for group use. For example, my first humor workshop was with the staff of a nursing home. They were to select a frustrating work experience shared in common as the theme for a song to the tune "Row, Row, Row Your Boat." They did it with zest and enthusiasm. Their subject was "Loose Bowels." I regret that I did not keep a copy of the lyrics.

The humor workshop can also be conducive to personal growth. One man, using the song method, picked up on his compulsive desire for recognition. Here's how the theme "played out" when he structured his thoughts to the tune of "A Bicycle Built for Two:"

> Lordy, Lordy, what am I to do
> I'm so busy trying to get mine, too.
> I'm after admiration
> A dandy reputation
> I'd give my all for a concert hall
> And a flattering review.

SYNTHESIS

As I have flirted with the relationship between humor and religion over many years, it seems to me that the goal of such flirtation is the achievement of a humorous attitude. A humorous attitude allows for the development of a particular frame of mind within which one can be simultaneously involved in and detached from life, a salutary stance amidst the dichotomies of the human condition. Techniques, methods, and approaches are validated for assisting individuals in gaining access to a comical viewpoint that is uniquely their own, and thereby achieving the humorous attitude.

An interesting phenomenon that I have repeatedly observed is the constant presence of laughter throughout the course of death-and-dying workshop sessions. This is despite the fact that each session involves facing the most profound and emotionally charged of human experiences. I puzzled over the significance of this occurrence for a long time. As I pondered the impact that such programs have upon the participants' lives, I understood that, in death-and-dying workshops, people are engaging the central values of their being, what some call "core values." They are re-ordering their living to be consistent with their inner values. I further realized that in the play and humor techniques I described, the same reordering occurs. Such reordering has a freeing effect, resulting in spiritual health and constructive personal growth.

Consequently, humor is the natural byproduct of living our lives in harmony with our own "core values." It is the realization and enactment of these personal values in everyday life that generates genuine humor. However, such genuine living is the ideal. Perfection does not appear to be a human characteristic. Therefore, the encouragement to develop the humorous attitude through methods and techniques is an enterprise worthy of our time and effort.

CLOWNING PROCESS WORKSHEET

Step 1. My focus thought is (the reader identifies a concern consistent with the given theme):

"I'm in a rut and would like to get out."

Step 2. My four life situations are (the reader selected these from associations made while reading the essay):

1. Lesson planning
2. Getting started for the day
3. Reading the daily newspaper
4. Looking at needed-to-be-done housework

Step 3. My clown's responses are (reader uses the clown viewpoint to examine the preceding situations):

1. The clown stands up tall taking on a proud and pompous stance.
2. Clown throws a bucket of cold water on my face while I'm still in bed.
3. Clown puts hand over its mouth and giggles as though it knows a secret about me.
4. Clown puts a model of the world on its shoulders and staggers around under the load.

Step 4. The significance of these responses is (the reader evaluates their meanings):

1. I feel the pressure in believing I must be profound in what I say and teach.
2. I'm using all my reserve energy in the necessity of keeping going.
3. I'm reading the paper in search of items to feed some of my resentments.
4. I see the burden side of most of what I do.

Step 5. My interpretation of these responses is (the reader determines the "message" of the comic viewpoint):

"I'm living from out of the heavy side of life, and it's taking its toll."

Step 6. My usual way of responding is (compares it with current behavior):

To go at it as though it is a burden.

Step 7. Period of Reflection (relate to "Focus Thought" in Step 1):

"I've chosen to act like Sisyphus. There's no good reason why I have to get the rock to the top of the hill."

The significance this has for my living is (write it if desired):

REFERENCES

Bernhardt, W. H. (1964). *A Functional Philosophy of Religion.* Denver, CO: Criterion Press.

Eberhart, E. T. (1984). *In the Presence of Humor: A Guide to the Humorous Life.* Salem, OR: Pilgrim House.

Eberhart, E. T. (1985, March). *The Playful Spirit: A Requisite for Humor and Wholeness.* Paper presented at The College of Chaplains Annual Proceeding, Boston, MA.

Eberhart, E. T. (1988). *Playlife: Rediscovering the Secrets of Childhood.* Salem, OR: Pilgrim House.

Fromm, E. (1966). *You Shall Be As Gods.* Greenwich, CT: Fawcett Publications.

Fromm, E. (1968). *The Revolution of Hope.* New York: Harper & Row.

Heimler, E. (1975). *Survival in Society.* New York: John Wiley and Sons.

Hyers, C. (1981). *The Comic Vision and the Christian Faith.* New York: Pilgrim Press.

Jung, C. G. (1963). *Memories, Dreams, Reflections.* New York: Pantheon Books.

Mikes, G. (1971). *Laughing Matters.* New York: The Library Press.

Mindess, H. (1978). *Laughter and Liberation.* Jacksonville, FL: Headwaters Press.

Polhemus, R. M. (1980). *Comic Faith.* Chicago: University of Chicago Press.

Zuver, D. (1935). *Salvation By Laughter.* New York: Harper & Brothers.

7

Humor in Relation to
Obsessive-Compulsive Processes

Allen A. Surkis

*In this chapter, the obsessive process itself becomes an obsession
for Dr. Surkis! In attempting to puncture the defenses of obsessive patients, Dr. Surkis uses the fly swatter of humor in a teasing, warm, and
compassionate style. He describes with delightful detail how the dreari-
ness of obsessive processes can be transformed into a veritable circus à
la Surkis where patients are coaxed into playing along with the show.
Through the use of a structured humorous-regressive clinical technique,
Dr. Surkis is able to bypass resistance and take patients back to important early childhood experiences where their obsessiveness originated,
while simultaneously providing them with a constructive and more mature framework to restructure their emotional experiences.*

*Allen Surkis, PhD, is Psychologist-in-Chief at the Montreal Gen-
eral Hospital and the Director of Professional Studies at the Argyle Institute of Human Relations. The influences that have shaped his professional journey have been psychoanalytic theory, client-centered core
conditions, psychodrama, methods and metaphors of Eriksonian hypno-
therapy, and neurolinguistic programming. These dimensions have been
integrated into his work and have resulted in a unique approach to psychotherapy. Dr. Surkis has presented numerous papers and workshops
on psychotherapy at the local, national, and international levels. In addition, he is well-known for his interest in group psychotherapy and is a
past president of the Canadian Group Psychotherapy Association.*

❖   ❖   ❖

THEORETICAL PERSPECTIVE

I was curious to understand how our language sets us up to
think about humor. So I ventured into the history of the word and

an interesting story unfolded. The word "humor" comes into contemporary language from Middle English. It arrived in Middle English from Old French, which took it from Latin, which probably took it from an Indo-European root. Back in that mist of history its ancestor seems to have meant "moist, moisten." During the course of time, it came to mean any fluid or juice of an animal or plant; especially any of the four fluids (cardinal humors) formerly considered responsible for one's health and disposition: blood, phlegm, choler (yellow bile), or melancholy (black bile). It then took on a more specific meaning, referring to a person's disposition or temperament, a mood or state of mind. In its contemporary usage, humor means "the quality that makes something seem funny, amusing or ludicrous; comicality" (Guralnik, *Webster's Dictionary,* p. 885).

In constructing an etymological path for the word "moist," I found that it followed a similar historical route, except that it cannot be traced beyond the Latin "mucus," meaning "slightly wet, damp." However, the word "mucus" does have an Indo-European anchoring - in a word meaning "slippery, slime, to slide." Today "mucus" refers to the thick, slimy secretion of the mucus membranes that moistens and protects them (Guralnik, *Webster's Dictionary,* 1984).

And so develops our sense of the word "humor," coming to us from the shared experience of many generations, as an idea that refers to a means of "defense." A defense protects the sensitive inner tissues of the body as well as the sensitive inner fabric of the personality. Humor as a mechanism of defense allows one to bear, and yet to focus on, what is too terrible to be borne (Meissner, 1985).

Vaillant (1977) has written that "mature mechanisms can be conceptualized as well-orchestrated composites of less mature mechanisms" (p. 116). For him, humor is a "truly elegant" mechanism of defense, a most potent antidote for emotional pain.

Many years earlier, Freud had already commented on humor as a defense. He wrote:

> The defense processes are the psychic correlates of the flight reflex and follow the task of guarding against the origin of pain from inner sources. . . . Humor can . . . be conceived as the loftiest of these defense functions. . . . Humor strives to bring . . . a pleasure which has really

been lost. . . . The euphoria which we are striving to obtain is . . . the state of our childhood in which we did not know the comic, were incapable of wit, and did not need humor to make us happy. (Brill, 1938, pp. 801-803)

One of the major arenas for the use of humor in psychotherapy is in relation to obsessive-compulsive processes, which we can observe across the spectrum of maladaptive functioning personality types. Although obsessive-compulsive processes may not represent the predominant pattern in a particular personality structure, they nevertheless play an important role in interactions with oneself as well as with one's psychosocial context.

Obsessive-compulsive individuals are cautious and deliberate, thoughtful, and rational. They prefer reason and logic to feeling and intuition and do their best to be objective - all this in order to avoid being swayed by their subjective reactions. Moreover, they maintain a rather reserved attitude toward change (Nemiah, 1985). Beneath the surface they struggle with the conflicts that erupt when libidinal and aggressive impulses clash with superego constraints. They then engage in such defense mechanisms as rationalization, undoing, blocking, displacement, suppression, denial, passive-aggressive behavior, and the isolation of emotions from content. One significant result of such defenses is the inhibition of spontaneity. Moreno (1971) describes spontaneity as an energy that propels a person toward an adequate response to a new situation or a new response to an old situation.

A major psychopathological affective state for the obsessive-compulsive is anxiety (nonspecific fear). Fear, as first seen in the infant, is a total body response to stress, or to any threat endangering physical survival. In order to survive threat, anger emerges in the form of infantile rage to respond to the threat. A more evolved and refined fear appears in childhood when there is active remembering and active fantasizing that manifests itself in anticipation. At this time the child is capable of deliberated prediction.

This more evolved fear results from a cognitively derived fantasy that anticipates aggression or destruction, and has at its base the emotion of infantile rage, which drives the fantasy that results in fear. This fantasy, this prediction, has a negative outcome. The child projects his or her anger into the world, and then reacts to it with fear. This phenomenon is repeated throughout the life cycle.

Clinicians hear the statement "I'm afraid of the unknown," and take it at face value. Most of us think we understand what is being said. We can identify with the experience, and it makes perfect sense. Therefore we have no need to question its meaningfulness and its validity.

In my clinical understanding, the mythical, awesome, and terrifying "unknown" of which we are afraid is, in fact, only an absence of information. Nature operates to fill its vacuums; so do people when they fill their psychological vacuums with fantasy in reaction to the absence of information. The fantasy has as its outcome injury or destruction of life or limb, of some aspect of personality, or of property. One imagines, for example, that if one goes out into the street something dreadful will happen. When pressed to elaborate what dreadful event will occur, the response can be such images as being hit by a truck, shot, or assaulted. One can imagine an authority figure being critical and shaming rather than appreciative. One can imagine losing a competition, or being fired from one's position. What is important is that these fantasies are future oriented. All of them are based on anger projected outward into people or forces in the world, which is then turned back unto the person who is now the "victim." The "victim" has no awareness that anger led to the fantasy that led to the fear, and that the anger originated with him or her.

In order to control anger and destruction, we develop defense mechanisms at both psychological and behavioral levels. These defenses aim to protect us, and others, as well as property. At times the result can be excessive control, with the manifestation of such traits as ideational inflexibility, rumination, and withdrawal of affect. We know that people with these traits laugh little, enjoy little, and are almost unable to please themselves or others.

Psychotherapy, particularly from a psychodynamic perspective, aims to work with the patient in order to explore the content and the processes of the patient's mind, to generate understanding, to evoke abreactions, and to possibly achieve catharses. Thus, energy is liberated from the bondage of neurotic conflicts and made available for more constructive and creative reinvestment.

The psychodynamically oriented psychotherapeutic process itself, with its explicit and implicit restrictions for both therapist and patient, is a fear-based, obsessive-compulsive approach to clinical intervention. The rituals of the more traditional approach are themselves obsessive in nature. Among them are repeated verbal self-examination, a repetitive narrative process, stress on verbalization rather than action, and repeated reliving of emotions.

Traditional psychodynamically oriented therapy establishes a safe environment for self-exploration because it imposes its own structure, permitting the expression of affect and impulse at minimal levels that are comfortable for the therapist. As a colleague and as a supervisor, I have had the opportunity to observe that therapists are often uncomfortable with the expression of intense affect or impulsive behavior, whether it is expressed by the patient or by themselves. This conservative approach to self-expression is rationalized because it serves to protect the therapist's own sensitivities.

It is advantageous to both patient and therapist to minimize the resistance to insight and change. It is true that most of us want to avoid pain. Yet the process leading to psychological change is often painful. Consequently we employ our defenses in an effort to keep stressful content and processes from reaching awareness and becoming therapeutic currency.

Humor can be used in psychotherapy to move a person from a position of isolation or opposition at the anal stage to a position of cooperation and initiative at the phallic stage. Cooperation is a consequence of the successful resolution of issues related to autonomy and competitiveness.

Killinger (1987) discusses how she became aware of the potential of humor as an adjunctive strategy for coping with obsessive-compulsive mechanisms:

> The humor I had spontaneously begun using in psychotherapy appeared to release patients from a narrow, ego-centered focus while loosening rigid, circular thinking. Thought processes that had become ruminatively stale and closed were interrupted through humor, and new, fresh perspectives emerged. . . . The shift in focus facilitated by humor may then serve to unlock or loosen the rigid repetitive view that individuals often hold regarding their particular situations. (p. 22)

Unfortunately, in the field of psychotherapy, there are no anesthetics to equal the potent chemicals used in surgery. This fact poses a significant challenge to the clinician: how to disengage the fear of the pain attached to the therapeutic process itself so that the patient will responsively receive the therapeutic interventions, arrive at understandings, achieve realizations, and effect changes. A principal protective and pain-reducing strategy that meets this challenge is humor. This means that the therapist is required to have "a sense of humor," to be able to laugh, and to be able to make others laugh. It is important for the therapist to recognize the value of humor in professional practice. A funny psychotherapist is not an oxymoron. Outside our offices, we remember that as children we experienced intensely painful emotions. As adults we can laugh about many of the childhood circumstances within which we felt them. The humorist laughs, and makes others laugh, over painful or embarrassing issues in adult life as well as during childhood.

As a defense, laughter and its concomitant excitation function to divert our experience away from fear. As discussed previously, our own anger, when projected outward in fantasies about the future, can result in us being afraid. Therefore, laughter can also be a manifestation of denial of anger. When we laugh at a prediction, or say "Don't be silly," on the surface we are reacting to the fear. However, at a deeper level we are defending against the fantasy of our omnipotence where it involves our anger.

A term that has puzzled me for some time is "inappropriate laughter." The way I think, there is no such phenomenon. We are all familiar with statements such as: "It's not funny. I shouldn't laugh," "I'm laughing because I am nervous," or "If I didn't laugh, I'd kill you." In each instance, laughter is a defense that both provides and expresses relief (experienced as pleasure), no matter how momentary, from an aggressive impulse. Laughter stimulates, energizes, and blocks negative emotion during its span of expression. One does not laugh and experience fear or anger simultaneously.

Laughing is reflexive. It is a response to pleasure and amusement. Babies smile. They laugh. They laugh when they feel "good," when they enjoy something or someone. They laugh when something amuses them or when they feel pleasantly stimulated at a physical level. They do not laugh when they are afraid, when they have gas, or when they are hungry. Adults do not laugh when they are assaulted, receive news that someone has died, or are told that they have cancer.

That anger and fear also stimulate is true. Both produce the condition of excitation. However, there is a difference. Fear moves the person away from others, resulting in isolation. Anger moves the person against others, often resulting in antagonism. Humor, on the other hand, moves a person closer to himself or herself and to others. The latter is true whether the humor is benign or aggressive. Some comedians employ aggressive humor, targeting members of the audience, and are nevertheless very popular - even with their "victims." My understanding of this phenomenon is that the audience perceives the humor to be, in the words of patients, "not-angry aggressive" or "friendly hostile." In other words, the comedian bears no personal animosity toward his or her victim. Thus, the expression and the reception of the exaggerated and caricatured anger occurs within a safe interpersonal context. The recipient of the comedian's aggressive remarks experiences the embarrassment (the exposure and injury to aspects of his or her self-concept) but also the fulfillment of a wish for attention and a sense of being special. The aggression tickles in the same way as when one tells a child: "I love you so much I could eat you up."

Having looked at the words "humor" and "laugh," we now give attention to the word "smile." Etymologically it relates to being astonished, which means being filled with sudden wonder or great surprise. "Astonish" relates to the word "thunder" which is a loud rustling deep noise (Guralnik, *Webster's Dictionary*, 1984). When one smiles or laughs, even in the midst of sorrow or anger, it reflects a moment of feeling "good," of being filled with sudden wonder or great surprise.

I concur with the notion that humor can be regarded as a protective lubricant. Through the utilization of humor as a defense and as a facilitator the therapist can reduce the pain that may be associated with the patient's productions or with therapist interventions.

The therapist can make interventions such as interpretations, clarifications, and empathic statements regarding the manifest content (that which the patient actually speaks about). The therapist can also make comments about process (the underlying psychological principles of functioning within the patient's personality structure). Both types of intervention can have an impact upon the patient's intellectual and emotional world. The patient can respond with much pain as heretofore unspoken conflicts, impulses, and self-experiences are brought to life in the therapeutic encounter. There can be much pain attached to realizations about transference reactions, repetition-compulsions, denial, intellectualization, projection, and other ways of engaging in self-protection.

In part, the patient's resistance in psychotherapy is a reaction to a method of clinical intervention which encourages the resurfacing of archaic, emotionally hurtful material. When there is pain with its accompanying sense of vulnerability, there is also a move to enlist anger as a defense to protect against the feared potential elimination of aspects of our psychological life. This anger provides a false sense of strength and courage.

Patients do not want to remember, let alone relive, traumatic historical experiences and emotions that have led to maladaptive processes. Maladaptations have their purpose: to allow the patient to continue living in his or her imperfect and hurtful world. The maladaptive processes have as their purpose the protection of the individual from the fear of taking new initiatives, from running the risk of failure or success, and from further pain.

Yet there is a window through which the therapist can enter the pain-sensitive areas of a person's life - humor. Colloquially, we use the expression "slip one in." Employing humor as the lubricant, the therapist can "slip in" or "ease in" an interpretation, a clarification, or a confrontation, bypassing and/or disarming the resistance. Employing humor as the vehicle for transporting an intervention, the clinician can assist the patient to regard experiences, content, and processes in new ways.

The patient, in the midst of laughter, may not be aware that self-protecting strategies have been circumvented. At times, after the laughter or the smile has ended - sometimes in a matter of seconds - the patient may say "That's not fair" or "You manipulated me" or "That was a dirty trick." Therapists can be very sensitive to guilt. Perhaps that is part of our training; perhaps part of our nature. We don't like being accused of misdemeanors. Consequently, we overly constrain ourselves with our own obsessive-compulsive processes, sometimes offering lofty rationalizations with which we attempt to anchor ourselves to an idealized theory or an idealized authority figure. I have seen Kubie (1971) cited on more than one occasion as presenting authoritative reasons for not engaging humor as a therapeutic strategy. My thinking is that the resistance to humor and other nonconservative adjunctive strategies in psychotherapy is based on the myth of the therapist's omnipotence. It is as if reality has not been tested, that experiential lessons have not been learned.

The therapist, through the power invested in him or her by the patient, can influence or "flow into" the patient. Although words are powerful, words do not either cause or cure illness. The therapist's words do not cause decompensation or resistance. Decompensation is a form of resistance related to an angry effort to escape the influence of a person or situation. The patient's response to the therapist's interventions is the choice, conscious or subconscious, of the patient. I put forth that the negative attitude toward humor as a means of facilitation is based upon a collusion between the therapist's fear of his or her imagined omnipotence and an assumption regarding the patient's imagined fragility. In that perspective, there seems to be a sharper focus on the patient's dysfunction than there is on his or her ego resources.

TECHNIQUE

When I refer to humor I refer to anything, verbal or nonverbal, that will produce a smile or a laugh. The therapist may be funny, sarcastic, facetious, ridiculous, or mocking. Humor may be expressed with words, facial gestures, voice tone, phrasing, or body language. Often the laughter has less to do with the content of the words than with the delivery. As comedians know, "Delivery is everything."

In order to address the patient's defenses during psychotherapy, the therapist can choose from three response modalities: reflecting the same developmental level as the patient, presenting a developmental level higher than that of the patient, or presenting a developmental level lower than that of the patient. Because of its nature, humor as a mature defense facilitates both regression as well as simultaneous access to higher developmental levels. The therapist, through a mirroring of the patient's anger with his or her use of "not-angry aggressive" humor can bypass or disarm obsessive defenses.

The therapist can also choose to analyze the resistances, to claim they don't exist, to confront them, to bypass them, or to disarm them. In conventional psychodynamic therapy, the method, in part, is to analyze them.

Bypassing and disarming the resistances facilitates a more rapid access to conflicts that originally necessitated the defenses. For example:

Patient:　I just don't feel confident. I'm anxious in social situations. I know people don't like me, but I don't know what's wrong with me. . . . Sometimes I feel like hiding from everybody. . . .

Therapist:　(In baby talk) Aw geee, you such a nice gool (ghoul). (A corruption of "girl")

Patient:　(Gives an immediate smile followed by a quick defensive response) That wasn't nice. You're making fun of me.

Therapist:　You angwy wif me. But you smiled, and I'm wondering why.

Patient:　You spoke in baby talk. You sounded funny.

Therapist:　It's funny when an adult, a therapist, talks baby talk? It ought to be embarrassing. It's not appropriate.

Patient:　You just sounded cute, but I think you were mocking me.

Therapist:　Imitating you!

Patient:　No, mocking me!

Therapist:　(In baby talk) You wanna fight wif me?

Patient:　(Smiles) Cut that out!

Therapist:　Okay, if you will. Now, tell me what did you really feel good about.

Patient:　I don't believe it. You called me a "ghoul."

Therapist:　You know, you have a weird sense of humor. That's an insult, not a compliment.

Patient:　(Smiling) Stop it. I'm not weird.

Therapist:　I didn't say *you* were *weird.* I said you were nice and that your sense of humor is weird. What are you smiling at. . . ?

Patient:　You.

Therapist:　Me? . . . me?

Patient:　You're awful. You know, I think I'm unattractive, and there is something about me that puts people off. When you called me a ghoul the first word I thought of was "witch." My mother called me that a lot when I was a kid. You didn't know that, did you?

One aspect of caricature is that it portrays features of a person in an exaggerated manner. Parody devaluates content, travesty devalues form or process. In the foregoing example, the obsessive, self-embarrassing, self-devaluing aspects of the patient are initially caricatured. In doing so the therapist intends to devalue both the content and the processes that she is introducing.

Caricature is aggressive in nature. In this case, it was used to "fight fire with fire," to engage the patient's anger in an interpersonal transaction rather than have it continue to be aimed at herself in an obsessive manner. The therapist, in his interventions, enacts the conflicted child within the patient which, when experienced by the patient, is recognized. The humor in the therapist's caricature adopts the patient's negative attitudes and self-destroying anger, liberating her to experience the pleasure of being aggression-free, conflict-free, for the moment. The aggression is now directed toward the therapist in a quasi-annoyed manner, and with pleasure. The earlier self-induced emotional pain is absent for the moment, and she has considerable difficulty maintaining her obsessive ideational processes. Continuing with humor, the therapist disarms the patient's anger both toward herself and toward the therapist. The obsessive process yields, and the result of these interchanges is the presentation for exploration of an earlier painful character-assassination experience.

A second caricature enactment became a dramatic turning point in working with another patient. Although the experience was painful for the patient, the conclusion was "funny" and "fun." I had been working with a young woman for about 8 months. She suffered from severely disruptive personality processes. Her reality testing in most areas of her life was poor, her emotions were highly labile, and her impulse control seemed inconsistent.

One day as we walked down the hall to the office for our session, she began kicking the walls. Once inside the office she became verbally explosive and stomped the floor. I chose to respond at the other extreme. I sat in my chair and moved into a fetal position. I remained silent. I began gesticulating with my hands in an autistic manner. I hid my face behind my hands, peering through my fingers. I remained silent. Within several minutes the patient began to notice me.

Patient: What are you doing? Who are you?
Therapist: (Remains silent, and continues the self-absorbed behavior)
Patient: Answer me. Who are you? What are you doing? You're scaring me.

Therapist: (Remains silent, and continues the self-absorbed behavior)

Patient: (Gets down on her hands and knees and crawls over to the therapist and clings onto his leg) Who are you? Answer me. I'm scared. Please answer me. Who are you? Are you okay?

Therapist: Don't touch me. You want to kill me. Go away. Don't touch me.

Patient: No I don't. Honest. Are you okay? What's the matter with you?

Therapist: You're lying. You don't care. Don't touch me.

Patient: (Begins to cry and then sob) Don't do that. Please don't say that. Who are you. I don't know you. Stop. Please stop.

Therapist: (Remains silent)

Patient: Do you want a candy? I have a candy. (She pulls over her purse and starts going through it)

Therapist: No. You want to kill me. It's poison.

Patient: No it's not. Honest. Please take a candy.

Therapist: What kind?

Patient: Oh, it's a Life Saver.

Therapist: A Life Saver. Are you sure it's okay? (The therapist begins to wind down the enactment)

Patient: I promise. Honest.

Therapist: Okay. That is really kind of you. Thank you.

Patient: Do you feel better?

Therapist: Thank you. I'm feeling better all the time.

Patient: (Smiles, then breaks into a laugh, hugs the therapist's leg, and exclaims "You're okay!")

Therapist: (She continued to sit on the floor at my feet, laughing and crying) What's happening? What's this all about?

Patient: (Breaks into a big smile, shows pleasure and excitement) You took on all my badness, and all that was left for me to experience was my goodness. (Begins to laugh)

Therapist: (Joins in the laughter)

Patient: I feel good. This is fun.

Therapist/Patient: (Share a moment of silence and contentment. Nothing more needs to be said.)

For Freud (Kris, 1965), that which is comic bears a close relation to infantile life. Its expression in words revives modes of expression employed by the child as he or she was developing speech responses. In the first vignette, the manner of speech and some of the words used were an invitation for the patient to return to childhood conflicts in order to work them into the therapeutic conversation. The patient felt pleasure and laughed because "you mimicked something I know."

PERTINENT ISSUES

I consider the use of humor with obsessive patients to be a way for introducing excitement, pleasure, an emotional tickle, into the patient's experience with the therapist. It also encourages an impressionistic response. Humor allows the therapist and the patient to respond to each other on a channel of affect rather than on an intellectual, reasoned, logical wavelength. Humor is generally considered to be palliative. It eases pain and suffering. It facilitates the emergence of personally relevant material. On the other hand, humor can be employed to arouse anger or anxiety. There are occasions when this is a desirable strategy. One example is when the patient is at a loss for something to say because there is no obvious distress. Another example is when the therapist wishes to evoke anxiety, fear, or anger, in order to yield potentially more productive material. In the aforecited examples of caricature, anxiety and anger were aroused. These emotions reflect a recognition that an element or trait of personality has been uncovered about which one feels ashamed or guilty. The attendant feeling of vulnerability results in fear and anger. Yet when the emotional cycle is successfully played out, there is pleasure and relief.

For now, we must rely upon our own creativity and intuition to sense the appropriate time for introducing humor into the psychotherapy session. As much as I would like to, I have been unable to formulate a reasonable or objective set of criteria for using a particular type of humor in a given circumstance with a patient. Sometimes the strategy to use humor, and/or the humor itself, bombs. Seeing the humor in that, and laughing, is in itself a good object lesson for the patient regarding how to respond to a failed effort.

CLINICAL PRESENTATIONS

CASE 1

A male patient stated: "I keep worrying that I ran over someone. I keep looking out the rear-view mirror. It drives me crazy. I can't drive. I do but . . . I probably knocked down some little old lady. How do I know I didn't? It doesn't matter who's in the car with me. I go strange."

Therapist: Vroom, vroom.
Patient: What are you doing?
Therapist: Vroom, vroom - vroom, vroom.
Patient: You crazy?
Therapist: Maybe.
Patient: Stop kidding around.
Therapist: Vroom, vroom. I think I knocked an old lady down. Oo-oo-ps, I mean maybe . . . (Pause) . . . I knocked her up.
Patient: (Laughing) You're nuts?
Therapist: Your nuts scare the devil out of you! Co-o-ome on, what are you smiling about?
Patient: (Laughs) You're telling me I knocked an old lady up!
Therapist: Maybe not *an* old lady!
Patient: Oh shit . . . *my* old lady.
Therapist: I didn't say that, but I'm willing to consider the possibility.
Patient: (Smiling) You're telling me that I am anxious about knocking down, or up, or whatever, my old lady, my mother! (Laughs)
Therapist: So what's so funny?
Patient: I don't know. I suddenly feel very sad. I don't know.

In this example, the patient is talking about an anxiety-loaded rumination. The impulse is aggression, and there is doubt. The therapist employs humor to dislodge the expressed anxiety from the aggression expressed in the rumination. The patient becomes anxious (feels threatened) and mildly angry in relation to what the therapist is doing. However, the therapist disregards the fear and its defense of anger, continuing with humor in order to present and facilitate the patient's acceptance of an impulse-superego conflict interpretation, the content of which is at a phallic (oedipal) level. The latter is accomplished by the use of "double entendres" or double meanings. Sadness is felt as the patient is suddenly in touch with feelings of love and loss.

In the midst of this clinical material I am inserting a short vignette to provide another illustration of the use of the "double entendres" to minimize anxiety in a situation of acute distress.

Mr. Kohin has had a heart attack and is being attended by a paramedic who has just covered him with a blanket.

Paramedic: Are you comfortable, Mr. Kohin?
Patient: Thank God, I make a living.

In an effort to deny the gravity of the situation, reduce the anxiety, and focus on life rather than possible death, the patient switches the sense of the word "comfort," and the effect is humorous.

CASE 2

The patient is in the midst of a long monologue: ". . . and I only want to do something I like. Trouble is, I can't decide what I would like to work at. I don't seem to have any choices. I . . . this is embarrassing . . . I try . . . to. . . ."

Therapist: Paul, enough. Tell me a joke.
Patient: What?
Therapist: Ya, I asked you to tell me a joke.
Patient: I don't know any. Besides, I always screw them up.
Therapist: Paul, someone at some time told you a joke, and it's somewhere in your mind.
Patient: I . . . I'm not sure how to tell this one. . . .
Therapist: I guess we're stuck then. (Starts to smile and then to chuckle as he looks straight at Paul)
Patient: (Starts to smile, then laughs) What are you smiling about?
Therapist: I'm thinking about something funny.
Patient: Okay, I think I've got it right. Do you want to hear it?
Therapist: Of course!
Patient: There was this rabbi and this priest and they were sitting beside each other on a flight. And the stewardess says, "Gentlemen, can I offer you something?" And the rabbi says - "I'll have a Bloody Mary." The priest

says - "I don't drink and I don't fornicate." The rabbi looks at the priest and motions to the stewardess, calling her back, and says - "Miss, I didn't realize I had a choice!"

Therapist/Patient: (Both laugh. The therapist always laughs, no matter how "bad" the joke, valuing the processes in the patient that produced it.)

Therapist: How do you feel right now?

Patient: Right now? Okay.

Therapist: Interesting. How come?

Patient: The joke is funny.

Therapist: What about it is funny for you?

Patient: You laughed too.

Therapist: I did. What's funny for you?

Patient: The rabbi's a lush and wants to fool around. You know what I mean?

Therapist: (In an amused manner) That's funny!? You enjoy the fact that the rabbi would rather make it with the stewardess than have a drink. The rabbi, a good upstanding, moral, ethical, and spiritual leader is ready to descend into the gutter, and you think it's a joke. What's the matter with you?

Patient: (Laughing) I'll bet you're no Mr. Kleen either.

Therapist: Thank you. I take that as a compliment, Paul. Interesting how we were talking about work, and now we're talking about fornicating; sex a mile high; and instead of obsessing, you're challenging. Paul, there is a difference between knowing you have a choice and realizing you have a choice. You chose the joke. And the joke was about choice, after you had been complaining that you had no choice. I think it was funny for you because you really are not interested in work right now. You don't want to conform to the demands of a job, a boss, a schedule, a dress code, productivity. You have other things on your mind - like . . . women, sex. . . ."

Patient: (Smiling) You're damn right!

Therapist: So!

Patient: (With new energy) Okay. First I can tell you, I'd be too embarrassed to ask a stewardess to go out. They meet so many guys. . . ."

The mutual experience of the comical, through the telling of a joke, affects the listener like "an invitation to common aggression and common regression." (In this example the therapist invited the patient to invite the therapist into this process.) The pleasure comes from a common regression and common utilization of infantile modes of thought (Kris, 1965).

This joke, with its sexual content, its focus on choice and initiative, paves the way for the patient to approach conflictual material. The patient shifted away from anal level obsessive-compulsive processing to seducing with a joke - which is a higher developmental phallic stage function. There is now a shift in attention away from uncertainty and ambivalence about work, toward the exploration of phallic level relationships with women. For the moment, the less mature defenses have been disarmed.

Humor is like a handshake. It attaches people to one another. It facilitates interpersonal alliances and evokes positive feelings between people. Especially significant for the obsessive patient is the fact that humor provides an experiential learning that attachment, problem solving, and self-awareness can occur in ego supportive, pleasurable contexts. With humor, obsessive patients may come to realize that learning, growing, and changing do not have to be constantly painful experiences.

When a constructive environment is established in therapy such that interaction between therapist and patient can be pleasurable, the patient looks forward to subsequent sessions, anticipates working, and may engage in positive activities in preparation for the next session.

Kris (1965) writes: "No clear line can be drawn between play and fun, and as early as the end of the first year both are expressed and understood. . . . Even in a child's second year, and in fully developed form in the third, fun is over and over again favored as the chosen means of mastering aggression, or more correctly, ambivalence. Even the attitude expressed by fun plainly shows that it has to perform the task of mastery and defense" (pp. 182-183).

When assessing a candidate for psychotherapy, I make a point of asking the person to tell me a joke. People are often self-conscious about telling a joke. They risk narcissistic injury if the joke fails. After all, the joke-teller wants the listener to find the joke funny. He or she wants to be liked and appreciated.

The freedom to laugh, to tell a joke, is related to the ability to function, even briefly, at a phallic (oedipal) level, which involves the capacity to take initiative, to seduce, and to be seduced. The patient's efforts to make the therapist laugh reflect an ability to initiate and participate in a cooperative interpersonal relationship. Stimulating another person to laughter touches a positive emotional chord and stimulates an initial, if brief, attachment. The ability to laugh is the ability to be aroused and to be spontaneous. Moreno's (1971) conceptualizing of spontaneity has it as a readiness, a precursor, for creativity. These considerations are significant in assessing a person's potential response to treatment.

SYNTHESIS

As an adjunctive technique in psychotherapy, humor is particularly aimed at the obsessive-compulsive processes and "is mainly concerned with the negative aspects of life. It is a form of criticism. While people can laugh easily at the absurd, the pretentious, even the mean, they are hardly likely to be sent into gales of laughter by the sincere, the upright, the noble" (Ausubel, 1951, p. XIX).

Some humor seems to take its energy from anger. The feeling of anger can be thought of as a defense against a sense of vulnerability and a feeling of fear. Anger gives one the impression of possessing strength. It is important to distinguish between infantile rage, a global undifferentiated body response seen in infancy, and early childhood anger. Rage is prelogical and not associated with verbal symbols. It involves gross motor movement, massive vocalization, and is a total body response aimed at physical survival. Out of this primitive energy emerges goal-directed anger and goal-directed aggression. This goal-oriented anger with its refinement, purposefulness, and verbal symbols, can further evolve into humor, given a context of emotional maturity.

We know that humor can be aggressive, and aimed at a particular person, group of persons, or institutions. Because it requires deliberation or planning as well as verbal and nonverbal symbols, humor can be thought of as a mature obsessive-compulsive defense. But humor goes beyond the obsessive-compulsive. It bridges the obsessive and hysterical processes. It aims to evoke emotionally intense responses. It often has as a context the nostalgic, the romantic, and the idealized. It aims to bypass intellectual processing. It is designed to hit its mark at the level of feelings. The patient is moved from a thought-oriented, deliberate, anger-related set of processes, to a response set that is feeling-oriented and "love"-related (Shapiro, 1965, pp. 111-118). Humor aims to touch the intuitive. As Saint-Exupéry (1943) wrote in *The Little Prince*, "It is only with the heart that one can see rightly; what is essential is invisible to the eye" (p. 70). Humor aims at the heart of what matters. It targets what is essential.

A longer range goal of using humor is to have the patient achieve an integration of both obsessive-compulsive and hysterical traits. With humor, defensive anger, which is maladaptive in our neurotic and psychotic patients, is rechanneled as a means of mobilizing positive attachment, trust, and hope. In turn, these feelings influence the thought processes so that one now considers positive options and takes new initiatives, making creative adaptations possible in the face of adversity.

I would like to end this chapter by presenting a patient's perspective with regard to the use of humor to disarm obsessive-compulsive processes. The patient is a 26-year-old married woman, now completing the requirements for her doctorate in psychology, with whom I am engaged in long-term reconstructive therapy. At this juncture of our work together, she often comes to our sessions with a toy - a white cat, similar to her pet at home. During times of stress in the sessions she has often taken it from her bag to caress it, or hammer it against her seat. Sometimes she has spoken to me through it. I recently asked her to make a brief note on the humor she experienced during our time together. At the session following this request, she presented me with the following eloquent note on therapeutic humor:

> What I consider to be humorous are generally experiences that hold a pleasant and unexpected element. During these times I experience what would be called "delight." A recent session with you when you pretended to be a small child, I think, was particularly pleasing, and I laughed throughout most of it. The humor emerged from the situation. During that hour the conversation and movement was spontaneous on both our parts. You spoke about the leaves and making a nest to sleep in and chocolate cows and "titties" and watching me play with my pussy. You spoke like an imaginative child who was "free" and happy. For me, it felt warm and good, and I felt free to participate in the generally spontaneous atmosphere. I am smiling now as I remember that afternoon.

Humor between us also emerges when you "creative-ly" connect with some aspect of myself. This quality of creativity is difficult to describe, because it is not primari-ly analytic or cognitive and because I am not particularly creative at an interpersonal level. A good example of it is last week when you said "Get your mother out of here," in response to one of my "shoulds." I wasn't aware that she was with us, and yet as you repeated it, I started to smile and then to laugh. You were so serious as you said it! Again there was an incongruity, an element of surprise, which gave space for freedom to experience my mother's presence in me, but I didn't feel criticized as I usually would had you spoken more conventionally. The humor came from your *SELF,* from your integration of thought, feeling, and imagination, from your capacity to visualize and your movements from abstract to concrete in a verbal ballet that I could not predict. When you connect with me at a meaningful level there is often an element of humor in the way that I "process" the message, despite my resist-ances.

REFERENCES

Ausubel, N. A. (Ed.). (1951). *Treasury of Jewish Humor.* Gar-den City, NY: Doubleday.

Brill, A. A. (Ed.). (1938). *The Basic Writings of Sigmund Freud.* New York: Basic Books.

Guralnik, D. B. (Ed.). (1984). *Webster's New World Dictionary of the American Language* (Second College Edition). New York: Simon and Schuster.

Killinger, B. (1987). Humor in psychotherapy: A shift to a new perspective. In W. F. Fry, Jr. & W. A. Salameh (Eds.), *Handbook of Humor and Psychotherapy: Advances in the Clinical Use of Humor* (pp. 21-40). Sarasota, FL: Profession-al Resource Exchange.

Kris, E. (1965). *Psychoanalytic Explorations in Art.* New York: International Universities Press.

Kubie, L. S. (1971). The destructive potential of humor in psy-chotherapy. *American Journal of Psychotherapy, 127,* 861-866.

Meissner, W. W. (1985). Theories of personality and psycho-pathology: Classical Psychoanalysis. In H. I. Kaplan & B. J.

Sadock (Eds.), *Comprehensive Textbook of Psychiatry/IV* (pp. 337-418). Baltimore: Williams and Wilkins.

Moreno, J. L. (1971). Psychodrama. In H. I. Kaplan & B. J. Sadock, (Eds.), *Comprehensive Group Psychotherapy* (pp. 460-500). Baltimore: Williams and Wilkins.

Nemiah, J. C. (1985). Obsessive-compulsive disorder (obsessive compulsive neurosis). In H. I. Kaplan & B. J. Sadock (Eds.), *Comprehensive Textbook of Psychiatry/IV* (pp. 904-917). Baltimore: Williams and Wilkins.

Saint-Exupéry, A. de. (1943). *The Little Prince.* New York: Harcourt, Brace, & World.

Shapiro, D. (1965). *Neurotic Styles.* New York: Basic Books.

Vaillant, G. (1977). *Adaptation to Life.* Boston: Little, Brown.

8

The Enlightenment
of Sisyphus

Waleed A. Salameh

In this chapter, Dr. Salameh picks up the allegory of Sisyphus where Albert Camus left off and addresses the issue of how to help Sisyphus with his nihilistic absurdity. Using various vignettes from Dr. Shamrock's inspirational stories, Salameh seeks constructive remedies to the absurd dilemmas of life presented by patients. His hope is that Sisyphus and Dr. Shamrock will become good friends while the Gods continue with their demonstration projects.

Waleed A. Salameh, PhD, is a clinical psychologist, organizational consultant, and international trainer in private practice in San Diego, California. He is the author of over 140 articles, presentations, clinical handbooks, and invited chapters in the areas of psychotherapy and effective communications. His book chapters on the subject of humor and psychotherapy include: "Humor in Psychotherapy: Past Outlooks, Present Status, and Future Frontiers" (1983); "Humor as a Form of Indirect Hypnotic Communication" (1986); "The Effective Use of Humor in Psychotherapy" (1986); and "Humor in Integrative Short-Term Psychotherapy (ISTP)" (1987). Dr. Salameh is the originator of Humor Immersion Training (HIT), a systematic approach to the development of humor skills.

❖   ❖   ❖

Sisyphus was getting tired. Carrying the rock up and down the hill was not his idea of a grand time. Whatever philosophical or spiritual meaning was meant by the Gods to be attached to his unending repetitive gestures was certainly beyond the pale of his understanding. Whatever latent meanings were supposed to emanate from his gestures seemed to quickly evaporate under the harsh sun of his daily toils. Wake up every morning, shave, position the rock as comfortably as possible over his shoulders, go up the hill, come down the hill, do it again, then do it over again all day long. He was simply fed up. Although the salary and benefits package was good, this thing was taking too long.

Up beyond the clouds, in the inner sanctum of God Land, the Gods noticed that Sisyphus was getting restless. They knew that they had to soothe his soul. Somehow, he needed to make sense of his predicament. Following an emergency meeting to address Sisyphus' discontent, the Council of Gods decided to send Tiara, the new Outside Sales Representative, to talk to Sisyphus. The Gods wanted the Sisyphus theme park to serve as a good demonstration project for the God Council's exemplification of the human condition. Tiara seemed to be the right person to work on the human resources side of the Sisyphus problem. If Sisyphus were dissatisfied with his existence, then surely Tiara could do something to attend to his problem.

Tiara happened to be a rather extraordinary being. During her sojourn on earth, she had been an amiable and extremely successful advertising executive. Due to her human condition, she had sought help from a system humans call Psychotherapy. The way the Gods saw it, humans had devised a unique program to change their human condition that they called psychotherapy. To the Gods, therapy was like a nonreligious religion, a way of cleansing the emotional system of impurities. It included a little bit of what humans call Science, a little bit of creativity, a little bit of the Spirit, a little bit of heaven, and a little bit of hell. While on earth, Tiara had seen a psychologist by the name of Dr. Shamrock. Dr. Shamrock used to teach her things by telling her stories about his interactions with different patients, especially the humorous interactions, because he felt that humor had inspirational value. Tiara thought that the best way to heal Sisyphus' problems was to tell him some of the inspirational humorous stories recounted to her by Dr. Shamrock. She reasoned that Sisyphus might take solace in the fact that he was not alone, that other people experienced similar issues, and, if he could laugh, there would be some liberation released with the laughter.

Tiara went down to earth to meet Sisyphus, who was arduously toiling as he carried his rock up the hill. She told him that she wanted to help, and that she understood his predicament. She told him about Dr. Shamrock and his inspirational humorous stories, all of which was of great interest to Sisyphus. She then proposed to walk up and down the hill with Sisyphus every day and tell him some of Dr. Shamrock's humorous therapeutic stories. Sisyphus gladly welcomed this unexpected change in his daily routine. Tiara related the stories to Sisyphus in exactly the same way that Dr. Shamrock had conveyed them to her, in the first person singular, to give them immediacy and intensity. Here are some of Dr. Shamrock's stories as told to Sisyphus by Tiara.

CASE VIGNETTES*

SURPASSING LIMITATIONS

A 45-year-old divorced woman related in group therapy that she was attracted to a 66-year-old man, who was also interested in her and had frequently asked her out. However, she was emotionally holding back with him because: "I don't know, about 66," to which I replied: "So he's 66? He's over the speed limit! Are you afraid you are going to get a traffic ticket for a *moving* violation?" to which both the group and the patient responded with hearty laughter.

THE CONSUMERISM TRAP VERSUS HUMAN INTIMACY

A woman was separated from her husband and was working with him in couples therapy to repair the marriage. She was invited by the husband during a therapy session to a long walk by the beach the next morning so they could comfortably talk to each other. She responded that she could not spend the next morning with him because the local department store was having their once-a-year sale, and she really wanted to "Catch the bargains." In response to their interaction, I visually imagined a cartoon scene that I conveyed to them: "I am just imagining the two of you in a Romeo and Juliet scene with Romeo serenading Juliet under her balcony, asking her to spend tomorrow morning with him. Juliet answers, 'I'm sorry honey, I can't see you tomorrow. I've got to go to the once-a-year sale at the piazza!' "

---

*In order to protect the confidentiality of Tiara, Sisyphus, Dr. Shamrock, and all the other protagonists, certain details in the stories have been altered to maintain anonymity.

SHOULD VERSUS IS

A divorced woman who happened to be Catholic was depressed because, prior to her divorce, she had an affair with
another man and lived with him intermittently while her then husband was traveling. Although her marriage had been declared
emotionally dead for a long time prior to the affair, she still felt
remorseful that, had she not had the affair, perhaps she and her
husband would have recaptured their love for each other. She
maintained this viewpoint despite previous revelations that her
husband had practically abandoned her early on in their marriage
and had pursued numerous affairs throughout the relationship.
During a session when this issue was brought up, I commented:
"So you were living in sin with this man while your ex-husband
was traveling?" which she answered semi-laughingly: "Yes, I
guess I was." I then told her: "Well, are you saying that you and
he were fornicating? You know how Catholicism views fornica-
tion, don't you!" The patient broke out laughing, saying: "Yes,
we were fornicating, but I suppose that's what I really wanted to
do. It was better than trying to revive a dead relationship," to
which I replied: "I do understand your feelings about shoulds.
You are looking at the product of 12 years of Catholic school."

FLOWERS BURSTING OUT OF THE TRUNK

A woman reported in individual therapy an interesting dream
that she had the night before. The dream was particularly relevant
because it coincided with the patient owning up to her true incli-
nations regarding a major life transition. The life transition involved her deciding to accept a lower paying job that was emotionally satisfying to her while simultaneously resigning from a
high-paying glamorous job that seemed stress inducing and highly
uncomfortable. As reported by the patient, the dream consisted of
driving down the freeway in her car with her boyfriend when she
noticed that the trunk was open. She pulled over to the roadside
to close the trunk when she suddenly discovered all kinds of mul-
ticolored and fragrant flowers bursting out of the trunk that were
forcing it to open. She then stated, laughing, that she tried to
close the trunk several times to no avail, even with her boyfriend's
help. Each time she would close the trunk, the tenacious flowers
inside would push it open. She reported that during her dream
she was laughing hysterically at this turn of events, wondering

where all the flowers came from and why she couldn't close the trunk. She would shut the trunk and it would pop open over and over again with the brilliant flowers gushing out of it. The patient was wondering what the dream meant, and commented that she thought it was "funny." In further discussing the dream with her, I responded that the dream was a rather eloquent symbolic message from her unconscious mind that was being conveyed through the medium of humor. The message was that no matter how often she tried to lock herself up in the trunk, her burgeoning, irrepressible Self with its gifts of fragrant and colorful flowers would time and again assert itself and pop the trunk open. The locked trunk represented her rigid character armor while the open trunk was a metaphor for her free, authentic Self. The flowers represented the new learnings and positive developments in her life that were now asking for recognition and inclusion in her total self-image. No matter how many times she tried to close the trunk on the flowers of Self, her genuine Self would still emerge, undaunted, gleaming, in full regalia. Moreover, the dream also constituted a humorous tip of the hat to the patient from her unconscious world to keep moving in the direction of authenticity and personal growth. Following this episode, the patient carried on with an onslaught of constructive life decisions and therapeutic breakthroughs that squarely thrust her in the direction of the flowering trunk, away from the closed repressed trunk. From then on, her "trunk" was open to the world, exposed to the sun, continuing the journey of authentic personhood. As of the last reading, the rebellious flowers were still blooming.

HIGH ANXIETY - BEYOND MEL BROOKS

A highly anxious patient was constantly worried about different items in his life. The weekly special would change, but the obsessiveness remained. I told him: "These obsessive thoughts keep patrolling your timeline. When you're depressed they go to the past, and when you're anxious they go to the future." He replied: "Moses is my teacher. He patrolled Mount Sinai for a long time, he was very worried." The patient then continued: "I can just imagine a historic encounter between me and Moses. My obsessive thoughts are patrolling my timeline and Moses is patrolling Mount Sinai. We meet each other somewhere on the slopes, and he is holding the Tablets in his hands. He gives them to me, saying: 'Here. Take two tablets and call me in the morning.' "

As the patient and I heartily laughed regarding his scenario, it dawned on me that much of his anxiety was related to the Ten Commandments - guilt.

SELF-IMPOSED IMPRISONMENT

A man revealed in group therapy that, when he interacted with women, he was mostly interested in the sexual aspect of the interaction, to which another group member replied: "You're locked up in a penistentiary!"

MOODINESS

A brooding, cranky man was complaining in marital therapy about different items not going well in his life, although the items did not seem to be so catastrophic. I asked: "What's the matter? Are you having your period?" The patient replied: "Yes, yes, I guess I'm having my period," to which his wife retorted: "Ask me! I know all about that! Not only is he moody, but he sees red at every turn, and at night it's the old 'not tonight, I have a head-ache honey!' "

THE TIMELESS CURE

A patient was making little, if any, progress in therapy due to his stubbornness and his refusal to experiment with new yet nec-essary changes in his life. At one point, it seemed that the only way to work with him was to ally oneself with his resistances, to move in the same direction as his oppositionalism. When he complained at one point about not making much progress since he started therapy, I replied: "Well, you know, therapy usually takes a long time. I'm not in a rush as far as you are concerned. What-ever can be done well in a short period of time can be done just as well in a long period of time," to which the patient replied: "I have been making regular contributions to the Therapist Retire-ment Fund." After the laughter, he was able to more comfortably explore his resistances and where he was getting stuck.

DEATH

During a psychotherapy session, a 77-year-old patient brought up the issue of growing old and his fear of dying. He stated that he examines the obituary section of the newspaper every day and had recently recognized some of the names in the obituaries as people he knew. He then commented: "You know, it's funny. Some people are dying now that have never died before."

BOUNDARIES

An impulsive man had difficulties controlling himself in different situations where his impulsivity seemed to be harming both his personal and relational life. I recounted this joke to him: "A man came to visit a friend in an apartment building, but could not find a parking space. Frustrated, he decided to park in a space earmarked for resident parking. After he parked his car, he looked up and saw a beautiful woman beckoning to him from a window on the third floor to come up and visit her. Curious about the situation, he went up to the third floor and knocked on her apartment door. She greeted him in an attractive negligee and seductively invited him in. He went in with great trepidation and as he reached out to her, she hit him, saying: "Stay out of my parking space!"

UNNECESSARY BURDENS

A female patient related during a group therapy session that she really liked gardening. She liked it so much, in fact, that she wanted to take a week off work to take care of her garden and trim her flowers. But she could not carry out this project because trimming the hedge on her property line might offend the neighbors whose properties surrounded hers. I commented: "Perhaps you should go around and have all your neighbors sign a petition that it is okay for you to trim your flowers." She responded with a half-smile. I continued: "Actually, this issue is so important that it should be on the next State of California ballot. The people of this state should be able to vote on how what you do affects the environment!" to which the patient and the other group members responded with uproarious laughter.

THE SECRET TELEPHONE NUMBER

A married couple came in seeking sex therapy because they experienced certain inhibitions regarding sexuality that could be

traced back to their dysfunctional upbringing in strict family milieus. They had difficulty creating sexual excitement and sexually
letting go with each other because they had not learned the language needed to describe their sexual needs and build up a stimulating sexual ambience with each other. In response to this problem, and in a rather serious fashion, I made the following sex
therapy assignment to them. The assignment consisted of each of
them calling the other partner at work at least twice a week during
the day, when they would not normally see each other. The caller
had to pretend that the person on the other line was a sexy respondent from a 900 number (900 numbers are for-pay telephone
numbers where callers pay to have a sizzling sexual conversation
with a supposed male or female sexpot). The assignment to the
couple was that when one of the partners called the other in this
manner saying: "Have I reached the 900 number?" the other person was supposed to answer: "Yes" and respond to the caller in
the same sexually provocative manner that is supposedly used by
the 900 number operators. For each minute that the respondent
was able to keep the steamy sexual conversation going on the
phone, the partner making the call was supposed to pay them $3
for the minute. Each of the partners was supposed to make a min-
imum of two calls per week to the secret "900 line." At first, the
couple found my assignment "unusual" because it did not fit within the realm of their prior experiences. Nonetheless, they did go
ahead and give it a try. The combination of the safety of using
the phone to say "dirty" things to each other coupled with the
funniness of the entire process made the assignment a rather enjoyable experience for them, especially because there was a mone-
tary gain associated with the length of each call. The longer the
respondent could keep their partner on the line with sexual fantasies, the more he or she stood to "gain" from the other partner.
After 2 weeks of this, the couple reported to me that they were
each richer by at least $150 and, as another benefit, had gained
much more insight about each other's sexual interests and fantasies. Out of respect for their growing sexual intimacy, I never
asked them about the content of their 900 number telephone conversations. Within another 3 weeks, they had developed an entire
ritual around the telephone calling, and their sexual problems
gradually dissipated as they discovered more about the humor and
excitement inherent in human sexuality.

THE FINE FOR IFFINESS

An obsessive-compulsive patient constantly qualified his emotional statements in group therapy with terms like: "It's possible, I guess, maybe, I suppose, it could be so but then again it could not be so." Exasperated by his emotional ambivalence, I informed him that, starting next group, he would have to pay each group member a dollar whenever he used one of the aforecited terms more than once within any given group session. During the next group, the patient reverted to his usual emotional iffiness and started using these terms again. When he used the term: "I guess so" once, I warned him: "That's one!" When he said: "I guess so" the second time, I then instructed him to give each group member a dollar, to which he readily replied: "I've got the money, I've got the money here," and started distributing a dollar bill to each group member. I then commented to the group: "Didn't I tell you that therapy would ultimately be good for you, that it would end up putting money in your pockets!" In the midst of the laughter, some group members experienced pangs of remorse for taking the patient's dollar and wanted to give it back to him, to the consternation and humorous disbelief of the impulsive group members! Despite some temporary confusion triggered by the framework shift, they all seemed to get the message: Emotional garbage is useless, it's okay to have fun, and therapy does end up being good for you.

GOD'S CONDO

A dissatisfied and overly religious individual was trying to make up for her dissatisfactions by following every church rule to the letter, and going to Mass on a daily basis. However, she was still dissatisfied with her life, in a way replacing the need for immediate action on this earthly plane with the promise that things would be better in an afterlife. She seemed to miss the point that the challenge of being on earth is to formulate a winning combination with what one has at hand. When she talked about her frequent Mass attendance during one session, I responded: "It seems that every time you go to church you get five dollars deposited in God's bank toward the purchase of your condo in Heaven. The more you go to Mass, the more expensive a condo you will get, a condo with a beautiful view in a nice neighborhood." Although surprised by my remark, she commented: "Well, there's got to be more to it than that. Besides, I'm not dead yet! I can enjoy my condo right now." To her smile of understanding, I replied: "So let's explore how you can enjoy some of heaven on earth."

GAMES IN RELATIONSHIPS

A patient who tended to be manipulative in relationships brought in a cartoon that he thought was very funny. The cartoon showed a man and a woman conversing on a date with the man saying: "And I like honesty in a relationship. I'm into playing games." I laughed about the cartoon, and then said to the patient: "You're right, I agree with you. If you want to be a phony, you might as well be honest about it."

GOING FAST NOWHERE

A patient said in group therapy that she could not figure out her life: "Too many things happening." This was due to her creating a crowded, busy world for herself where many things seemed to be going on, whereas in reality nothing meaningful was happening. She had too many appointments, too many friends, too many people to see, and too many dates to do different activities. Realizing this, another woman in the group told her: "You really need to slow down so you can read between the lines of your life. That's the reason they don't have posters on bullet trains."

THE BURNING BUSH

An anxious patient was discussing in detail the price of his anxiety in terms of everyday casualties and failures caused by the anxiety. I shared with him a joke I had just received in a letter from a psychologist colleague. The joke was as follows: "A patient with two bandaged ears went to a psychologist for hypnosis to regenerate tissue growth. The psychologist asked him how he managed to sustain such an unusual burn injury, only to his ears. The patient replied: 'I am an easily stressed person; the slightest change in routine upsets me. The other morning I was running late for work and suddenly discovered I didn't have an ironed shirt. I became upset and began ironing a shirt while worrying about being late. Suddenly, the phone rang and I immediately put the iron to my ear.' The psychologist winced and indicated how he could see what happened to one of the ears. He asked about the other one. The patient looked at him with some frustration and said: 'Well, I had to call the ambulance, didn't I?' "

DEUS EX MACHINA

A woman patient described how she and her boyfriend were having sexual difficulties. She said she had complained to her boyfriend that he seemed to treat sex mechanically, to which he had retorted that he thought *she* was mechanical during intercourse. I responded to her: "It sounds like two robots accusing each other of not being human."

MEETING AT GROUND ZERO

When I worked at a psychiatric hospital, I was once asked by the Program Director to do an intake interview with an inpatient who was described to me as a paranoid schizophrenic with delusions of being Jesus Christ. I started the interview by asking the patient when his birthday was, to which he replied: "The 25th of December. It's a well-known date all over the world. Everyone wants to celebrate my birthday with me." I tried to control my laughter and moved on further in the interviewing process. When I asked him about his family and parents, the patient replied: "Everyone worships my mother, and they all think that my dad is their dad." When I later asked him whether any events or situations made him uncomfortable, he replied: "Well, I haven't particularly enjoyed being crucified for no good reason with one thief on each side of me." At another turn during the interview, I asked the patient what his hobbies were; he retorted: "Raising people from the dead," at which point we both broke out in solid, uninterrupted laughter.

WISDOM IN A BOTTLE

At different junctures during the course of treatment, I have used timeless stories from different cultures to communicate crucial messages that may have otherwise gone unabsorbed by patients if conveyed in a conventional interpretive mode. I particularly relish the following three stories:

1. I shared this story with a patient who exhibited a rather oppositional and negativistic frame of functioning: "A company

needed to employ a new executive secretary. They placed an advertisement in the newspaper asking for an executive secretary who was computer literate, could type at least 80 words per minute, and could speak French and Spanish. A woman called about the position and showed up for an interview. When the office manager interviewed the applicant, she asked her if she could type 80 words per minute as specified in the advertisement. The interviewee answered that she could not. The office manager then asked her if she spoke either French or Spanish, and the woman again stated that she did not. She finally asked the applicant if she was computer literate, and she answered 'No.' Feeling rather frustrated, the interviewer then angrily asked the applicant, 'in that case, would you please explain why you showed up for this interview,' to which the woman replied, 'You see, I just came to let you know that you should not count on me.' "

2. Another patient was complaining about being unable to please the people around him no matter what he did. I told him a story about a man and his son who had to travel from one side of the mountain range to the other side with their donkey. On their way to the other side of the mountain range, they had to cross five villages. As they crossed the main square of the first village with the man riding on the donkey and his son following him, the people in the village square started to laugh and point at them. The man asked them what they were laughing about. They responded: "We are laughing at how inconsiderate you are! You are a strong, fully grown man and your son is still a child and here you are, riding on the donkey and letting your son walk." The man thought that the people's observation may have been well-taken, so he got off his donkey and let his son ride it as they entered the second village. As they crossed the main square in the second village, the people in the square again started to laugh and point fingers at them. The man again asked them what they were laughing about. One of the people in the main square answered, "We are laughing about how you could let your youthful and vigorous son ride the donkey while you, an older and respectable man, walk behind him." So the man got on the donkey with his son as they rode together into the third village. As they crossed the main square, they were again the subject of ridicule from the village folk. The man asked them what they were commenting about. They answered: "We are laughing about how you and your son are so insensitive to overburden

this poor donkey and overtax him with your combined weight." Feeling exasperated, the man got off his donkey and asked his son to walk beside him as they escorted the donkey into the fourth village. As they crossed the main village square, another group of people started to point fingers at them. The man asked them what the remarks were about. The people answered: "We are laughing at how silly you are. You have this donkey available for your use and yet here you are both walking beside your donkey instead of riding him." At that point, the man pulled the donkey up on his back and ran with his son into the fifth village!

3. A patient came in expressing many unnecessary worries about different subjects. So I told him another donkey story about Goha (or Mulla Nasreddin), the perennial Middle-Eastern Schlemiel. The story is about the prince of Goha's town who had a beloved donkey that he greatly cherished. So he put out the news around town that he was seeking someone to teach his donkey how to read and write. The teacher would be immediately granted 500 gold pieces in order to carry out the task. However, if the teacher was unsuccessful in teaching the donkey how to read and write, then he or she would be decapitated as punishment. Goha presented himself at the prince's court as the sought-after donkey teacher. He told the prince that he could indeed teach the donkey how to read and write, but that he needed 10 years to complete such a time-consuming and challenging assignment. The prince agreed and gave Goha 500 pieces of gold, instructing him to return the following day and begin the reading lessons with the donkey. When Goha got home and informed his wife about what had happened, she started to wail, scream, and pull out her hair. She told Goha that he was such a fool to accept this assignment because he knew that he could not teach a donkey how to read or write and would therefore end up being decapitated by the prince. Goha answered her: "Calm down. In 10 years, one of three things could happen: Either the prince could die, or I could die, or surely the donkey will die!"

Sisyphus felt very soothed by Tiara's narrative. Through Dr. Shamrock's inspirational stories, he realized that it was not just he who had to carry a rock up the hill. Slowly, the truth was beginning to dawn on him. He realized that the rock he was carrying could be anything, anything at all. There were different kinds of rocks embodying different kinds of problems, a rock language with its own hieroglyphs. There would always be rocks in the lives of human beings. The rock was a symbol for burdens, for the trials and tribulations of life. The trials of life simply represented a string of unending initiation rites within the long human procession toward awareness, sacrifices at the altar of understanding. That, thought Sisyphus, is the stuff that holy sweat is made of.

Sisyphus was starting to discern that what was more important than the rock was its projected shadow in his own mind. The shadow he created in his mind could alternatively make the rock evil, ominous, neutral, redemptive, inviting, or simply another way station on the road to enlightenment. What is the rock made of anyway? Is it a paper rock made of paper mâché? Is it a balloon filled with helium? Is it a pillow full of feathers or a round bag of tricks? Is it a volcanic bubble or is it a crystal ball? Is it made of chocolate? Or is it a vanishing Vanitas Vanitatum, as evanescent as a desert mirage?

The gods wanted humans to discover the meaning of life after birth rather than be preoccupied with life after death. Sisyphus realized that individuals like Dr. Shamrock were like renaissance artists of the psyche, helping humans uncover meaning in their lives. And this was the purpose of what humans call psychotherapy. The rock was simply a seed, a germ, a beginning, an attempt to trigger some curiosity on the part of human beings about the meaning to be found in this world. Sisyphus finally understood the meaning of the rock. Everyone was carrying their own rocks. He could even feel some camaraderie among all the rock carriers, each engaged in a valiant and ultimately meaningful struggle. That made him feel better. Tiara was happy, and the members of the Council of Gods were also satisfied.

From the other side of the hill, Candide, the protagonist of another demonstration project initiated three centuries ago, yelled to Sisyphus: "We must cultivate our own garden!"

Sisyphus smiled. He knew that, from now on, he would never be the same.

HUMOR IMMERSION TRAINING™

Dr. Salameh is the developer of *Humor Immersion Training™*, a systematic approach to the development of humor skills. HIT workshops are conducted nationally on a regular basis. For more information on arranging for a workshop to address specific organizational needs, please contact: W. A. Salameh, PhD, 1335 Hotel Circle S, #207, San Diego, CA 92108. Telephone: (619) 260-1014. Fax: (619) 291-1985.

9

The Role of Humor
in a College
Mental Health Program

Gerald Amada

Dr. Gerald Amada has devoted his professional career to working with students, as humorously as possible. During their turbulent identity-forming years, students undergo many crises that tend to make their lives difficult. Dr. Amada chooses to work with the resistance, often using humor to alleviate the sometimes volcanic rages experienced by students and helping them to remove their blockages and graduate into adulthood. He simultaneously may turn the humor magic on Counseling Center staff and faculty journeymen working with students. And, behold, the whole Zeitgeist changes in the direction of productive interactions.

Gerald Amada, PhD, is Director of the Mental Health Center at the City College of San Francisco. He is a recognized author in the area of student counseling. His books include A Guide to Psychotherapy *(1985) and the edited volume* Mental Health on the Community College Campus *(1985).*

❖   ❖   ❖

When I was approached by the editors of this book to write a chapter on the role of humor in a college psychotherapy program, my first thoughts harked back to a pivotal episode in my own college career. After spending 2 dreary years enrolled in a business administration program, I had become thoroughly disenchanted with my lack of academic purpose and progress. One day, late in the spring semester of my sophomore year, I wandered about the corridors, eavesdropping on some of the lectures that could be overheard through open classroom doors.

Glancing into one of the classrooms, I observed a very attractive psychology instructor begin her lecture with a joke. The students had evidently been accustomed to this instructor's rib-tickling pedagogical methods since they were all smiling and attentive. I can no longer recall the content of the joke, but I do recollect that it was quite witty, risqué, and pregnant with psychological significance. At the conclusion of the joke, the class laughed uproariously. I went away somehow profoundly affected by this fleeting event.

The soul-searching that followed this episode raised important concerns and considerations in my mind. I was finding my pursuit of a business career to be a monotonous and dismal treadmill. Suddenly I had been exposed to its delightful antithesis in the form of a psychology course that was being taught with humor.

Early on, toward the end of my freshman year, I had already become aware of a budding interest in psychological studies. But I was definitely further catalyzed in this direction by the not altogether warranted belief, based upon my brief eavesdropping experience, that psychology courses were generally taught with stimulating and engrossing humor. With that provocative thought in mind, I went to see the university psychologist about my academic quandary. He administered a battery of aptitude tests which, as I had anticipated, confirmed the fact that I was disastrously ill suited for a business career. Conversely, the tests revealed that I seemed to possess the requisite skills and interests to successfully pursue a career in the field of human services. On the strength of this discovery, I transferred into the university's department of arts and sciences in my junior year, majored in psychology, and, as the saying goes, the rest is history.

It would of course be façile and naïve of me to suggest that the single positive experience of overhearing a good joke told in a psychology course could, in itself, affect the entire direction of my career. There were naturally far more overarching reasons for my decision to change majors and careers at that juncture of my life, such as, for example, my boredom and atrocious academic record while in business school. But, in retrospect, I view that brief but memorable experience outside the classroom of a jocose psychology instructor as one of the truly pivotal moments of my college years.

I have introduced this chapter with an autobiographical vignette in order to illustrate a point. If, as my story suggests, even an accidental encounter with humor can catalyze a student's academic and maturational growth, should we not reasonably expect that the timely, selective, and ongoing use of humor in psychotherapeutic work with college students could yield significant reparative results?

THEORETICAL PERSPECTIVE

There has been much written and said about both the psychological vulnerabilities and developmental opportunities of college students (Margolis, 1989). Because college students are at the developmental crossroads of embarking upon relative independence from their families and pursuing what is likely to be a lifelong professional career, they are beset by many demands and pressures for personal and scholarly success. As all college psychotherapists are well aware, the unique demands of college life often lead to a wide range of psychological and interpersonal difficulties. Depression, alcoholism, substance abuse, unwanted pregnancies, date rape, and an impulsive, live-for-the-moment orientation are problems that are endemic among contemporary American college students (Amada, 1985b).

On the positive side, students are generally eager and ripe for new or enriching experiences. They attend college to enhance their knowledge of both themselves and the complex world in which they will soon function as independent adults. Because students are accustomed to learning from instruction, they are apt to turn to a college psychotherapist to be educated about themselves and about life in general. Therapists can teach students about themselves through a wide variety of modalities, interventions, and orientations, including cognitive, behavioral, didactic, environmental, and psychoanalytic approaches.

My own orientation is psychoanalytic, and, consistent with this theoretical model, my clinical work emphasizes such factors as the student's psychogenetic history, diagnosis, unconscious motivations, fantasies, and the quality of the transference relationship that develops during the course of treatment. There seems to be a general agreement among mental health practitioners, regardless of their theoretical orientations, that the indispensable cornerstone of psychotherapy is the development of an empathically connected, positive therapeutic relationship (Ducey, 1989). An integral component of my own psychotherapeutic perspective is humor. Humor as an adjunctive yet essential clinical tool can be invaluable in two comprehensive respects. First, it can be used as a versatile and fairly reliable diagnostic instrument. The quality and vitality of a student's sense of humor will probably provide some measure of how well he or she will weather emotional storms (Amada, 1985a). Frequently, for example, the presence, availability, and quality of a student's sense of humor can be a dynamic index of the depth and potential reversibility of his or her state of depression or anxiety. On a deeper level, the presence or absence of a sense of humor can, when evaluated in conjunction with other relevant factors, illuminate much about a student's character structure, family dynamics, and the social milieu in which the student was raised.

For example, a therapist initially encountering a student whose life and personality are quite devoid of humor can usefully test several important hypotheses. Is the absence of humor in the student indicative of a reactive depression? Or, is it more a manifestation of a certain deficit, rigidity, or depressive feature in the student's character structure? Does the absence of humor perhaps reflect and befit a social norm and value that prevailed within the student's family and social culture? In other words, was humor simply neglected or unused by the student's family as a potential mode of healthy, problem-solving communication? Was it somehow considered socially unbecoming or offensive? These are some of the questions and hypotheses that can be investigated for important diagnostic purposes.

A second, and more important, purpose for utilizing humor in psychotherapy with college students is to foster and effect positive therapeutic change. As pointed out by Salameh (1987), humor is more than just a technical tool. It reflects an attitude and a way of being. Therefore, it has the potential, if used wisely by the therapist, to promote positive transformations both within the therapeutic relationship and in other realms of the student's academic and personal life.

The positive effect of humor has been extensively discussed in the literature. Klein (1989) has noted the power of humor to heal and to release afflicted persons from grief, sorrow, disappointment, and loss. Fine (1983) has discussed the potential of humor for enabling groups to deal with forces that might threaten or disrupt them. He has also alluded to the power of humor for building confidence in groups as humor helps group members realize that they are in the same situation. Humor can be especially effective in helping persecuted groups deal with tragedy by providing them with a vehicle with which to poke fun at their oppressors.

The power of humor to persuade others when more serious means have been abortive has also received attention (Blumenfeld & Alpern, 1986). Furthermore, humor can be especially helpful in conveying a therapist's humanness to a patient when other, more traditional, therapeutic methods have been unsuccessful (S. Edwards, personal communication, 1989). Fay (1978) has highlighted the therapeutic efficacy of humor for pointing out dysfunctional aspects in the behavior of psychiatric patients without putting them on the defensive. Humor has been credited with the power of enabling an individual to overcome adversity by acquiring a sense of mastery (Lefcourt & Martin, 1986). One researcher (Vaillant, 1977) has even "honored" humor by designating it as one of the "mature" defense mechanisms.

TECHNIQUE

In this chapter I will highlight two principal therapeutic uses of humor. The first is the rather specific, limited application of humor as a means of resolving therapeutic impasses. The second is the employment of humor as a general framework for conveying optimistic concern, goodwill, and respect for student patients.

Obviously, the use of humor to melt a therapeutic stalemate and its more general use as an effective means of conveying regard, nonhostility, and respect for the patient often go hand in hand. Most clinicians have had the experience of resolving an impasse or conflict with a patient by injecting appropriate humor into a session precisely because the therapist's use of humor was correctly perceived by the patient as a sensitive and respectful attempt to establish mutual goodwill and understanding. Because humor can be a potent vehicle for transmitting empathy and understanding, its judicious use in psychotherapy may certainly be expected to enhance the overall quality of the therapeutic relationship and play a vital part in the entire therapeutic enterprise.

The students who use the City College of San Francisco Mental Health Program represent a broad range of ethnic groups, ages, and personality types. Some are well functioning moderately depressed or anxious individuals who seek treatment for rather transient and easily resolvable crises. Others suffer from more serious and chronic conditions such as severe character disorders and schizophrenia. Despite the diagnostic diversity among the student population, it has been my experience that most students, irrespective of their particular personality types, are responsive to humor as a therapeutic technique when it is used in a timely, sensitive, and dynamic manner. In my view, humorous interventions are most effective when used to address and alleviate the patient's central concerns and fears.

In order to determine the patient's primary concerns, therapists are advised to formulate, at least tentatively, a diagnostic (or dynamic) impression of each patient's personality. Assuming that the therapist's diagnosis will be relatively accurate and valid, it can serve as an important dynamic instrument with which to determine when and how to strategically intervene with humor. For example, obsessive-compulsive patients who, to their own detriment, typically ignore or repress recurrent forbidden thoughts, may at times benefit from humor that focuses on the "unacceptable" unconscious impulses or fantasies they have diligently sought to repress. Paranoid clients, who tend to suffer from persecutory delusions and severe interpersonal conflicts, may favorably respond to humorous interventions that address and allay their fears of having their thoughts controlled or manipulated by others. Depressed patients, who are usually afflicted with feelings of low self-esteem and hopelessness, can appreciate and derive comfort from a therapist's humorous perspective of their exaggerated sense of gloom, provided of course that the therapist's lighthearted viewpoint is not intended or perceived as ridiculing or dismissive.

Therapists who are well attuned to their patients' core concerns can use their humorous interventions to illuminate and objectify those concerns. Naturally, all therapeutic interventions, whether humorous or deadly serious, have the potential for backfiring and producing unwanted and undesirable results. Sometimes, the undesirable effect of a humorous intervention can be attributed to the guarded and intractable mood of the patient. At other times, the failure of a humorous intervention can be ascribed to poor timing, clumsiness, or the denigrating quality of the therapist's humor.

In the next section of this chapter I will illustrate how I have therapeutically used humor with college students either to troubleshoot a difficult impasse in the therapy or to address and explore an acute concern manifested by the student patient. I will attempt to explain with each example of a humorous therapeutic intervention why it did or did not succeed as I had hoped. Following that discussion, I will illustrate other pertinent uses of humor with students, faculty, psychological interns, and support staff in order to demonstrate the varied and significant role that can be played by humor in the daily operation of a college mental health program.

CLINICAL PRESENTATIONS

CASE 1

An extremely morose and volatile student was generally regarded as belligerent and intimidating by his college peers. This man came to therapy irregularly, but usually following an incident in which his hostile behavior strongly offended or frightened someone at the college, causing him to be warned or disciplined by one of the administrative staff. Because this unfortunate man had little control over his moods and behavior, I thought it necessary to be very sensitive to the terrible distress these campus predicaments caused him. Throughout our interviews he would rant lengthily about perceived violations of his moral rights. Although he seemed partially trustful toward me, he gave me little opportunity to share my point of view about his problems. Overall, he was largely impervious to my attempts to lighten his angry and depressed mood.

Toward the end of one of our sessions he angrily asserted that no one respected his intelligence or acknowledged his academic accomplishments. He was, after all, a geology major, and a damned good one. Upon hearing this news, I asked him, "Since you're a geology major, what would you say if I told you that's gneiss (a granite rock, and homophone of the word 'nice')?" A broad smile broke out upon his face, the first that I had ever seen, and he sprightfully responded, "I'd say, 'gee,' that's a good joke, since it (gneiss) starts with a gee." The two of us erupted with a good belly laugh and during the following moments, we shared a closeness that had not been there before. His mood, which I could not dent by other means, began to lift after it was reached through humor. I suspect that this humorous intervention succeeded because it reflected my respect for the patient's intelligence and accomplishments as a geology student while also conveying my willingness to respond to his anger with a gesture of unmistakable friendliness.

CASE 2

Humor played a crucial role in defusing a potentially explosive situation with a very disturbed and hotheaded student. The student entered my office loudly proclaiming that she had been grievously wronged by friends, co-workers, and several of her college instructors. As the student plunged forward with her tirade against a menacing and conspiratorial world, she began to decompensate even further. Watching her shout and leer at various objects in my room, I apprehensively expected that she would pick up some object and hurl it at me. Just as I was making up my mind about how I would extricate myself from impending danger, the student suddenly looked up at the wall and, seeing a photograph of my three adorable Shar-Pei dogs, smiled and said, "Are those your children?" Surprised and delighted at this sudden but very friendly digression, I seized the opportunity by replying, "Not exactly. The big one is my daughter. The other two are my granddaughters." The student laughed heartily and the conversation then turned to the emotionally safe and neutral subject of raising dogs. By the time the session was over, the student was relatively calm and rational. She even agreed to see me again, which she did on several subsequent occasions. As expected, she remained prone to rapid and dramatic regressions under stress, but she fortunately felt safe enough with me to return to the clinic for timely assistance. The humorous exchange that took place between us seemed to have a positive effect because it related to an emotionally neutral and pleasurable subject (pets) while also revealing an important aspect of our basic humanness through the discussion of our common fondness for dogs.

CASE 3

By contrast, an attempt to enlist humor as a means of resolving a therapeutic impasse once resulted in abysmal failure. A 19-year-old student who was exasperated with her overbearing and hypercritical mother requested that I meet with the two of them in order to mediate their disputes. After a few sessions, it was evident that the disputants were unbudgeably committed to their respective positions and entirely lacked respect for each other's viewpoints. Each looked to me to invalidate her adversary's opinions.

Having been incapable of resolving their irreconcilable differences through interpretation, explanation, empathy, or even sheer exhortation, I decided to try humor. Taking into account that these patients were Jewish, I thought it apropos to tell them a Jewish folkloric tale of which I am extremely fond due to its wit and wisdom.

The story is about a disputatious married couple who went to see their esteemed rabbi for advice. The wife, who was the first to consult the rabbi, told a long tale of woe about an insensitive, selfish, and uncouth husband who was entirely to blame for their marital problems. The rabbi sagely and patiently listened to the woman's long harangue and then said, "You know, I think you're right." Feeling vindicated, the wife left. The husband, who next consulted with the rabbi, excoriated his wife by referring to her as an inconsiderate, unkempt, and half-witted shrew who was entirely at fault for their marital difficulties. The rabbi once again listened with forbearance and then replied, "You know, you're right." The husband then left the rabbi's office feeling quite satisfied. Soon after the couple had left, the rabbi's wife entered his study in a state of obvious distress. She said to the rabbi, "I overheard what happened when you spoke to that couple. When the wife blamed their unhappiness on her husband, you said she was right. When the husband blamed all their problems on his wife, you said he was right. You know, they both can't be right." To which the rabbi replied, "You know, you're right."

I had hoped that the forbearance and moral relativism displayed by the rabbi would provide a positive example through which my two patients could begin to examine their own intransigence toward one another. To my disappointment, however, they each looked at me as if I had just committed some terrible *faux pas*. Dismissing this wise tale as if it had not been told, they immediately resumed their useless and endless squabble.

I believe that this example illustrates an important point regarding the use of humor in psychotherapy. It is important to recognize that a humorous intervention may be perceived as irrelevant or insulting by certain patients, due to either their particular personality formations or their current life conflicts. Obviously, a therapist cannot always predict the eventual outcome of a humorous intervention. Therefore, it is generally advisable that therapists who are inclined to use humor with their patients philosophically accept the fact that certain individuals are simply not

amenable to it. Therapists who are ordinarily empathically attuned to their patients are usually, although not always, able to determine when it is appropriate to use humorous interventions. In
this regard, it is probably helpful to bear in mind that the therapeutic use of humor is a form of risk-taking behavior that, due to
its potential to inflict psychic pain upon patients, can strongly test
a therapist's empathy. However, the same could be said regarding
any other potent therapeutic technique.

CASE 4

A more positive example of the therapeutic use of humor occurred at the very outset of a session with a student. The student,
a 35-year-old gay man who worked as a part-time librarian came
to me in crisis, immediately following the breakup of a longstanding love relationship. Although he desperately wanted to tell me
about his grief, he could not initially overcome the expectation
that I would view a gay relationship with contempt. He thought I
would discount the depth of his grief by regarding his mournful
reactions to be less painful than those experienced by heterosexu-
als when their love relationships dissolve. He began his first session with an angry challenge. He said, "Look, before I can tell
you anything about what I've been through, I've got to know, what
do you think of homosexuals?" I must admit that for a moment I
had no idea how to answer such an accusatory challenge. I then
collected myself and said, "You know, I guess how I feel about
homosexuals is a bit like Mark Twain when he was asked how he
felt about Jewish people. He said that Jews were human beings
like everyone else. And he couldn't imagine anything worse that
could be said about a person."

The student laughed easily and, disarmed of his hostility, soon
proceeded to disclose the recent difficulties he was having with
his lover. Although my use of this quotation was extemporane-
ous, it has always been a favorite because it effectively says that
no group of people should be vilified, or for that matter, glorified,
for its differences. I had hoped that the patient would accurately
interpret my use of this quotation. Perhaps what was most telling
was my eagerness to respond to this patient, not with anger or
with an apologetic discourse on the plights and rights of gays, but
with a humorous quotation from a great and compassionate author
whose humane values would be well known to this librarian.

CASE 5

A student recently entered therapy in a state of disorganizing confusion and panic. His gay lover had left the country for a few weeks on a business trip, saddling the student, who was 21, with the formidable responsibility of caring for the lover's 16-year-old daughter. The daughter was a very testy adolescent who was involved with a highly sadistic man. Her father and the student had done their utmost to remove the girl from this destructive relationship, but to no avail. She refused to heed their advice and repeatedly exposed herself to psychological and physical danger as a result. The student feared that, during his lover's absence, his rebellious young charge would either run away from home or be seriously injured by her boyfriend. To add to his woes, he dreadfully anticipated that, when his lover returned from his trip, he would be blamed for whatever catastrophe befell his lover's daughter. While the student spoke about these matters, I noticed that his speech was sprinkled with a great many jocular asides accompanied by frequent nervous giggling. I also noticed that practically all of the student's attempts at humor were self-disparaging and not in the least amusing. Consequently, I neither laughed nor smiled at his joking remarks.

As the student disclosed his personal history it became apparent that his exaggerated sense of responsibility for the care and welfare of his lover's daughter had been an outgrowth of his lifelong tendency to please and appease others at his own expense. While discussing this topic, he alluded to the fact that he had managed to cope with a miserable childhood by acting clownishly with his parents and other adults, such as his teachers. Toward the middle of the session, after having tried to amuse me with his self-deprecating humor for the umpteenth time, the student turned to me and said with evident annoyance, "Don't you ever smile? You make me anxious by being so serious." I replied by telling him that I often smiled but thus far it seemed to me that the brand of humor he used was rather defensive and self-victimizing. I asked him if he felt compelled to act comically as a means of covering up certain painful emotions. The student then began to cry without restraint. When he finally stopped, his manner became calmer and much more natural. He went on to acknowledge that he was often annoyed and frustrated with himself for constantly resorting to self-humiliating forms of humor when faced with personal adversity. Gradually, as he was able to reveal and accept

the depth of his painful emotions, he once again spoke humorously about his predicament. His manner, however, had changed
dramatically. It was no longer forced or self-deprecating. In response to this positive change, I became more openly responsive
to and encouraging of his humorous comments.

This example illustrates the need for therapists to exercise
care and discretion in response to a patient's use of humor. When
patients castigate themselves through humor, it is generally unwise for therapists to deliberately encourage such behavior. By
smiling or laughing with patients who ridicule and humiliate
themselves, therapists are apt to reinforce this self-punishing form
of behavior and therefore compound their patients' feelings of low
self-esteem. Obviously, to do this would be contrary to the basic
objectives of psychotherapy.

CASE 6

There are many women students who have entered therapy
with rather gruesome tales about the men with whom they live.
Many of these men are described as neglectful, selfish, amoral,
brutal, and parasitic. Clinical research (Wild, 1989) indicates that
many of the women who tolerate and endure chronic and severe
abuse from men suffer from a borderline personality disorder. An
important characteristic of the borderline personality is the proclivity to use primitive defense mechanisms such as splitting and
denial (Goldstein, 1985). A clear example of the use of denial
that I have observed in abused women students is their tendency
to wait and hope for miraculous personality transformations in the
men who have chronically mistreated them. After describing how
their lovers or husbands have long betrayed and beaten them,
spent their earnings on dangerous drugs, and punished their aspirations for success and fulfillment, these women often state in the
next breath that their partners are not really harmful to them, and,
after all, they just may one day change dramatically and become
good partners.

Therapists who encounter such patients may experience intense countertransference feelings of frustration and anger toward
them for putting up with such sadistic men. It may be clear to the
therapist that such men are unlikely to change quickly or radically
and that the patient's life, if she chooses to remain with the man,
is likely to go from bad to worse. However, the borderline patient's intense fear of abandonment causes her to cling to the rela-

tionship despite chronic and even savage abuse. In my work with abused women students I have used a wide range of techniques including interpretation, confrontation, empathic support, environmental manipulation, and humor. One of the humorous interventions used aims at calling attention to the patient's denial of the immutable abusiveness of her relationship. The following vignette is a rather typical example of how this intervention is used:

Therapist: You've told me that he beats you, steals from you, cheats on you, uses the money he takes from you for drugs, and has even threatened to kill you. And, furthermore, this has been going on for 5 years. What's keeping you in this relationship? What are you waiting for?

Patient: Well, I love him. And I'm afraid of being on my own. Besides, he's promised to change. Every so often he does something nice, like bringing me flowers. I think to myself that if I am patient enough he will someday overcome his problems and treat me well. And I always think that I can make him change if I only try hard enough and stand by him. What do you think?

Therapist: I think I might have a solution to your problem.

Patient: You have! What is it?

Therapist: Well, it's a magical potion. It will make you live to be 700 years old. You see, you're going to have to live at least that long in order to see your boyfriend change. (In response to this intervention, many clients smile or laugh. Others will wince or cry out of a sense of regret over my wry and pessimistic depiction of their plight.)

Patient: I don't think I'd even want to live that long, especially if he doesn't change.

My deliberate use of a humorous intervention referring to a magical potion that prolongs life touches upon two principal defenses of the borderline patient. First, it addresses the patient's rigid denial of the immutably destructive nature of her current relationship. Second, it exposes the omnipotent and magical thinking that is a common hallmark of the borderline patient (Searles, 1986). Often, the borderline patient's magical belief in his or her own omnipotence and superhuman powers can cause him or her to grandiosely and endlessly aspire to transform and rehabilitate abusive partners. A humorous intervention that calls attention to the patient's proclivity for denial and magical thinking can animate his or her interest in facing and understanding their inner thought processes as well as the outer reality of their social world. By using the silly example of a magical potion, the absurdity of magical thinking is brought to life in a safe and comical manner that enables the patient to integrate the significance of the intervention without excessive fear.

Of course, the defense mechanisms of denial and omnipotent thinking are not peculiar to the borderline personality disorder. Therefore, the previous example of the therapeutic use of humor to address these particular defense mechanisms can probably be applied with variation to many other types of personality disorders.

CASE 7

In my work with college students, I naturally encounter a great many who cannot discuss their parents critically without inordinate guilt. One of their favorite ways of dealing with the guilt they experience over their angry and critical feelings for their parents is to say, "Well, how can I be angry with them? After all, they meant well." When I hear this oft-used, hackneyed expression, I will perhaps teasingly reply, "You know, saying that someone meant well is just about the worst thing you can say about them."

The astonished student will of course ask why I would say such an outrageous thing. "Because," I reply, "when you go out of your way to say that someone means well it suggests that you can hardly think of any other good thing to say about them." By joking about students' sugarcoated descriptions of their parents in this way, I am often able to uncover the compensatory, guilt-laden quality of their remarks. This quite commonly leads to a frank and essential discussion of the student's true feelings toward his or her parents.

Many students who have grown up in homes where severe family discord was an everyday phenomenon will glibly describe their parents and families as perfect and totally problem-free. In dealing with such students, I am apt to feign great astonishment and exhilaration while saying, "This is quite remarkable. I've worked for many years as a therapist and have talked with literally thousands of students. But you are the first one I have ever met who has been reared in a perfect family. Your family is definitely a rarity."

Because my remarks are generally spoken in a laughing, joking manner, students quickly grasp that I am joshing with them. At the same time, they hear me restate in literal, albeit very exaggerated, form what they have told me about their family's alleged perfection. As a result, the distortions that stem from their idealized views of their families are farcically exposed and then discussed in the benign atmosphere induced by the humorous intervention.

A great many students who have been severely traumatized during their childhoods will vehemently deny that their current psychological problems have even the slightest relationship to their pasts. As far as they are concerned, they have come away from their miserable upbringings largely unscathed. From their perspective, any problems they may presently encounter are simply the result of how their personality functions now, not how it developed over the course of many years.

When dealing with such students in therapy, I may be inclined to kid them in the following manner. "You say you've had problems studying for years, your personal relationships have never been especially satisfactory, and you've always lacked self-confidence. Yet, you claim that your current academic and social problems have nothing to do with your past. I think I understand what you mean."

The student replies, "You do?"

"Yes. From what I can tell, years ago you were hatched from an egg in some remote forest and grew up without any human contact. That explains why you have no recollection of your life being influenced by emotional experiences within a family environment."

This parodistic intervention usually arouses a laugh and, at first, a defensive reaction such as, "Well, I didn't exactly say I didn't have a family or that my family didn't affect me in some respect. I just meant that I'm pretty much responsible for the kind of person I am today."

With these slight admissions from students that early family life has indeed made some contribution to their current difficulties, the students and I are then able to begin exploring their rather grim past within the lighter therapeutic atmosphere that was just induced by the humorous intervention.

PERTINENT USES

Beyond the strictly clinical uses of humor, there are an infinite number of ways in which humor can be effectively used by the staff of a college mental health program outside the consulting room. For example, each semester I am requested to lecture to several health education classes on the subject of psychological defense mechanisms (Amada, 1983). The instructor assigns each class to read the textbook chapter dealing with this subject a week before my lecture so that the students can be relatively conversant with the material by the time I arrive.

I usually begin my lecture by mentioning that the instructor informed me about assigning the defense mechanisms chapter for the class to read. "Is that true?" I query the class. In unison, almost everyone nods their head with an agreeable smile. I then continue, "Then I suppose. . . ." When I pause, the students usually begin nodding their heads even more vigorously, expecting that I will finish my sentence by saying, ". . . you've all read the chapter." Instead, I say, "Then I suppose *none* of you have read the chapter." Upon hearing this unexpected, incredulous statement, the students laugh knowingly. As I well know from past experience with these classes, most students indeed do not read the chapter beforehand as assigned. To make sure of the accuracy and fairness of my surmise, I quickly and good-naturedly poll the students. A show of hands usually indicates that no more than 5 students out of a class of about 35 have actually read the assigned chapter before I have delivered my lecture. By taking this humorous tack I have discovered something that I can usefully incorporate into my lecture on defense mechanisms. I first remind the students that I will be further discussing their disinclination to do the assigned reading later in the lecture when we get to the topic of psychological repression. When I subsequently describe and explain the defense mechanism of repression, I first talk about how people forget such things as doctors' appointments, the names of familiar persons, bringing their textbooks to school, their parents' requests to take out the garbage, their keys, and so on. The class usually finds these examples interesting and amusing. Then I remind the class that they "forgot" to do the assigned reading for today's lecture. Because we had already discussed some of the dynamics of repression, I ask them, "Why do you think you forgot to do today's assignment?"

Because this issue has been handled with levity, the students are psychologically open to discussing some of their heretofore hidden motivations and many, not surprisingly, admit without much embarrassment that they did not do the assignment because they simply did not like it and, therefore, unconsciously forgot to do it. Together, we laugh about the way repression is often connected to feelings of anger, defiance, and rebellion. The humorous and modulated tone of the discussion enables the class to grasp some important psychological concepts that might be difficult to emotionally assimilate in a more serious, untempered academic atmosphere.

As I am sure many lecturers have discovered, humor not only fosters the receptivity of listening audiences, but helps to relax the lecturer as well. Therefore, when I lecture to college classes I usually try to think of a few good jokes to bring along with me. If they turn out to be too corny and the class boos or hisses, I then make fun of myself for inflicting such cornball on them.

Occasionally, a student will ask a question that will prompt me to play an impromptu gag on the class. For example, I was once asked by a student if I practiced hypnosis. I replied with pretentious seriousness that I did (I did not) and that, as a matter of fact, I had, without their knowledge, placed the entire class under a hypnotic trance about 20 minutes earlier. For a brief second, I could see several credulous students stare at me with expressions of fear. Then with a smile I added, "Now if you will all pass your wallets to the front of the room." Most of the students find this gag quite funny. However, if I become aware that someone in the class still does not seem to understand that I was merely joking (e.g., a paranoid student who was hypersensitive to the possibility of mind control), I then simply make my intention absolutely clear to everyone.

As a college psychotherapist I have countless contacts with faculty and support staff each day. With many of these individuals I will stop to have a brief chat and tell a joke. I have found this to be an excellent way to overcome the sometimes stilted and stuffy atmosphere of academia and a great medium for getting to know my colleagues. It has been a source of interest and pleasure to me to discover that many of my colleagues now seek me out whenever they hear a good new joke. Unquestionably, these humorous, pleasurable exchanges help to improve and cement important professional relationships between the Mental Health Program and other members of the college staff.

For example, a member of the faculty recently called me to seek assistance with a professional matter. We chatted several times on the phone that same week and then arranged to meet. She asked what I looked like and I told her that I bore a strong resemblance to Burt Reynolds. Since I have very little hair on my head, this was clearly a lie. Nonetheless, the instructor chuckled with enjoyment. The next time we spoke she said that she had seen a photograph of me and that I really looked like Paul Newman instead. This light banter made our conversations easy and pleasant. When we finally met in person at a faculty meeting I presented the instructor with a bagged gift. It was a jar of Paul Newman's salad dressing which I claimed to have prepared myself earlier in the day. This opened our meeting on a note of hilarity that was very conducive to the discussion that followed. The next day I received a lovely potted plant from the instructor. Attached was a picture of Jane Fonda and a note that said, "From Jane." The humor we shared throughout our interactions enabled us to form an excellent professional relationship that I am sure will be of significant future benefit to our respective programs.

Most colleges and universities employ large numbers of so-called classified personnel who work as telephone operators, gardeners, carpenters, janitors, and secretaries. For social and cultural reasons, this group of workers - who occupy positions on the lower rungs of the organizational hierarchy - may be ignored or disregarded by the instructional and administrative staffs of the college. This is extremely unfortunate since the work performed by these individuals is essential to the successful implementation of the educational services of the college and, therefore, those individuals are certainly entitled to respect and acknowledgment. After all, instructors cannot adequately teach in classrooms that are improperly cleaned, heated, or lighted.

Due to the nature of my assignment as administrator of a college mental health program, my own contacts with the college's classified staff are minimal. Therefore, when I have a passing encounter with a member of the classified staff, I often take the opportunity to tell a joke or pose a riddle to them. I think this is a marvelous way to convey my interest in and appreciation for them. Also, like many of my colleagues, because I often turn to the classified staff for professional favors, I think the personal touch of humor enables me to convey that I appreciate their assistance and do not somehow regard it as my due by virtue of my supposedly superordinate position.

The following represents a fairly typical encounter I have had with one of the college telephone operators just before I requested that she place a call for me.

Amada: What do Jack the Ripper and Winnie-the-Pooh have in common?
Operator: I don't know. What?
Amada: They have the same middle name.

After a brief pause, the operator laughed raucously. For weeks after this brief exchange she mentioned how she and her husband repeated and enjoyed this riddle with their friends. In my view, humorous and pleasurable interactions of this kind can do much to bridge otherwise unbridgeable professional gaps between college employees whose contacts with one another are ordinarily very scant and impersonal.

In addition to providing high-quality clinical services, I think it is also essential that a college mental health service maintain a warm and inviting facility for staff and students alike. To some extent, the warm and welcoming quality of a clinic can be reflected in the decor and furnishings of the facility itself. However, the extent to which a college clinic will be seen in a favorable light will largely depend upon how well people are treated when they come in to utilize the clinic's services.

The City College of San Francisco Mental Health Program is located in the on-campus Student Health Services building. Student Health Services offer both medical-nursing as well as psychological services, primarily to students. However, many faculty members come to the clinic at the beginning of each semester to have a tuberculosis (TB) checkup. Normally, they have to wait several minutes before seeing a nurse, during which time they either read a magazine or twiddle their thumbs.

On occasion, when seeing a faculty member waiting for his or her TB test appointment, I walk over and have something like the following conversation:

Amada: Here for your TB test? I can help you with that.
Instructor: You can? I didn't know you handled things like that, Jerry.

Amada: Of course. Ready?
Instructor: Sure.
Amada: Okay. Who was the first person to contract TB?
Instructor: Huh? How the hell do I know?
Amada: Don't know, huh? Well, who was the physician who invented the cure for TB?
Instructor: I haven't the foggiest idea.
Amada: Don't know that either? Sorry, but you just failed your TB test.

Usually, this ridiculous gag evokes some derisive but friendly laughter and then serves to ignite a further exchange of jokes or some friendly conversation. I have repeatedly discovered that many faculty members will arrange to take time every now and then to come to the clinic, tell me a joke, and schmooze a bit. Evidently, a college clinic whose staff can display genuine humor is likely to be viewed as a warm and hospitable context within which to receive personal services.

By virtue of my administrative role, I am frequently confronted with the need to notify the clinical staff of changes in policy and practice. If disseminating information by word of mouth is too time-consuming, generally the handiest alternative is a quick memo to the staff. In sending and receiving such memos for many years, it has been my experience that they are usually written in boilerplate prose that is quite dry, overly serious, and disagreeably authoritative. In order to counteract some of the disagreeable aspects of transmitting memos to staff, I have recently begun to write them in a lampooning style. The following is an actual example of such a memo.

To: The Metal Hearth Staff

From: Dr. Amoeba

Because the clinic secretaries' assignments have become increasingly hectic, please check the waiting room for your patients if you have not been notified of their scheduled arrival by Gloria or Wendy. Remember, a bird in the hand is worth two good scrubbings.

The following is a memo I sent to the staff soon after receiving complaints that some persons were inconsiderately leaving bread, fruit, and other foods on the sink and table of the lunch room, evidently expecting someone else to clean up after them.

To: Student Health Staff

From: Arnold (The Exterminator) Schwartzbagle

The lunch room has begun to look pretty seedy lately, that is, from the human standpoint (it's beginning to arouse ant ipathy and ant agonism, and enc roach upon the hygienic rights of the tidiness-minded among us). So please, if generosity has prompted you to bring in a refreshment for the staff, please remove it before it becomes moldy and attacks us.

It has been my impression that humorous memos of this kind generate wholesome amusement. They are also read with greater interest and willingness to comply with their stated directives than are serious or authoritative memos.

Each year the Mental Health Program provides psychological internships to doctoral students from nearby graduate schools. These interns, who usually serve in the program 3 days a week, provide direct psychotherapeutic services to City College students, for which they are supervised by the senior staff. Before accepting these interns into the program, their résumés are carefully reviewed and evaluated. Each intern is then invited to have a personal interview with the staff in order to allow us to more precisely evaluate his or her levels of clinical sophistication and interpersonal skills. During the course of these personal interviews, I am often asked by the interviewees to explain what particular qualities or qualifications I deem most desirable in prospective interns. In response, I candidly allude to such qualities as personal warmth, a capacity for self-disclosure, introspectiveness, a genuine interest in psychodynamic theory and practice, sincerity, intellectual curiosity, and a capacity to cope with and learn from constructive criticism and adversity. What I do *not* tell these interviewees is that I am also highly interested in the depth and quality of their sense of humor and, to the extent that such a quality can be determined in the course of only one interview, their teasability.

My interest in an intern's teasability partly relates to the fact that during the course of supervising interns I will use a light and easygoing manner of teasing them, especially during times of excessive difficulty. Times of difficulty arise for interns when they report their technical mistakes and countertransferential overreactions to clients, often with guilt, anxiety, and embarrassment. My own teasing reflects my attitude that the commission of errors and blunders in performing clinical services is largely unavoidable and forgivable, especially among neophyte therapists. If dynamically understood, errors and blunders can become a valuable wellspring of learning and growth. Additionally, by my teasing interns about some of their mistakes in judgment, technique, or conceptualization, I am giving them the opportunity to realize that, because their supervisor can be philosophically nonjudgmental about their fallibility, perhaps they too can forgive themselves for and learn from their mistakes. This would in turn help them to develop a tolerant attitude toward their own patients.

Obviously, gross errors in judgment, such as deliberately violating the confidentiality of a patient, may need to be dealt with in an entirely serious manner.

I value a sense of humor and a capacity for teasability in psychological interns because of my belief that interns who can appropriately laugh, joke, and be teased will develop a better coping ability than interns who approach their work with unrelieved seriousness. A sense of humor can ease the tensions, crises, setbacks, and disappointments that normally occur in a college mental health program. Having provided clinical supervision for more than 20 years at City College, I am fully convinced that a resilient and versatile sense of humor is a most desirable trait to identify and strengthen in the psychological intern.

Because of the inherent imbalance of power and the evaluative nature of the supervisory relationship, interns often approach their supervisory sessions with an appreciable degree of trepidation and guardedness, at least initially. For this reason, I sometimes like to start a supervisory hour by telling a joke that I have recently heard. Not infrequently interns will respond by telling me one themselves, and a mood of friendliness and humor is thereby immediately engendered. Frankly, this tack also helps me to relax because I, too, frequently approach my supervisory responsibilities in a mood of unease and hypervigilance.

Quite often, in my supervision of interns, I seize the opportunity to turn an overly serious discussion into a light and humorous one. I will illustrate this point with a recent example. At the beginning of our supervisory hour, I informed an intern that I would need to reschedule one of our supervisory sessions. Since the rescheduled time seemed to be even more convenient for her, the intern asked if we could *always* meet at the new hour. I replied, "Do you mean even after you have terminated your internship here?" We both laughed uninhibitedly over my deliberately literal interpretation of her question, a pleasurable interlude that set a very warm and positive tone for the remainder of our session.

In 1988, I was asked by the campus newspaper, *The Guardsman*, to write an advice column called "Ask Amada." Since that time the column has appeared regularly. According to the feedback I have received thus far, it enjoys a fairly wide and faithful readership among students and faculty alike. In answering the letters submitted to me by students, I have tried to mitigate the heaviness of the advice and information presented in the column by infusing my replies with humor. For example, I received a letter from a student whose girlfriend's son was exhibiting sexual curiosity by poking at him in the area of his genitals. The student wrote that his girlfriend advised him to tell her son that this was his "pee-pee" and should be left alone. After suggesting certain guidelines for dealing with this situation, I wrote that it was perhaps okay to use the term "pee-pee," but "to paraphrase Gertrude Stein, a penis is a penis is a penis." Such light touches of humor appear to be appreciated by readers of the column who will sometimes requote them to me at a later time.

Finally, this chapter would not be complete without at least brief mention of my mutually teasing and bantering relationship with the two Student Health Services secretaries. These two fine individuals are responsible for greeting and scheduling students, answering the telephones, and generally keeping everyone on their toes. Although we, of course, have our very serious moments, our sense of teamwork and camaraderie is definitely enhanced by the opportunities we take each day to exchange amusing personal tales or play innocent jokes and tricks on each other. My favorites have been to shake hands with one of the secretaries with my middle finger folded into my palm and then apologize for the "wart." Or, I would walk over to the other secretary and ask if I could count on her. When she says "Yes," I begin drumming on her shoulder with my index finger while counting, "One, two, three, four." As indicated earlier, silly but meaningful interactions of this kind help to lighten the social atmosphere of the workplace. Such interactions break down the sense of separateness and tension that may exist among college mental health staff who are usually preoccupied with exigent assignments. In the end they undoubtedly work toward enhancing staff morale and improving the overall quality of clinical services to students.

SYNTHESIS

In this chapter, I have attempted to demonstrate the central role of humor in the daily administration of a college mental health program. As illustrated previously, humor has played a crucial role in my psychotherapeutic work with college students due to its capacity to transmit dynamic insights, defuse potentially explosive situations, and resolve therapeutic impasses. It also serves as an effective means of conveying empathy, understanding, goodwill, and optimism.

I have attempted to show how humor can play a very important role in the nonclinical activities of a college mental health program. Humor can help to bridge the social gap between the psychotherapy staff and other members of the campus community. Within the college psychological service itself, humor can engender camaraderie and teamwork. In the supervision of psychological interns, humor can be used as a counterweight to the anxiety-producing imbalances of power that normally characterize a supervisory relationship. Among the clinical staff, humor helps to attenuate feelings of separateness and interpersonal tension. In short, humor, if used judiciously, can be an indispensable helpmate to college psychotherapists in carrying out almost any clinical or administrative function.

A caveat is in order before concluding this chapter. I would like to clarify that my strong emphasis upon the use of humor in this chapter does not mean that I advocate a one-sidedly playful or hedonic approach to the practice of psychotherapy with the college student. My colleagues and I take our work very seriously. During those times when we realize that the use of humor would be either inappropriate or offensive, we generally avoid using it. Nevertheless, I like to think of the wise and creative use of humor as a splendid leavening force that can raise the qualitative level of my clinical and administrative work, and, for that matter, my life. Finally, for those readers who may wish to write to me regarding this chapter, I would like to mention that I welcome all letters, provided, of course, that they are highly flattering.

REFERENCES

Amada, G. (1983). Mental health consultation on the college campus. *Journal of American College Health, 31,* 222-223.

Amada, G. (1985a). *A Guide to Psychotherapy.* Lanham, MD: Madison Books.

Amada, G. (1985b). Organizing a community college mental health program. In G. Amada (Ed.), *Mental Health on the Community College Campus* (pp. 1-12). Lanham, MD: University Press of America.

Blumenfeld, E., & Alpern, L. (1986). *The Smile Connection.* Englewood Cliffs, NJ: Prentice-Hall.

Ducey, C. (1989). Academic underachievement. In P. Grayson & K. Cauley (Eds.), *College Psychotherapy* (pp. 166-192). New York: Guilford.

Fay, A. (1978). *Making Things Better by Making Them Worse.* New York: Hawthorn Books.

Fine, G. (1983). Sociological approaches to the study of humor. In P. McGhee & J. Goldstein (Eds.), *Handbook of Humor Research* (pp. 159-181). New York: Springer-Verlag.

Goldstein, W. (1985). *An Introduction to the Borderline Conditions.* Northvale, NJ: Jason Aronson.

Klein, A. (1989). *The Healing Power of Humor.* Los Angeles: Jeremy Tarcher, Inc.

Lefcourt, H., & Martin, R. (1986). *Humor and Life Stress.* New York: Springer-Verlag.

Margolis, G. (1989). Developmental opportunities. In P. Grayson & K. Cauley (Eds.), *College Psychotherapy* (pp. 71-91). New York: Guilford.

Salameh, W. A. (1987). Humor in integrative short-term psychotherapy (ISTP). In W. F. Fry, Jr. & W. A. Salameh (Eds.), *Handbook of Humor and Psychotherapy: Advances in the Clinical Use of Humor* (pp. 195-240). Sarasota, FL: Professional Resource Exchange.

Searles, H. F. (1986). *My Work with Borderline Patients.* Northvale, NJ: Jason Aronson.

Vaillant, G. (1977). *Adaptation to Life.* Boston: Little, Brown.

Wild, E. (1989). *Borderline Pathology in the Chronically and Severely Abused Woman.* Unpublished doctoral dissertation, California School for Professional Psychology, Berkeley, CA.

10

Humor and Spirituality in Psychotherapy

John McKiernan

In this chapter, Dr. McKiernan starts from a broad humanistic base to address the role that humorous spirituality may play in psychotherapy. He discusses the rich legacy of humorous spirituality and how it can elegantly enrich the psychotherapeutic process. His work offers an almost poetic dimension as he engages in felicitous psychotherapeutic work with hungry souls.

John McKiernan, PhD, DD, was born in Ireland in 1933. He received the Licentiate in Philosophy (1953) and the Doctorate in Theology (1961) from Maynooth College in Ireland. He spent 4 years as a priest in the barriadas of Lima, Peru (1961-1965) and 4 years as a priest in the Province of Mindanao in the Philippines, where he was Chancellor of the Diocese of Ozamiz (1965-1969). He received his Doctorate in Clinical Psychology from United States International University in San Diego in 1974. He lives with his wife and daughter in San Diego, California. He is currently Chief Psychologist at the San Ysidro Health Center and also in private practice in San Diego.

At first sight, humor and spirituality seem to belong to very different worlds. And yet, one of the greatest spiritual journeys of written record began with a laugh. It is the story of the Hebrew people, in the very moment of their call by God, through the promise to Abraham of a son to be born to his wife Sarah.

God said to Abraham, . . . "I will bless her and give you a son by her. I will bless her and she shall be the mother of nations; the kings of many peoples shall spring from her."

Abraham threw himself down on his face; he laughed and said to himself, "Can a son be born to a man who is a hundred years old? Can Sarah bear a son when she is ninety?" . . . "Your wife Sarah shall bear you a son, and you shall call him Isaac" (which means, "he laughed"). (Genesis 17:15)

All the long history that followed, with its searching and struggling, intrigues and deceptions, victories and betrayals, hopes and despairs is surely one of the great images of the personal journey of Everyman. The personal journey of Everyman, in turn, is what claims the interest of both spirituality and psychotherapy.

THEORETICAL PERSPECTIVE

A common predicament that frequently brings someone to therapy is the realization that the resources at hand are not adequate to deal with some current crisis.

One of the most exciting experiences in therapy is precisely this: to meet the challenge of a current impasse by discovering an access to some secret skill - one perhaps that had been practiced at an earlier time in life and then put aside or even forgotten.

The possibility of a hidden treasure of forgotten skills became very real to me during the days I watched my 5-year-old daughter deal with life. I marveled at her skills, her persistence, her myriad experimentations. I frequently found myself wondering - was I like that once?

It gives a newness to the ancient words of Christ - "Unless you become as little children, you cannot enter the Kingdom of Heaven."

What do we have to do to become like little children? We could search through the theological refinements of centuries of Western spirituality. Please continue reading; I am not going to do that. The other way is to go directly to the world of the child and explore its secrets. This way is certainly less boring, though any parent who has not long since succumbed to the drowsy numbness and vacant stare of the maturing adult knows that it is a journey fraught with perils of the gravest sort.

I have discovered three stashes of secret treasure in the child's world.

First, surely one of the most impressive skills of the child is the ability to let go of things. The hurts and rages of yesterday will not even be remembered tomorrow. Even "surprises" can be rehearsed and recycled, reappearing each time with all the intrigue and bated breath of a new creation. "Let's do that again" triggers the magic power of wiping out all memory of and credit for what you have just staggered through - for the umpteenth time! The technical theological term in Western spirituality for this cute little trick is "detachment" - the freedom of not being attached to things, the ability to let go, start again, and move on unencumbered.

Secondly, there is the child's aliveness to the world with all the eagerness to explore all sorts of new places, new ideas, new ways of doing things. My little daughter asked me one day if mommy and I were going to get a divorce. Being an old hand at the therapy business, it was a matter of moments for me to zero in on the child's insecurities and fears and mobilize my most reassuring affect and concern. "No," I said; "your mother and I love each other; believe me, we are not going to get a divorce!" "Why not?" she retorted. "We could have two houses. I would like a house with an upstairs." We adults have our dull "why" questions. The child has the shattering "why not" questions that never end. It is "Man's Search for Meaning" with a vengeance, having that special added intensity that comes with not having to bother about answers!

The third astonishing spiritual energy that permeates the world of the child is the awareness that the outer world facing us with its stony fixed stare of reality is not by any means the whole story. There are all sorts of worlds to be tried out and all sorts of roles to be tried on in play. From this a second world takes shape within the child through story and fantasy - a splendid and powerful inner world with its own light. This allows the child to look back upon the outer world with a magic eye and find there a truly marvelous creation.

Wordsworth (quoted in Williams, 1951) speaks of this light, which fades as we move further away from childhood:

At length the Man perceives it die away, And fade into the light of common day. (p. 317)

This experience represents a truly religious aspect of the child's world that evokes mythology. The purpose of mythology is not to tell a story in order to explain how the world began. Rather, the purpose of mythology is to explain how some great and present mystery could possibly have come about. It says "Something marvelous must have happened to have led to this." The "great and present mystery" that mythology addresses goes far beyond the naked world of rocks and stones and trees. It includes the world as seen by the child - a world of mystery. "Mystery" is only a grown-up word for "secret" - something hidden.

For this reason, the great creation myths and the great religious myths in general, when properly told, have about them the magic of the child's "let's pretend." And so as if by magic (and indeed it is by magic), the child learns to go beyond the world of appearances. He or she learns to look at things and say "There is more to this than meets the eye!" Western spirituality calls this religious experience "transcendence."

Simply put, a little child instinctively practices the same three great motifs of Western spirituality that have taken centuries of theological refinement to crystallize: (a) detachment, (b) the search for meaning, and (c) transcendence.

What happens to these amazing endowments of the child's spirituality as he or she grows up? That is the story of each person's life and the stories are legion. Frequently, these spiritual traits are weakened or lost through divergent programming that takes place either in the family setting, at school, or in the community at large.

It may also happen that the spiritual life of the child is seen as something separate from everyday life. Like the child's education or the child's health, the spiritual life is entrusted to the professionals - to organized religion.

Like any other competitive enterprise, churches frequently have their own agenda, with conformity of the members a matter of high priority. Any particular organized religion may take these three great skills that are the natural endowment of the child and substitute rote performance for any true voyage of discovery.

One by one, the lights go out.

In place of "detachment" or the ability to let go of things, it is possible to substitute "guilt" which will insure a permanent bonding with the most dismal aspects of one's past life.

There is a strong element of mistrust in Western religious tradition, because the world is seen as contaminated by sin. Here the model for detachment would be the old monks of the Scythian desert as they wove their rush baskets all day long. They would unweave them during the night, happy to pass their time without sin, as they waited for an eternity elsewhere.

There is a style of morality that encourages avoidance of sin by using "detachment" as a sort of anesthesia. It may seem as if one is walking around in a world bathed in the true odor of sanctity whereas one in fact is simply suffering from a paralysis of the olfactory nerve.

I described the second spiritual gift of the child as an eager aliveness to the world. This "search for meaning" aspect can be successfully blocked by any religious dogmatism that effectively sets up a situation similar to the television game *Jeopardy.* Here the game host gives the answer and the player is supposed to guess the question. This system constitutes a very effective way to limit the spirit of free inquiry. I am reminded of a cartoon I once saw of a procession of protesters. At the head of the procession came a placard with the inscription "Christ is the answer." There followed various placards with varying inscriptions. At the end of the procession came a placard with the inscription "What is the question," rather like the aforecited game show. This cartoon was not at all antireligious. It was protesting the violence of aborting a question before it could come to full term so that answers, in turn, were stillborn and without life.

Platitudes are a bad habit. They drain life from questions so that finally one question sounds as good as the next, like the Irishman who viewed the first highly successful demonstration of the steam engine. "Well," he said, "we now know it works in practice. But the question is - does it work in theory?"

The third gift of the child was described as the ability to look beyond the world of appearances and experience transcendence. It is not necessary to specifically deny transcendence in order to severely curtail people and stop them from wandering all over the place. All that is necessary is to insist that individuals stick to the straight and narrow path. This can be reinforced by placing "Keep off the grass" signs at all the good spots, which will put a stop to any temptation toward transcendence. In organized religion, this objective is frequently achieved by minutely prescribing what one may and may not do. An illustration that comes to mind in this respect are the kits available in supermarkets that teach painting by numbers. Such kits make it possible for someone with the least possible skill to paint a perfectly good horse. Unfortunately, another individual with the greatest skill paints the same perfectly good horse if he or she uses the kit. In fact, everybody ends up painting the same unfortunate horse.

The demand for conformity is truly surprising in the light of the persistent insistence on a healthy agnosticism across all great religious traditions. In the Hebrew tradition, we do not know for sure how to write the vowels in God's name (Yahweh? Jehovah?) because God's name was not allowed to be pronounced - God the Ineffable. Thomas Aquinas begins his Summa Theologica by saying that we do not know what God is; we know rather what God is not. Zen gives the same tradition - "Before heaven and earth, there was something eternal, the Mother of all things. I do not know its name, I call it Tao" (Matthiessen, 1987, p. 77). In this tradition, the purpose of theology is not so much to reveal a set of truths about God as it is to highlight the inherent limitations of our mind in our search for God (Colledge & McGinn, 1981). The mystic becomes speechless before the Mystery of God:

> I said to the almond tree:
> Sister, speak to me of God;
> And the almond tree blossomed.

I wonder if God would nod approvingly at the picture of the good old "draw-it-by-numbers" horse, which begins to look more and more self-righteous as one contemplates it further. Or would God nod rather approvingly by the fire dreaming some old dream about being a child at Christmas, muttering about - "a painting book in which I could make the grass, the trees, the sea and the animals any color I pleased, and still the dazzling sky-blue sheep are grazing in the red field under the rainbow-billed and pea-green birds" (Thomas, 1954, p. 17).

To paint the spiritual landscape by numbers leaves little room for the Spirit. The Greek word for spirit is the same as the word for the wind - "The wind blows where it wills; you hear the sound of it, but you do not know where it comes from, or where it is going. So with everyone who is born from spirit" (John 3:8). It takes great courage to make our life a true experiment, open to what we might find around any given corner as we take our one walk on the face of the earth. This profound truth is reflected in the words of John Middleton Murry:

For the good man to realize
that it is better to be whole
than to be good
is to enter on a straight and
narrow path compared to which
his previous rectitude was
flowery licence. (Richards, 1989, p. v)

I now remember with pleasure the shock I experienced years ago on hearing a famous spiritual director describe a self-righteous priest friend of mine. "What that man needs," he said, "is one good mortal sin!" That thought seemed rather audacious - to prescribe a deliberate breach of God's law! These were the days predating the advent of "paradoxical intention"! Today it doesn't sound too outlandish - to leap up with the glad cry and hurdle a few of the "Keep off the grass" signs!

So it can happen that people's religious development some-times separates them from the original spiritual endowment of their childhood. The gift of detachment, the eager search for meaning, and the spirit of transcendence fade into the light of common day. It is easy to become attached - stuck in the looping of old recurrent response patterns that we call symptoms. The fresh new wine of life's mysteries dries up and the old wineskins crack.

Perhaps, in time of crisis, individuals may come to feel iso-lated and lost, deprived of guidance or overall direction in their lives. In this situation, when they turn to psychotherapy, individ-uals may say things like - "I have lost my religion" or "I don't go to church anymore." This does not call for any immediate repri-mand or other signs of approval or disapproval on the therapist's part. However, they may go on to say things like: "But I think I am a spiritual person," and may add something like - "But I'm not sure what that means." In this instance, I would certainly recom-mend that the therapist explore what such statements might indeed mean and what techniques might be available to reconnect the patient with those childhood stashes of therapeutic treasure that I described earlier in terms of childhood spirituality.

TECHNIQUE

When the great Rabbi Israel Baal Shem-Tov saw mis-fortune threatening the Jews it was his custom to go into a certain part of the forest to meditate. There he would light a fire, say a special prayer, and the miracle would be accomplished and the misfortune averted.

Later, when his disciple, the celebrated Magid of Mezeritch, had occasion, for the same reason, to intercede with heaven, he would go to the same place in the forest and say: "Master of the Universe, listen! I do not know how to light the fire, but I am still able to say the prayer." And again the miracle would be accomplished.

Still later on, Rabbi Moshe-Leib of Sassov, in order to save his people once more, would go into the forest and say: "I do not know how to light the fire, I do not know the prayer, but I know the place and this must be sufficient." It was sufficient and the miracle was accomplished.

Then it fell to Rabbi Israel of Rizhin to overcome misfortune. Sitting in his armchair, his head in his hands, he spoke to God: I cannot even find the place in the forest. All I can do is to tell the story and this must be sufficient." And it was sufficient. (Shea, 1978, p. 7)

The technique of the therapist is to create an atmosphere for someone's story to unfold in a way that allows the story to change in the telling. Old acts may need to be dropped. Long forgotten plots may need to be revived. Our particular focus here is how to rediscover spiritual attitudes and powers that naturally belonged in the world of the child.

I have found four specific techniques to be particularly useful for this purpose: (a) humor, (b) hypnosis, (c) play therapy, and (d) storytelling.

HUMOR

Here I mean a "sense of humor," a friendly atmosphere as opposed to one of solemn formality, creating a space where the child in us can be at home. Such a stance carries with it a permission not to take ourselves too seriously. They say that the fallen angels fell from heaven through the force of gravity! However, the humorous attitude also creates an atmosphere within which transactions of the most serious nature can take place.

A useful image from the child's world can help us visualize this atmosphere. It is the image of the circus. Here, transactions of the most serious nature take place - walking on high wires, flying throughout the air with abandon, looking closely at the tonsils of tigers! And yet the circus is a place where the clown is at home. The role of the clown in the circus is not only to create laughs. Clowns come in between acts, not just to amuse the audience while the ring is being cleared, but to encourage "detachment!" Their role is to loosen the grip of the previous breathtaking act so that the audience is ready afresh for new wonders.

In therapy, the therapist's sense of humor plays a similar role, creating a friendly place so that we can have the confidence to let down our guard and be open to new learnings. The same principles apply in hypnosis with its regressions and its gifts of surprises from the unconscious, and in the processes of play or storytelling.

HYPNOSIS

1. Hypnosis may be utilized to connect with childhood experiences through regression to a childhood experience of the therapist or of the client, as in the following example. This particular example will illustrate the power of the spiritual quality of detachment and how a little playfulness can allow some serious communication to take place.

   Jimmy was a 9-year-old boy who was "brought" for therapy. I knew only that he had experienced much physical abuse in his background with an alcoholic mother and a violent father who had abandoned the family early on. Luckily, we were both wearing green sweaters. "Hey!" I said. "We are both wearing green sweaters. We must like each other." It is never too soon in the session to start a little trance logic.

   He grudgingly admitted that he was 9 years old, but that seemed to end the conversation. "I have a 5-year-old daughter," I said. "She would certainly think you were pretty old. Can you even remember when you were 5?" "I dunno." His replies seemed to suggest a preference for "brief psychotherapy."

   A regressive trance was induced by way of a story. I told him that I could remember when I was 9 years old. In fact, I could remember a particular day in our kitchen and I could see exactly what everyone was doing. I then described in detail a scene that ended with my father throwing a bread knife in rage across the kitchen. I could hear it thudding against the wall. By now regression was well under way for both of us. "Did it stick in the wall?" he asked. "No," I said. "It fell to the floor. I was glad when my father left the house one day and never came back." "Me too," he said.

It had not been an easy task for me over the years to learn that I can possess those early memories without feeling that my whole identity is defined by them. This achievement is an example of the quality of detachment that I am presenting as an aspect of spirituality. It is just as relevant for the therapist as it is for the client. In the present example, my own detachment provided a conducive atmosphere for Jimmy to arrive at some measure of acknowledgment and validation of his own experiences without being overwhelmed by them.

"Do you want to see something weird?" I asked. Within the atmosphere of the trance, playfulness comes naturally. "What?" he said. "A 50-year-old scar" I boasted. We examined it carefully, still there on my thumb, and relived the story of how I got it. He showed me one of his. I had another pretty good one on my shin, though not as well preserved. He had several, better than mine with the livid freshness of youth. Mine were of the more subdued vintage brand. At the end he said: "I have been hurt so much, I don't feel anything anymore." At that moment, I felt he knew he was speaking about all the hurts of his life. When he rose to leave, he said: "Maybe I'll come back. Are there any kids around here to talk to?" I hope he wasn't being sarcastic!

2. The regression experience can also be used as a resource to help deal with present trauma. The following example illustrates the spiritual power of transcendence - to find the secret hidden in the world around us. The example also illustrates what Frankl (1963, p. 68) discovered amidst the horrors of a concentration camp: "Humor, more than anything else in the human makeup, can afford an aloofness and an ability to rise above any situation, even if only for a few seconds."

I was working in therapy with a young man named Mark who was dying. One of the things he agonized over the most was whether his 4-year-old daughter would remember his love for her.

We used trance in our therapy to induce regression just to give some momentary relief through a reliving of the playful time he had as a young boy. Here there were scenes of Christmas and snow, of the old farmhorse pulling the sleigh to town, of smells of food and woodburning fires, of laughing and fighting in the snow.

The purpose of the regressions was to build up a repertoire of images and stories that would provide, as it were, a place of relief. This useful technique is frequently used by children when they ask for a story to be told again and again or when they engage in endless replays of an exciting activity. Mark called on this resource many times as his illness progressed.

However, for Mark, this experience was turning out to be something more than just memories. Among all those topsy-turvy images of snowdrifts and laughing and Christmas, one little girl began to stand out. It was his sister who in later years had become closest to him of all his family. He came to realize that her love for him began when she was a little girl playing with him during their childhood. I asked him how old his sister had been when her love for him had first taken hold. He thought a while. "Four years old," he said.

The foregoing is an example of the inner search that leads to a new light being cast on the outer world. This light is lit through an inner experience of story and fantasy. It must be an inner experience, not just an intellectual statement about how things are. In this case, Mark was able to transcend his fearful brooding on the question of whether his 4-year-old daughter would be able to remember his love for her. The truth he discovered based on his own trance experience was that yes, love begun at 4 can be well remembered!

I later stood by his coffin and looked at a small crumpled bunch of flowers laying on top of the coffin. Beside the flowers was a drawing of trees and grass and flowers with the word "daddy" in crooked letters. This was certainly no "draw-by-numbers" picture, and I knew from looking at it that love was well begun by 4.

PLAY THERAPY

We described the second spiritual gift of the child as the ability to explore all sorts of new places, new ideas, and new ways of doing things. Play is a great way to enter into this exploration and constitutes a powerful technique in therapy. Its therapeutic purpose goes far beyond just having fun - though fun may certainly be a part of it. Play may in fact be used to discover just how little fun we are having, as the following example illustrates.

I was working with a family where the mother had recently remarried. She and her three children had moved into the home of the new stepfather. She had two boys - a 15-year-old and a 17-year-old, and a girl of 11. The husband refused to come for family therapy.

Things seemed to be very strained at home. The house and everything in it clearly belonged to the stepfather. Rules were expected to be observed with no questions asked. The mother felt that respect for the stepfather and his home demanded compliance. Discipline was very arbitrary. All instructions to the children were given through the mother. Even simple things like asking for more salad dressing were interpreted as critical of the household and a sign of defiance. The stepfather would make the appropriate protest to the mother later in the evening, and it was her duty to convey it to the guilty party. This style of relating was similar to the way the mother had been brought up in her own family, and she felt that her children had no other option but to comply with her husband's ways.

She was unable to understand just how enraged the children were, and at what profound spiritual level they were being disrespected. I designed a play therapy session where I hoped the playfulness would allow the strong family defenses to relax long enough to open up new perspectives.

I had the family sit around a table - myself at the head, in my most arrogant manner. We would play Mr. Wiggly. It was my game, my table, my chairs, my house, and we would play Mr. Wiggly by my rules. I made that clear. I made them change places a few times during the game, suddenly and for no reason. I went through the cards and picked out the good ones for myself. I sometimes disallowed the children to have their turn. I had very little direct interaction with the children but gave all my instructions through the mother.

The game was fun for a little while, but then became painful; so painful in fact that the mother finally burst into tears. That was a very poignant moment for everyone. The mother seemed to understand what was being communicated through this therapy experience: "I didn't realize what I was doing to my children." She had finally come to understand how seriously the children's spiritual rights were being violated and how deeply hurt they felt.

Play may be fun but we can come to understand some very serious realities through it.

STORYTELLING

Storytelling must surely be as old as language. One of the most persistent early requests of the child is: "Tell me a story!" There is a long tradition of storytelling in the history of spirituality - whether it be the oral myths, the stories of Zen, the parables of Jesus, or the stories of the medieval miracle plays.

Storytelling has also come to be recognized as a highly effective natural technique for psychotherapy (Gilligan, 1987). Its purpose is to utilize the powerful process of indirect communication through the use of a story that can work as an extended metaphor for some element in the therapeutic situation.

The "indirect" aspect of storytelling is something we are all familiar with. It is the old "I have a friend who has this problem" technique, which diverts any personal defensiveness that might interfere with an objective discussion of a particular situation. Therapists sometimes use the "I have a story" technique in a similar way.

Of course, the context for storytelling in therapy needs to be prepared and the story ought to have a point. Hopefully, the therapist would not launch into long stories about his recent fishing trip before the client has had a chance to speak. Nonetheless, I have a vivid memory of doing something just as silly, albeit in a reversed sort of way.

It happened a long time ago. I preface the story with that remark by way of excuse. I was in the midst of an interview with a patient in a psychiatric hospital where I had recently begun my internship in clinical psychology. I was supposed to do a psychological evaluation. The woman had suffered a traumatic loss, attempted suicide, and was quite stunned and self-absorbed. I can still see myself, holding up a dull old gray picture from the Thematic Apperception Test and saying to the woman: "Tell me a story." She looked at me blankly and said with great deliberateness: "I have tried to kill myself, I am in a mental hospital, I don't know where my car is, and you want me to tell you a story?"

Individuals sometimes have a good laugh when I tell that story as it helps to break the ice in therapy. Stories can become just that - good ice-breakers. Stories can be useful because we come upon a lot of places in our therapy journeys where defrosting is needed.

PERTINENT USES

In early times in Japan, bamboo-and-paper lanterns were used with candles inside. A blind man, visiting a friend one night, was offered a lantern to carry home with him.

"I do not need a lantern," he said, "Darkness or light is all the same to me."

"I know you do not need a lantern to find your way," his friend replied, "but if you don't have one, someone else may run into you. So you must take it."

The blind man started off with the lantern and before he had walked very far someone ran squarely into him. "Look out where you are going!" he exclaimed to the stranger. "Can't you see this lantern?"

"Your candle has burned out, brother," replied the stranger. (Reps, 1957, p. 79)

I like this story. It reminds me of the fact that our original spiritual endowment is frequently extinguished, without our realizing it. This happens when guilt is substituted for detachment; religious dogmatism for any real search for meaning; conformism for any real search for personal integrity.

I have outlined some techniques for reconnecting with these lost spiritual habits. Their recovery provides resources that have many applications in the work of psychotherapy. Detachment will frequently be called upon to loosen the hold of guilts that tie us into looping patterns of old symptoms. Escape from rigid dogmatism in our belief system and from artificial conformism in our code of action nourishes the possibility of freedom, of mobility, of growth in the therapy process (Richards, 1989).

Individuals doing psychotherapeutic work often speak of a disillusionment with formalistic or conventional religious systems. It is useful to recognize that such disillusionment can open the way for reconnecting with more meaningful spiritual attitudes.

The understanding that disillusionment can lead to growth is beautifully illustrated in one of the initiation traditions among the Hopi Indians. The initiation rite begins with increased activity of the Kachinas, the gods in wonderful masks and costumes who visit the village at special times. They treat the children to be initiated as special - with secret stories, dances, and celebration. At last the children are taken into a special hut to await the final visit of the Kachinas. They hear the Kachinas approaching. Excitement mounts as they wait for the dancing gods to enter. But to the children's amazement, the Kachinas enter without their masks and reveal themselves, not as gods but as members of the village (Shea, 1978). The children are thus initiated into the magic that belongs to everyday reality.

CLINICAL PRESENTATIONS

I would like to illustrate my approach by presenting an actual therapy case. I shall call him John - a bright, sophisticated man in his early thirties in a good marriage with two children, a boy and a girl. He was a successful engineer and had all the intellectual focus and precision we might expect from his training. Due to his work, he had been away from home a good deal on business trips.

He initially presented his situation as follows: "I'm here because my son is having problems! I'm sure it's my fault. It's not fair that he should have a problem because of me." It did not take him long to set aside his initial presentation and agree that he had work of his own to do for his own sake.

As we proceeded with our work, I found out more about John. He had been brought up in a very strict Southern Baptist religious tradition. But no - he didn't think he had taken the idea of God very seriously. However, he was also able to describe with emotional blandness how, as a child, he was very aware of the large black book where God wrote down every bad deed of his. I had personally made several prominent appearances in the same black book (though in a different edition, because I was Catholic). I had paid large sums of money to various therapists over the years in an effort to have my name edited out of it. So I doubted that the issue was as matter-of-fact as it sounded!

Again, no, he didn't think his father had a significant impact on his early years. In fact, John felt that his father was not very involved in his upbringing, because his work took him away from home a lot. On the other hand, John was able to calmly articulate early connections to violence of a most traumatic kind in relation to his father. In actuality, the father's violent history had culminated in imprisonment for murder.

It was clear that, for John, the image of his father was highly encapsulated and was an area where there was going to be great difficulty in effecting a breakthrough into affect. I had a keen sense of Watzlawick's words:

"It may be a useful simplification to postulate that whoever comes into therapy signals in one way or another: Anything, except that. By this I mean that emotional suffering creates a willingness to do anything for its alleviation, except one and only one thing: and this "one thing" is exactly what causes his suffering. (1978, p. 139)

My own structuring of the problem was as follows:

1. John's strict early religious training had led to rigidity of thought and affect. He was very proficient in the art of rationalization. The spiritual "searching for new meanings" had long been curtailed.
2. John was unable to acknowledge his father's rage. This left him bound into his own helplessness which was connected to that rage. Guilt had long since replaced the resilience of detachment.
3. I suspected that the initial complaint was in fact symbolic of the real problem. "I'm here because my son is having problems" can point to John's unconscious awareness that in his own case too, the problems of the son come from the father.

I spent several sessions helping John pay attention to his dreams and teaching him to utilize the trance experience in therapy. As his therapy progressed, his dreams began to change.

Finally he came in distressed. "There is something wrong with my dreams!" he said. Earlier they were straightforward, with a beginning, a middle, and an end. "Now I can't understand them. They are becoming disconnected and seem to lead nowhere."

The most straightforward thing to do was to ask the unconscious about this new style of dreaming. I used the simple induction method of having him go into trance by holding his index fingers apart and having them slowly come together, going into a trance when they finally touched.

He had used this method before without difficulty. On this occasion, the hands came together until the fingers touched. However, the left hand floated to his thigh. But the right hand remained cataleptic, index finger stiffly pointing! John spent some time in his trance, hopefully allowing his unconscious mind to give him some hints as to what was happening with his dreams.

Finally he opened his eyes to find his right hand still poised, finger pointing. What was going on? "I feel - this finger - so rigid! So rigid!" was his response. What might it mean? "It's like it's pointing." The finger was pointing up toward his face. He suddenly burst out laughing. "We talk about my left brain and my right brain. My God! My left brain! It's so rigid!" He now understood the meaning of what we had been working on in therapy. Over a period of time his dreaming intensified and he became more open to nonverbal, symbolic processes.

At a later session, he returned with another dream. In this dream, he was going to take a picture of his mother. He was on a hill and it looked like she was too small in the viewfinder. He changed positions but now she was too big. He couldn't get her in the frame of the viewfinder. He got a tripod. The idea was to take a time exposure; he would click the camera and run around to join her. The tripod would slip. He never did get to take her picture. But he was able to understand that some unconscious process was going on affecting his relationship with his mother. He was also able to appreciate the image of "reframing" as a joke from his unconscious.

In time, John's relationship with his father came to be the focus of his therapy. During one of these sessions, he went into a trance that turned out to be an experience with immense emotional turmoil. During the trance he was on a beach. Things clouded over and there came the image of a military steel helmet, and the beach was enveloped in storm and fury. He came back out of the trance in tears and desolation. For John, this was a new opening into affect - frightening, powerful, and intensely real. I thought it appropriate at this juncture to allow the separation of intellectual and emotional sets to continue, without any immediate effort to link history to affect.

However, it was clear to him that his experience with this trance was not complete. I had John return to trance and he found himself once more on the same beach. He began a journey from the beach through a narrow place. It was a frightening journey. There were three main images, which he described as follows. First there was a wall, its base murky with fungus and old damp decay - a foreboding place. He moved along and came to an old window that opened into nowhere, dark and covered with dust and spider webs. The journey continued to yet another place with a dark and ominous opening into the earth, from which he drew back. He then withdrew from trance, again shaken and at a loss.

Things were still clearly unfinished and he did not wish to end the session like that. We agreed that he would go back into trance and if possible, find the beach and retrace his footsteps on that strange journey.

However, this time he was to imagine that his two children were with him, and he was to go on his journey hand in hand with them. He did so, as he reported afterwards. He was led again through the images, this time taking the hand of each of his small children - who laughed and played their way through the grim imagery and defused it. He came to the wall, and the children laughed and played in the sand. As they played, the place lost its foreboding atmosphere; the fungus and damp decay at the base of the wall became simply the wet that any wall has at a beach. They romped along and enjoyed themselves at the old window, writing their name in the dust and trying to run around and do their children's grimacing at each other through the old window. The dark frightening opening into the earth became just a hole in the ground and the children played in and out of it. And then the trance was over and was indeed truly finished.

In this case, hypnosis proved to be a useful technique. It allowed John to experience his own unconscious with its sense of humor. This in turn allowed him to stop taking himself too seriously.

The hypnosis also allowed the friendly influence of his children to free John from his connection to his father's rage and thus dissociate himself from his longstanding helplessness. For him, this was truly a lesson in detachment.

This breakthrough was not the end of therapy but it brought the therapeutic process to a new stage. After this experience, John dropped many aspects of his self-depreciation and started to let go of his crippling need for control.

John's name had finally been dropped from God's black book. A whole new spiritual journey had begun for him with a new-found freedom to ask questions about life without needing to have all the answers. It was a true initiation into the magic that can indeed belong to everyday reality.

SYNTHESIS

This chapter has reviewed three aspects of spirituality: spirituality as detachment, spirituality as the search for meaning, and spirituality as transcendence.

Spirituality as detachment shares with psychotherapy the energy that allows us to let go of old attachments. Humor, as C. S. Lewis (1982) notes, involves a sense of proportion and a power of seeing oneself from the outside, the perfect idiom for detachment.

Emphasis has been given in this chapter to the healthy agnosticism that is part of all great traditions of the spiritual search for meaning. For man, the search is the meaning. There is no cognitive capture of God. We carefully map the coastline of our island because that is the only way we have of charting the boundary of the ocean. In this outlook we join the tradition of Zen, where enlightenment comes after the road of thinking is blocked. The same process is manifested in the therapeutic technique of reframing. Humor, like the clown in the circus, has a special power of enchantment to move us through transitions.

Materialism gives priority to outer arrangements. Spirituality places us within the framework of living things. Here life does not proceed mechanically, adding years from without as one might add candles to a birthday cake. Here life proceeds from within. Here paths cross with psychotherapy in the inner search. There is a spontaneity to life that moves more lightly through humor than through the gravity of reason.

The technique of the therapist is explored as that of the compassionate witness, allowing humor to temper the atmosphere with friendliness so that someone's story may truly unfold. Humor, hypnosis, play therapy, and storytelling are given their place in such a process.

Three stashes of secret treasure can be discovered in childhood spirituality. One of the most exciting experiences of therapy is to discover a new access to these skills that were once practiced at an earlier time in life and then cast aside or forgotten.

The case presented dealt with a violent earthly father and a heavenly Father with a big black book. In this case, the "let's pretend" of children worked its magic and the candle that had gone out was lit again.

REFERENCES

Bateson, G. (1988). *Mind and Nature.* New York: Bantam Books.

Carroll, L. (1962). *Alice's Adventures in Wonderland* and *Through the Looking Glass.* New York: Macmillan.

Colledge, E., & McGinn, B. (1981). *Meister Eckhart, The Essential Sermons, Commentaries, Treatises, and Defense.* New York: Paulist Press.

Crossan, D. (1975). *The Dark Interval.* Niles, IL: Argus Communications.

Erickson, M. (1983). *Healing in Hypnosis.* New York: Irvington.

Fox, M. (1983). *Original Blessing.* Santa Fe, NM: Bear & Company.

Fox, M. (1988). *The Coming of the Cosmic Christ.* San Francisco: Harper & Row.

Frankl, V. (1963). *Man's Search for Meaning.* New York: Pocket Books.

Gilligan, S. (1987). *Therapeutic Trances.* New York: Brunner/Mazel.

Joyce, J. (1976). *A Portrait of the Artist as a Young Man.* New York: Penguin Books.

Lewis, C. S. (1982). *The Screwtape Letters.* New York: Macmillan.

Matthiessen, P. (1987). *Nine-Headed Dragon River.* Boston: Shambhala.

O'Connor, F. (1981). *Collected Stories.* New York: Knopf.

Progoff, I. (1973a). *The Death and Rebirth of Psychology.* New York: McGraw-Hill.

Progoff, I. (1973b). *Depth Psychology and Modern Man.* New York: McGraw-Hill.

Progoff, I. (1973c). *The Symbolic and the Real.* New York: McGraw-Hill.

Progoff, I. (1973d). *Jung, Synchronicity and Human Destiny.* New York: Delta.

Progoff, I. (1977). *The Well and the Cathedral.* New York: Dialogue House Library.

Progoff, I. (1978). *The Cloud of Unknowing.* New York: Delta.

Radin, P. (1972). *The Trickster.* New York: Schocken Books.

Ram Dass. (1978). *Journey of Awakening.* New York: Bantam Books.

Reps, P. (1957). *Zen Flesh, Zen Bones.* New York: Anchor Books.

Richards, M. C. (1989). *Centering.* Middletown, CT: Wesleyan University Press.

Rossi, E. (1988). *The Psychobiology of Mind-Body Healing.* New York: W. W. Norton.

Rouse, W. H. D. (1970). *The Complete Texts of Great Dialogues of Plato.* New York: New American Library.

Saint Exupéry, A. de. (1943). *The Little Prince.* San Diego: Harcourt Brace Jovanovich.

Shea, J. (1978). *Stories of God.* Chicago: The Thomas More Press.

Suzuki, D. T. (1964). *An Introduction to Zen Buddhism.* New York: Grove Press.

Teilhard de Chardin, P. (1969). *Human Energy.* New York: Harcourt Brace Jovanovich.

Thomas, D. (1954). *A Child's Christmas in Wales.* New York: New Directions Publishing Corporation.

Watzlawick, P. (1978). *The Language of Change.* New York: Basic Books.

Wilber, K. (1986). *Up from Eden.* Boston: New Science Library.

Williams, O. (Ed.). (1951). *A Little Treasury of British Poetry.* New York: Scribner.

Zeig, J. (Ed.). (1982). *Ericksonian Approaches to Hypnosis and Psychotherapy.* New York: Brunner/Mazel.

11

Kierkegaard's Humor and Its Implications for Indirect Humorous Communication in Psychotherapy

Julius E. Heuscher

In this unique chapter, Dr. Heuscher explores the hidden games human beings play to prevent the true Self from unfolding. Using Soren Kierkegaard as an "anonymous" guide to the Amazonian recesses of being, Dr. Heuscher explores how the Self can be dissimulated under the rubble of thinghood or behind the dance of the seven veils as individuals develop various stratagems of self-deceit to avoid facing the limpidity of being. Heuscher then examines how the Self can be resuscitated through humor, as humor raises the Self from a state of emotional death into living vibrancy.

Julius E. Heuscher, MD, is the author of A Psychiatric Study of Myths and Fairy Tales *(1974) and numerous articles, many of which focus on subjects of Existential Psychiatry. He is currently an Emeritus Clinical Professor of Psychiatry at Stanford University.*

❖   ❖   ❖

THEORETICAL PERSPECTIVES

The *Concluding Unscientific Postscript to the Philosophical Fragments* is Kierkegaard's most important philosophical work. It was written in 1846 under one of his numerous pseudonyms, Johannes Climacus, who likes to describe himself as a "humorist." As indicated by its title, Kierkegaard meant this to be the last work of his prolific authorship. Interestingly and significantly, his first major work was his thesis *The Concept of Irony* (1841/1965). His authorship seems to move from irony to humor.

At first, I wrongly suspected that the pseudonyms responsible for most of Kierkegaard's books published between *The Concept of Irony* (1841/1965) and the *Concluding Unscientific Postscript to the Philosophical Fragments* (1846/1941) were brilliant literary equivalents of Sybil's (Schreiber, 1974) artistic multiple personalities. They are not. Nor is it sufficient to view them as effective sophisticated devices for expressing different or conflicting feelings and reflections. Their meaningfulness resides primarily in Kierkegaard's awareness and conviction that in matters of human existence, of values and beliefs, direct communication is of limited value. Thus only methods of indirect communication offer safeguards against ideas being forced upon the readers and awaken the readers' freedom to find the truth. Kierkegaard's pseudonyms refer to almost unknown individuals. They tend to remove themselves from, or even disavow, their own views. They may insist that they are just humorists. In this manner, they challenge readers to accept full ownership for whatever truth emerges for them as a result of reading these volumes.

Kierkegaard's aim in his authorship was first and foremost the concept of *psychotherapy*, if by this term we intend any and all efforts to help the individual in gaining or regaining a genuine sense of Self. Such psychotherapy would assist the individual in expelling all "evil spirits" - philosophical, scientific, familial, neurotic, social, and even religious - that would eventually define or drown the Self. Since this "evil spirit" metaphor may smack of witch hunting, we may say instead that Kierkegaard's approach consists in an indefatigable uncovering of the numerous ways by which we human beings have forgotten what it means to exist in genuine selfhood. Kierkegaard calls himself an undercover agent, a spy, and he addresses not so much the crowd, but each single individual for himself or herself. His concerns are echoed almost a century later by Martin Heidegger (1961) in more sweeping and dramatic statements reflecting a sense of increased urgency characteristic of the 20th century. Heidegger proposes that we have forgotten what it means to be a Self, a "Being-There" (or Dasein). He also advances that we have become forgetful of *Being*, of a *Being* that gives continuity, cohesion, and meaning to all that exists. According to Heidegger, the individual's authentic aim must be a renewed and more aware concern with Being, and the fate of the entire Western Civilization hangs on how we meet this challenge.

This may sound too philosophical and too ominous. However, we cannot ignore that this focus on forgetting is at least partly reflected in the forgetting that Freud, Jung, and many others had in mind when they spoke of repression, of denial and projection, of archetypes and scripts, and of various levels of unconscious functioning. Most therapists' background, training, and social milieu inclines them to acknowledge the harm of forgetting only in the case of patients who consciously suffer (neuroses and psychosomatic disorders), who harm the environment (sociopathies), or who become dysfunctional within society (psychoses). Kierkegaard, Heidegger, Buber, and Sartre, however, speak of forms of forgetting that occur in individuals seemingly free of such symptoms. Well-adjusted, respected, and successful, such individuals can be just as unauthentic as the "officially" identified patients. They live in hidden despair or out of touch with their true Self like others who wear a psychiatric label. Although there are valid theoretical and practical reasons for distinguishing "sick" and "not-sick" people, our being aware of how tenuous this distinction is will improve our therapeutic stance.

Humor is the most universal, simple, and ephemeral reminder of our freedom, of our ability to reshape or recreate our world. Psychotherapy usually tries to "re-mind," to reverse the process of forgetting, whether the focus is on forgotten feelings or memories or, more fundamentally, on the lost experience of oneself (one's Self) as an existing, responsible, creative human being.

Before we examine how humor may be of value in psychotherapeutic reminding, I need to comment briefly on four closely related questions: What does it mean to be an "existing human being?" What is implied by the term "creative?" Are there only negative features to "forgetting?" And what are the possibilities of "reminding?"

Maybe *Genesis* offers the best image of what it means to be creative, when it tells us that the human being was created in the image of the Creator. We commonly forget the enormous implications of this, but this forgetting can be seen as purposeful inasmuch as it helps us to focus, and keeps us from being excessively flooded by options, desires, expectations, and doubts. The secret of a good memory, a wise old man once told me, lies in forgetting the unessential. Yet the narrowing of one's options or desires easily leads human beings to experience themselves as fully determined by their constitution, innate drives, and parental, social, or religious norms. Any teaching, advising, preaching, or philosophizing would be seen as tending to further alienate individuals from their Selves. The patient, the "sufferer" must patiently find his or her own truth, which is relative mainly in the sense that each one of us can apprehend only a very restricted view of the world.

It would ill behoove (let alone bankrupt) a therapist to put up a sign at his or her office entrance stating: "Find your own truth!" In what way, then, can the therapist assist a patient? Ancient and recent stories tell of saints, gurus, or yogis visited by pilgrims. They silently greet the supplicants and quietly sit with them during many hours. Though no words are uttered, the supplicants depart feeling tremendously enriched. Although our patients would hardly be willing to pay for this type of approach, we must ask what truth such anecdotes contain. It would be beneficial to examine how such a system can be incorporated into a therapeutic relationship in conjunction with the technical features of interpretation, analysis of dreams, of transference, and of humor. Indeed, the polarities and paradoxes of human existence also pervade psychotherapy. Therapists may occasionally have to remind themselves that they can do little for a certain patient, but that rejecting some patients, or not charging them for the visits, would be even worse. Therapists must sense and keep in mind that the very fact of their being present without needing to manipulate the patient's world can *re-mind* the patient that he or she is an "infinitely valuable," irreplaceable, unique Self. The patient may further realize that the Self is neither determined nor comprehended by any of his or her measurable, quantifiable, "positive" or "negative" feelings, qualities, assets, talents, and so forth. This unique Self tolerates no definition:

> "What are your names?" farmer Jones asked two odd creatures emerging from the flying saucer that landed in his field. "We have no names," one replied, "we know who we are!"

But this unique Self postulates another Self (or other Selves) to whom it is related. In fact its existence is unthinkable without such a relationship. Kierkegaard viewed this "other Self" primarily as "the Power that posits the Self," as God. This loving relatedness to the ground that sustains us would then be the source of our caring bonds to our fellow human beings. Whether the other human being or God is primarily experienced as "thou" may indeed be irrelevant, because "God is wherever two human beings genuinely meet," and because a genuine relationship with God brings with it an unselfish love for others. If an individual should fail to sense, accept, or cherish this other-related quality of the Self, he or she may become alienated from the creative powers of the Self. The therapist must first and foremost remain aware of this often ignored and rejected quality of the patient's Self: Kierkegaard views such rejection, such avoidance of one's openness for the infinite value of the other's Self, as a form of "despairingly not willing to be a Self."

In the United States, it was Carl Rogers who most effectively pointed toward the need to deal with this avoidance in psychotherapy. Though unfair, the sarcastic jokes about his approach remind the therapist that he or she must be more than an accepting, passive, nonjudgmental person reflecting the patient's thoughts and feelings. Yet how can the therapist be active without becoming another factor that forcibly tries to shape the patient's world, self-image, or behavior?

Kierkegaard's view of "indirect communication" becomes useful here. The gist of any such "indirect communication" is that its "author" is withdrawn from it as much as possible. As a result, the patient is left alone with the communication and must freely decide what to make of it. Kierkegaard communicated indirectly by using pseudonyms, by retracting or contradicting previously expressed views, or by having the pseudonym call himself a "humorist." In addition, he freely used humor, metaphors, and parables. Even in his later years when he launched his direct attack upon Christendom, Kierkegaard shifted the responsibility for truth to his readers. He repeatedly emphasized that he was speaking "without authority," that he himself was not a Christian, and that he was but a "corrective" - namely something like a spice that is not to be taken in as such but is to be mixed with food grown tasteless or unappetizing.

Indirect communication is indeed a hallmark of all effective psychotherapy. The psychoanalyst's procedure, for example, encourages indirect communication inasmuch as it allows the patient to project all kinds of "pseudonyms" (or transferences) upon the therapist who then disavows ownership of whatever the patient hears from or experiences in regard to these "pseudonyms." Interpretations are usually also offered in the form of indirect communication. They are not "objective truths" discovered by the shrewd therapist. Not unlike jokes, they are merely tentative and often ambiguous new ways of viewing things that patients are challenged to examine, accept, or reject. Feeling unconditionally accepted, patients begin to sense that their view of the world is based on many self-chosen presuppositions. Chosen at an early time for good reason, these presuppositions and prejudices have become part of their manifest identity. In psychotherapy, patients sometimes dare to step back and reexamine some of their assumptions. This stepping back is salutary not so much because patients end up choosing alternative views (in fact they may not) but because the stepping back from their manifest identity awakens within them what they have forgotten. They have forgotten that they are not - or rather not only - definable persons in this measurable world. They have forgotten that they are existing human beings that relate creatively and freely to what they have fashioned of themselves and the world.

Interpretations, explorations of options, explanations of dreams, and appropriate humorous comments are therapeutically more effective if they are rooted in the recognition that we all have a hand in the way we appear to ourselves and the way our world appears to us. What patients discover in psychotherapy is that they keep clinging to their ways of being-in-the-world for personal, usually well-concealed, reasons.

Indirect modes of allowing the patient to step back from his habitual world include humor, role-playing, guided daydreams, the use of parables and folklore themes, as well as comparing how other individuals have experienced and dealt with somewhat similar situations or conflicts (Heuscher, 1974, 1981b). These and other procedures indirectly offer new perspectives or options without lessening the patients' obligation to make their own choices. Sensing the rich meanings and powerful imaginative language conveyed in folklore and parables, Kierkegaard was particularly fond of using these methods to relate his messages to readers.

This contribution focuses on the relevance of humor as a form of indirect psychotherapeutic communication. Humor surreptitiously undermines the recipients' customary views and often introduces unexpected options. It is never a direct judgment or statement. It tends to be ambiguous and (in the form of jokes) anonymous. Therefore, humor is exceptionally well suited to *remind* the patient of feelings, views, and potentials that he or she never knew, repressed, or forgot.

"Re-mind" is a fortunate expression, implying that the primary therapeutic purpose is to help patients regain their own mind, their Self. The resulting responsible commitment to new or rediscovered values and views is a consequence of the patient's willingness to step back from a concertized, objectified, fixed picture of oneself and one's world. The trouble with forgetting is not so much that we forget part of the world, but that we forget our Self. Remembering how we became who we are and gaining insight into our present life do not necessarily increase our awareness of our creative, responsible Self.

The concept "Self" is nebulous, because over two millennia of Western civilization have produced a pervasive, one-sided interest in *things,* thus enabling our gigantic scientific and technological achievements. The cost has been a temporary dulling of the appreciation of *meaning* and *subjectivity.* However, various thinkers gradually began to focus upon what has been lost as well as upon the ultimate concerns of human beings. "What does it mean to be an *existing human being*?" was Kierkegaard's essential concern. "How did we forget 'Being,' especially our own 'Being-There,' our 'Self'?" asked Heidegger (1961). Husserl (1953), who was Heidegger's teacher, was radically empirical in his approach. He attempted to show the reality of the Transcendental Ego (or Self) that stands in creative contrast against a constituted Empirical Ego and Empirical World. This *Transcendental Ego* corresponds to what Goethe already intuited as *New Ego* and what Jung described as *Self.* Essentially related to a *body* and to an external world, the Self contains the potential for freedom, unconditional love, commitment, and the genuine "Will" (Yalom, 1980).

In addition to threats leveled at the Self from the natural sciences, the Self is equally threatened today by a tremendous volume of well-meaning talk about "self-assertion," "being Number One," "individual rights," "doing-your-own-thing," and so forth. Most of this seems to lack seriousness. Just as numerous individuals attend church at least on Christmas and Easter because they are baptized Christians, many individuals participate in Jungian and Gestalt treatment, Erhart Seminar Training, and Growth or Encounter groups provided they only temporarily shed the comfortable security of their collective middle-class status. When it is convenient, they may even become "existentialists," doing what they please and discarding whoever is offended by their narcissistic enlightenment or is unable to share their glory.

Yet now an inner voice admonishes me: "If you are so smart that you can afford making fun of your fellow human beings, then explain what is this Self you keep talking about?" Thank you, inner voice, for reminding me that I am indeed just as guilty as the ones I have ridiculed. I am also unable to fully experience and live this innermost Self. I must turn to Kierkegaard for help. Reluctant as he was to speak as an authority, he struggled his entire life not only to describe but to *be* an "existing-human-being" as well. I largely quote Kierkegaard when I tell patients that their irreplaceable Self, whether it be experienced, ignored, or denied, is of unlimited value. I may point out to them that a person becomes vaguely aware of the Self not at a time of success and praise but when he or she has failed, feels alone, or is powerless. At these moments, one can nevertheless sense that despite many bleak outward signs, one remains unique and unchanged in one's innermost being. We often tend to err by confusing our worth with outward, concrete, so-called "positive" attributes that we excessively identify with. Intelligence, blue eyes, friendliness, good grades, potency, Treasury Bills, clothes, lack of body odor, or even humility are supposedly sought-after goodies. Unless we become aware that such attributes are, at best, valuable reflections of the Self - and at worst pitiful substitutes for the Self - such one-sided focusing constitutes further evidence of having forgotten what it means to "exist as a human being." When we begin to view the sum of all our personal achievements and skills as "all-that-we-are," then we have started to lose our Self. Without this Kierkegaardian view of the human being, humor is inconceivable!

My focusing on the role of humor in psychotherapy is the result of a stepwise development. Early in life, I received solace from wise parental messages that helped defuse negative emotions: "Do not worry, it will turn out wrong anyway!" or "Against stupidity even gods fight in vain!" or "Don't do today what you can put off 'til tomorrow!" However, my coming of age could not be put off 'til tomorrow. My parents offered me the choice of either studying medicine or going to work. I chose the lesser evil, but soon defected to psychiatry and psychotherapy which promised more opportunities for daydreaming and philosophizing. Soon this nourished a growing interest in the existential meaning of folklore, and its relevance to psychotherapy.

It was William Fry who, aware of my interest, encouraged me to write about humor in fairy tales as far back as when he wrote his delightful book *Sweet Madness* (1963). Later, this prompted me to reflect more broadly on the philosophy of humor and humor's possible roles in psychotherapy. My fondness for folklore had gone hand-in-hand with attempts to gain more radical insight into human nature from existential thinkers. And finally it was Kierkegaard (1846/1941, 1841/1965) who furthered a more profound understanding of the meaning of various forms of wit. For the justification of the use of humor in psychotherapy, his distinction between *irony* and *constructive humor* is particularly helpful. To these forms of wit we may add *cynicism and sarcasm* as a third category.

Kierkegaard's views of the function of humor are best illustrated in his three stages of existence: *esthetic, ethic,* and *religious.* When living exclusively in the first, the human being is not aware of his or her ongoing Self. Lost in the esthetic stage, one is a victim of fate and arbitrariness in a world valued solely for its momentary sensuous and intellectual satisfactions. Yet, lacking a sense of true temporal continuity, the person existing in the esthetic stage is assailed by boredom whenever he or she is not distracted by physical or mental activities. The individual lives from one moment to the next, trying to avoid the nothingness in between, viewing his or her world-and-Ego-definition as an unalterable, unquestionable reality. Eventually, cynicism and sarcasm may contribute to the esthetic existence becoming more desperately rigid or monotonous: "In the United States," a Russian visitor claims, "man exploits man; in my country, however, we do it the other way around."

On the other hand, Kierkegaard shows that irony again and again questions any predefined world. For example, there is the story of Churchill being invited to a party by the Trumans. Knowing that Churchill was still smarting because of his recent defeat by Clement Attlee, Truman had warned the guests not to bring up the name of the new Prime Minister. Yet a thoughtless guest could not restrain himself and asked Churchill what he thought of his successor. Churchill replied succinctly, "There is less there than meets the eye!" A bit embarrassed, Truman tried to ease the situation by injecting, "but Attlee seems to be quite a humble person!" to which Churchill quipped, "Certainly, he has a lot to be humble about!" Although a nonironic statement might have proven offensive, Churchill's indirect, humorous communication challenged Truman to explore the relativity of his own worldview which had blindly assumed that humility - especially in politicians - always implies competence. Irony reveals that what we considered to be absolute ways of looking at things are but possible ways.

As we question our views of the world and of ourselves, we become aware of the "no-thingness" behind them. We have gained a sense of identity from those seemingly reliable structures, but now irony makes us insecure and anxious. Yet if we face and accept these pleasant feelings, the experience of being a Self dawns deep within us. The Self that emerges from the "no-thingness" provides human beings with a sense of continuity and freedom, leading us toward personal responsibilities, toward commitments, toward Kierkegaard's "ethical stage." One reaches this "ethical stage" not because one has chosen the good, but because one recognizes oneself as the chooser, and grasps the true meaning of the ever-present *either/or* (Kierkegaard, 1841/1959).

Kierkegaard's ethical human being, aware of irony's power to undermine all structures and aware that he or she *must* choose, becomes resigned. At this stage one aims for some of the accepted moral values of society and may become anything from a generous, kindly ironic burgher to a pompous, self-righteous, bitterly sarcastic Pharisee. This ordinary ethical human being requires creative humor in order to attain greater authenticity. Although irony dispels our illusions and points toward the Self - which is "no thing" - humor shows that the either/or is not simply the ability to choose between given alternatives, but the power to create worlds that we thought impossible. In the ethical stage the human being is, at best, a responsible part of the "universal" humanity; he is not yet an independent individual. In the eyes of his culture he is likely to be a highly moral person and a fine member of the church. But he has not yet reached what Kierkegaard calls the "religious stage;" a Christian he is not.

May I insert here that Kierkegaard's use of the terms "Christian" and "religious" has been frequently misunderstood. He points with these terms to the extremely difficult task of acting out of one's own Self, fully considering but not being controlled by personal needs or social prejudices and demands. Because Christ expressed this task in his life, and inasmuch as we strive to assume the same degree of responsibility for *our* choices and actions, the term "being a Christian" is to that degree synonymous with "freedom from despair" or with "authenticity."

Psychotherapy can be viewed as having both a socializing and an individuating role. These two goals are furthered only very little by direct communication. Both goals require that the therapist, as authority, disappear, and that the patient become aware of his or her own responsibility. The rationale for using humor in psychotherapy hinges on the fact that irony conveys indirectly that our world *can* be deconstituted. This awareness leads to the experience of our basic humanity and the appreciation of the crucial importance of relationships. The "irony" of a natural catastrophe consists in the fact that people often act more responsibly and helpfully toward each other after they have witnessed the destruction of all that on which they have tried to base their prestige and security. Their relationship, now, tends to be Self to Self, rather than doctor to lawyer, rich to poor, producer to consumer, bright to stupid, and so on. From overly clinging to externals, to the esthetics, these persons have moved toward the universal ethical stage.

However, the rationale for using humor in psychotherapy also hinges on the fact that creative humor indirectly conveys that our world can be reconstituted in previously unthought-of ways. Humor encourages not only our socially sanctioned ethical behavior, but also our individual ability to make meaningful, creative, moral choices. This third Kierkegaardian stage does not render obsolete the ethical stage any more than the latter makes obsolete the esthetics stage. In fact, the development of the higher stages integrates the lower ones in such a way that they gain in charm and significance (Kierkegaard, 1841/1959).

Humor indirectly conveys all this not so much by its content, which in fact may be offensively crude, primitively violent or erotic, and quite unsophisticated, but by its basic form and process. Its ability to unstructure and restructure our world makes us realize that we possess an ongoing, indestructible identity, a Self, which is meaningfully and creatively related to a world, but not determined by it. Dreams, parables, philosophical reflections, and psychological formulations also further the insight that we have defensively narrowed our world. But the laughter elicited by the punch line of a joke or the smile provoked by gentle humor provides us with the spontaneous experience of this freeing toward greater social responsibility or toward heightened individual creativity.

Let us look at a very simple, old joke, in which the punch line produces the experience of a sudden reversal of reality similar to that produced by the well-known picture of two profiles facing each other which, as figure and ground are reversed, turn into a vase:

The teacher wants to impress the class with the dangers of drinking, puts two glasses on a table, fills one with water and the other with vodka, and places a worm in each. As you would expect, the worm in the water keeps wiggling around, while the one in the vodka shrivels up and dies. And when the teacher asks the class (which he expects to respond in terms of Kierkegaard's universal-ethical stage) about the meaning of the experiment, Johnny gets up, declaring confidently, "If you drink enough vodka, you won't get worms!"

Although such a punch line reversal has nothing to offer in terms of shaping our current conduct, and certainly has little to do with lofty, authentic, religious values, it nevertheless contributes toward an increased awareness of the finest creative functions of the Self. I believe it is for this reason that Kierkegaard sees in humor an opportunity to transcend the universal-ethical stage toward the individual-religious stage.

By its ambiguous statement, "This is serious - this is play," humor conveys a message that is almost immediately taken back, so as to lead the recipient of humor to draw his or her own conclusions. Thus we hear Johannes Climacus, the pseudonymous author of Kierkegaard's (1846/1941) *Concluding Unscientific Postscript to the Philosophical Fragments* call himself a humorist. Speaking through a pseudonym is in itself a form of indirect communication; but this pseudonymous writer, after voicing crucial ideas about what it means to be an existing human being, takes back everything he said. He intends to keep the reader from accepting any suggestions on the basis of the writer's authority, thus activating the reader's Self to take full responsibility for what he or she experiences as truth.

In psychotherapy, we find that direct communication carries the risk that patients reject whatever appears novel and uncanny, or that they accept what they hear as just one more piece of knowledge to be added to the world of ideas, things, and obligations that govern them. Therefore the sense of Self, of personal responsibility, freedom, and creativity can be successfully evaded or forgotten. Behind the patients' screen of increased knowledge, of pseudo-insight, and of social adjustment, lurks despair, because they may have forgotten more and more what it means to be an existing human being, and may have ignored their infinitely valuable Self, their unique creativity.

With the help of Kierkegaard we have shown humor's profound implications for the Self, and the rationale for considering humor a potential psychotherapeutic agent. Now we must examine whether, when, and how humor can enter meaningfully the psychotherapeutic relationship, and whether its potential usefulness outweighs the risks of adverse effects.

TECHNIQUE

The literal translation of the Greek term *therapeuo* = "To serve" or "To show one's self helpful" may suit us well in defining therapy, and especially psychotherapy with an existential-analytic orientation. It does not presuppose definitions or criteria of sickness and health, but simply refers to a situation or a happening between human beings, wherein *one* displays an attitude of helpfulness, while the *other* is more or less free to enter the relationship. The psychotherapist, then, would act in such a way as to help the other human being, the "patient," to explore and to realize his or her existence (Heuscher, 1964). The patient may bring symptoms to be elucidated, dreams to be explained, attitudes to be interpreted, and problems that call for the consideration of options. Humor can arise in many forms during psychotherapy: jokes, puns, humorous remarks, irony, sarcasm, and so forth, the content and purpose of which may or may not be focused upon. All therapeutic procedures, be it noted again, are not primarily meant to change patients, but to help them experience themselves as unique human beings capable of closeness. Therapeutic procedures help patients see themselves as human beings who for good reasons chose to experience themselves and the world in a particular way, and who can become aware of their creative center and thus experience greater freedom to unstructure and rebuild their world (Yalom, 1980).

Everything the therapist does or does not do - even if he or she is simply "present" to the patients, without judging, with unconditional positive regard, while absolutely respecting the patients' right to be whatever they want to be - will have a direct effect upon patients. The therapist's behavior will be experienced by patients at best as a good technique or at worst as a manipulation. The realistic therapist will recognize and remain aware of this inescapable technical aspect of his or her approach. Paradoxically, psychotherapy is a relationship replete with technical aspects that simultaneously aims to transcend all technical aspects toward a relationship of two human beings who experience themselves and each other as free or autonomous. This, I believe, is the ultimate goal, albeit never fully attainable, of therapy.

With the preceding in mind I will discuss some technical or procedural aspects of humor in psychotherapy. First, I shall discuss the crucial importance of being aware of the quality of the therapeutic relationship in order to properly deal with humor. Secondly I shall consider various approaches to, or uses of, humor when it arises either spontaneously or deliberately in therapy. Finally, and most importantly, we must attend to the question of what to avoid, of what not to do so that humor in psychotherapy will not be counterproductive.

Psychotherapy, like most human relationships, usually begins on a rather conventional, formal, or impersonal level. It will hopefully evolve into a trusting relationship in which the care for the other is no longer strictly correlated with, or conditioned by, the momentary performance of the other. Humor tends to be appreciated much more in a setting in which an unconditional, trusting atmosphere has been established. The judicious use of humor can further the development of such a positive atmosphere. Therefore, the judicious, sparse inclusion of humor early in psychotherapy can be of some help in fostering an ambiance of trust and mutual respect. This kind of light, warm humor may sometimes be appropriate at the beginning or end of a session. It represents an expression of, and invitation for, trust, but may easily fail to produce the intended result if protracted, because every patient knows deep down that he or she does not come to therapy to be humored or entertained. Thus, this type of humor is simply a part of the more casual dialogue that commonly takes place between two people when they meet or leave.

Aided or unaided by this casual but tactful humor, the development of the type of relationship in which patients experience the therapist's unconditional caring sets the stage for a much more specific therapeutic use of humor. Such a relationship allows patients to risk experiencing the world in other than their usual ways. They can now be committed to their therapy, less frightened by the arousal of positive or negative feelings, and less impacted by either the wisdom or blunders of the therapist. Steadied by the relationship, patients become more willing to experience new existential dimensions that are revealed in dreams or as a result of the therapist's interpretations.

Only now can the analysis of spontaneously occurring humor, humorous remarks or jokes, introduced by either member of the therapeutic dyad, become effective. However, before he or she decides to introduce or to comment upon a humorous theme, the therapist must sensitively assess the patient's receptivity and the witticism's relevance to the particular situation with which the patient is dealing at the time. The therapist must furthermore remain cognizant of the implications of a humorous theme, as he or she continues to be responsive to the patient's genuine interests, to aroused anxiety, or to irritations.

In a favorable therapeutic relationship, I would address any spontaneous or accidental humor in the same way as I would address humor that is deliberately introduced by the patient or by myself. Usually this requires at least two steps. First there must be a genuine and shared appreciation of the humor. Only subsequently is the humorous incident or joke reflected upon in terms of its revealing novel views or attitudes and feelings, whether pertaining to the patient's everyday life or to the psychotherapeutic relationship.

When he or she is with a patient, the therapist becomes aware of innumerable feelings, observations, interpretations, suggestions, and options. Some will appear untimely, some inaccurate, some unimportant. The therapeutic skill largely consists in carefully omitting those comments that would not be profitable for the patient. Similarly, there may be many humorous remarks, witticisms, or jokes that occur to the therapist while being fully attentive to the patient. Of these, he or she occasionally selects one that seems unusually appropriate and introduces it into the dialogue in order to emphasize an unexpected emotion, an unusual view, or an optional behavior. Once the therapist has introduced a humorous theme, he or she is committed to rephrasing it seriously and following in depth whatever new ways of being-in-the-world it may open up for the patient.

When the patient deliberately says or does something witty, or when something humorous occurs unintentionally in the course of a meeting, the therapist can sensitively select for reflection those instances that are most likely to reveal new existential possibilities to the patient. Humor, especially in psychotherapy, is like a spice: If not overused, it can improve the entire process. Too much humor, just as too many interesting dreams or too many vivid childhood memories, may reflect defensiveness and therefore become counterproductive.

Of particular interest are witticisms that occur in a patient's dream, since dreams themselves can be viewed as portraying alternatives to a person's everyday "world-design." Puns, jokes, or witticisms in dreams seem to lend emphasis to such alternate "world designs."

An ex-nun, for example, fearful of any physical affection, but desperately looking for support and genuine male friendship, dreamed of stumbling down a stairway in a large church, only to fall into the arms of an ex-priest whose name happened to be Armstrong. Macabre humor manifested itself in the repetitive dream of a Christian Science lady who kept assuring me that she had never hated anyone. Yet in her dreams she prepared her tyrannical husband's breakfast tray. When she finally placed the salt shaker on the tray, the label would always read, to her great surprise, "Arsenic." Finally, there was an obese lady who forever decided to start dieting the next day. She dreamed of receiving a telephone call by a stranger who kept insisting that he was "Tom Morrow." Exasperated, she finally woke up and burst out laughing when she recognized her own pun.

It is of utmost importance that the therapist not only enjoy the humor, but that he or she underline its seriousness by rephrasing it and by pointing out its pertinence in the patient's current manner of being-in-the-world. A therapist would not allow a dream or a slip of the tongue to be sidestepped with remarks like, "It's only a dream" or "I just used the wrong words." Similarly, it would not be therapeutically beneficial to allow a joke to be dismissed by the patient as "only a joke."

There are also occasions where it is helpful to focus upon a patient's favorite jokes. The preferred joke of a slightly paranoid engineer who had many professional failures was that of the psychiatric patient who persistently brushed imaginary fleas from his suit. When he explained to his therapist what he was doing, the latter replied, "Okay but don't brush them all off on me!" This led to a fruitful exploration of this engineer's feelings of inadequacy and his using projective defenses in most of his interpersonal, including therapeutic, relationships.

Levine (1977) stresses the rebellious quality of humor that represents a *voluntary* withdrawal from "reality" (I would prefer: "from the everyday, accustomed, socially imposed, blindly accepted, or chosen world") in contrast to the *involuntary*, pathological, and maladaptive withdrawals of neuroses and psychoses. He sees humor as an intrinsic and essential component of the normal growth process and thus stresses its use in psychotherapy as a means of facilitating profound insights. Additionally, Hershkowitz (1977) sees the use of humor in psychotherapy as a way of presenting ambiguities that are acceptable, even sought after, which may serve to make the patient tolerate a world that is not always an either/or world.

Because humor is a first, fleeting attempt at revealing new and wider horizons, it can further the growth of the person who is able to integrate some of the new vistas. However, there must always be considerable spontaneity in the use of humor.

The more systematically humorous themes are introduced, the less effective they are likely to be in some instances. In fact, there are important caveats regarding the technical use of humor. Keen must be the therapist's insight into inauthentic or defensive factors that prompt him or her to focus upon a witty remark or joke. Such factors range all the way from attempts at warding off anxiety-producing situations, to veiled manipulations, to inordinate needs to be liked and admired. Humor can be easily inauthentically used to avoid change when the joking individual pretends to be open to wider options - deceiving himself or herself and others - while rapidly reverting to his or her habitual, narrow "world-design." In psychotherapy this becomes a kind of "playing at change" that allows therapists and patients to retain their uneasy security in their unchanging existence, rather than to risk facing meaningful consideration of genuine options. It is always the depth and quality of the psychotherapeutic relationship that determines whether humorous features become "holdfast" or "growth-enhancing" forces, whether they are attempts to hide problems or conflicts, whether they are veiled putdowns, or whether they are genuine suggestions that the patient is free to integrate in his or her lifestyle.

Inasmuch as humor is always revealing some aspects of the humorist's personality, its use by therapists tends to interfere with their being a blank screen for the patient's transferences (Kubie, 1971; Reik, 1962). Thus, humor will be expressed more readily by therapists who value sharing their own experiences, feelings, and views to the extent that they deem them therapeutically useful. The blank-screen therapist is likely to deal with humor expressed by the patient in a strictly interpretive way which would certainly discourage me from joking if I were the patient.

Just as the patient's choice of humor often reflects his or her feelings and transferences toward the therapist, so the therapist's wit may reflect his or her feelings and countertransferences towards the patient. A near "fatal" incident occurred not long ago when a patient of mine kept profusely apologizing during the session for many tiny or presumed mistakes. I was unaware of my growing irritation, and when, upon leaving, she delayed me by apologizing in the most friendly and protracted way for having taken too much of my time, I ushered her out with a seemingly equally friendly, "teasing" remark to the effect that I might consider forgiving her in a few years. Fortunately, the patient was later able to tell me how angry she was at my not taking seriously her need to belittle herself. Thus, we had a chance to explore together her compulsive apologizing and its negative effect upon most of her human relationships.

On the other hand, the patient's misuse of humor is certainly not confined to psychotherapy. Excessive laughing, smiling, and irony are often defensive measures against intimacy with Self and others. Even more destructive or inhibiting is the force of sarcasm or cynicism. In contrast to gentle humor, sarcastic remarks seem to freeze the status quo. For example, a long-married couple plays over and over again the deadly game of his responding to her seemingly exorbitant wishes with the crushing sarcastic remark, "What have *you* ever contributed to this marriage? You're just like Marie Antoinette!" Then she feels shattered and angry, withdraws and cries, while he is consumed by guilt. Now, no longer feeling taken advantage of, and eager to get rid of his guilt, he accedes to her wishes. Yet at that juncture she is no longer in the mood. And even if he prevails in convincing her to let him satisfy her wish, neither one can achieve any genuine satisfaction. I explained to them that sarcasm and cynicism are somewhat grotesque forms of clinging to one's established existence, whereas gentler irony can loosen the chains tying us to our world, and funny jokes can enrich it.

Cynicism reveals its defensive purpose in psychotherapy. Cynical and sarcastic remarks served this husband solely to maintain a precarious and tragic marital relationship. Becoming aware of the lack of self-worth and trust underlying his cynical attacks, and helped by his wife's greater understanding as well as by the therapist's support, he began to express his feelings and needs more directly.

Sarcasm and cynicism may strike us as funny because, in contrast to other humor, they absurdly affirm what *is*. In this context we must be sensitive to the fact that cynicism, even more than sarcasm, is a grotesque negation of genuine love, often hiding the all-too-common deep fear of love's implications. I heard a story about Oscar Levant returning to the television studio after one of his nervous breakdowns and being greeted by a "welcome back party." Upset, he muttered that the party was obviously given by his enemies. When a charming young lady tried to assure him that everyone loved him, he walked away, retorting, "That's just what I meant, because when they love you, you have to love back!"

Inasmuch as humor, even more than dreams, is only an ephemeral doubting of the everyday world and a playful revealing of alternatives, its significance may be easily forgotten after it has been reflected upon in psychotherapy. As with certain dreams, there are occasions in which repeatedly returning to a humorous episode leads to lasting insights and, more importantly, to new commitments in everyday life. A very inhibited young woman dreamed of me as a teacher of insects. When I asked her whether this meant that she wished me to be a teacher in sex, she readily recognized her pun. However, at her next visit she retaliated with another dream in which a "talking duck" was the main character, as if wanting to protest that the "doc" talked too much. At the same time the new pun led back to the theme of the previous one which she obviously wanted to pursue. Referring back to the meaning of previous humorous themes thus enables patients to gradually incorporate important hidden potentials into their everyday world.

Humor must be judiciously introduced by the therapist, but he or she should not be overly worried if it slightly misses the mark. The content of the joke is often less important than the sharing of the therapist's implied conviction that options are available to the patient. Just as a standard interpretation may be of help not so much because it is "correct" but because it questions overly rigid assumptions, jokes may be effective primarily by insisting that most accepted views can be subverted or replaced with a number of other views. Both in interpreting or in introducing a joke, the therapist must be aware that his or her role is not so much that of helping patients to better deal with harsh realities, but that of making them aware of their creative center, their freedom, and their responsibility. Even the nonfitting joke and the nonfitting interpretation still point to the Self.

In fact, there are many links between wit, jokes, or witty remarks on the one hand, and interpretations on the other. An example is my remark to a 54-year-old man disabled by coronary artery disease who for the past 12 years had become increasingly anxious at being unable to finalize a divorce from his wife so that he could live in peace with his mistress. He spent much of his time going to doctors and procrastinating. One day, without trying to be funny, it slipped from my mouth: "There seems to be a race between your heart and your divorce." This struck the patient as extremely humorous, and we were then able to talk more openly about his fears of death and their relationship to his procrastinating.

I find some of Victor Frankl's logotherapeutic techniques to be similar to humorous interpretations or indirect communications. I attended a seminar in which he interviewed a young, confused, rootless woman who explained to him that she was trying to "find herself." Frankl responded by getting out of his chair, roaming around the room, and protesting loudly, "You can never find yourself by going around looking for yourself; there's nothing to find, you're here!" Similarly, his "treatment by paradoxical intention," as when he instructs a patient who is afraid of fainting to "faint thoroughly," has a humorous aspect while containing an indirectly communicated, important truth.

Freud introduced the story of Oedipus to interpret basic developmental events. Similarly, many other epic or folklore fragments can be used to liven up an interpretation. When such tales have humorous connotations, they are even more effective. I occasionally use the story of Ulysses and Polyphemus to illustrate to patients what motivation might be hidden behind their Self-denial. Captured by the giant Polyphemus, Ulysses told him that his name was "Nobody." After being blinded, while sleeping, by Ulysses, Polyphemus appealed for help from his fellow Giants in order to recapture the escaped prisoners. Yet when he told them that "Nobody" had blinded him, they understandably refused to do anything, and Ulysses managed to flee from the Giant's island.

Humor in psychotherapy arises in every gradation, from the hilarious "canned" joke to the most subtle and comical implications of verbal and nonverbal communications. The latter can only be fully captured on videotape. However, as much as possible, it is important that the therapist be aware of them.

Let me close my comments on technique by emphasizing a few of the salient points:

1. It is self-understood that the therapist's response to, or introduction of, humor must always be in the service of the patient. Otherwise, it becomes a belittling or destructive betrayal.
2. Humor can increase an atmosphere of acceptance and trust.
3. Within this atmosphere of trust, humor can reveal options, expose defenses, illuminate transferences, and strengthen interpretations.
4. Humor can be an ideal indirect communication that leaves patients maximally free and responsible in either affirming their current ways of being-in-the-world or choosing alternatives.
5. Focusing upon humor must always carry the implication that insights further authenticity only to the extent that they are actively incorporated in one's life.
6. Humor must be neither overly premeditated nor manipulative. It can be viewed as a technique only because all human interactions, no matter how spontaneous, have technical connotations. It seems appropriate to quote an old Chassidic saying: "The external help as such is not what counts; this external help is but a cloak which hides and makes possible the internal help" (Buber, 1949).

PERTINENT USES

In almost any psychotherapeutic endeavor, including in the use of humor, the "technique" of using technique as little as possible is salutary. Total freedom from technique is an illusory, though very worthwhile, goal (Heuscher, 1964).

All therapists, wittingly or unwittingly, use wit in psychotherapy. I never plan it, but I monitor it carefully. It arises spontaneously in my or my patient's consciousness. The task, then, is to decide whether, in which instances, in what form, with which patients, and at what point during the session it can be profitably used.

With some of my patients, the expression of and focusing upon humor, either theirs or mine, has been quite rare. With some others, the use of humor has been frequent. We shall shortly see that a patient's diagnostic grouping is one of the factors affecting humor use. First, and more generally, I would like to state that my inclination to focus on humor tends to be stronger with relatively humorless patients, just as I am prone to focus on the dreams of patients who rarely dream or discount dreams, to use existential formulations with psychoanalytically minded persons, to introduce folklore themes in illustrating the dynamics of scientific souls, or to recommend behaviorist techniques for creative idealists.

Though there are many exceptions to this broad guiding principle, the reason for it is obvious. Human beings commonly tend to structure their world according to increasingly rigid views, be they scientific, fatalistic, deterministic, psychoanalytic, mystical, or existential. This tendency resides in the need for security, in the wish to avoid ambiguity, and as Erich Fromm (1971) already stressed, in the fearful desire to escape freedom. Thus some patients may stifle their growth in psychotherapy by bringing in an overabundance of magnificent dreams, others by discovering ever new powerful infantile memories, and others by having ever new meaningful insights. Other patients yet describe their experiences with innumerable, colorful, symbolic, and poetic metaphors, or by recognizing ever new humorous analogies and alternatives to their dilemmas. In doing so, they remain unaware of being caught in their own rigid world.

These one-sided generous offerings are but patient defenses against stepping back from their structured world toward their true, creative, free Self, the Self which, in Kierkegaard's words, is Spirit (Kierkegaard, 1848/1954b). The therapist's considered assistance in helping patients to let go of habitual ways of being-in-the-world, be it only by bringing humor to the humorless, or by supplying seriousness to the Pollyannas, offers patients an opportunity to experience themselves as the responsible originators of their rigid world-designs. And even if patients should choose to commit themselves to their previous world-design after such an experience, they will now do so with a greater sense of freedom and responsibility, with somewhat greater authenticity.

A patient's diagnostic classification provides only very vague guidelines to the use of humor. I can think of no condition - except unconsciousness - in which humor might not be valuable at certain times. Yet it is rather plain that humor must be used with great caution with patients suffering from severe depressions or from paranoid disorders, mainly because of their difficulties in establishing trusting relationships.

However, once some confidence has been gained, it can be strengthened by the therapist's willingness to risk focusing upon humorous features of various symptoms or complaints. If such an intervention is carried out with genuine warmth and respect, patients may then feel enabled to establish some distance between themselves and their depressive or delusional convictions and to see the humorous absurdity in some aspects of their symptomatology. I once explained to a depressed elderly nun who despaired over her salvation that if God sent her to hell I would gladly join her there since in this case the devil would be more agreeable company than someone who took delight in sending someone like her into eternal suffering because of some minor imperfections.

Schizophrenic thought disorders frequently have punlike connotations. The patient may be made aware of these, once he or she has developed some confidence in the therapist. An insecure, shy, unmarried young woman had delusional fantasies about being in love with a Victor Truman. Eventually we were able to discuss how this name was like a humorous riddle hiding her wishes and fears concerning dependability and truthfulness in men.

To the general public, the most comical neuroses are the obsessive-compulsive disorders, as attested by the popularity of *The Odd Couple*. This television series capitalizes upon the peculiar behavior of an individual, totally ignoring the suffering entailed in such a disorder. Obsessive-compulsive persons know only too well how odd their behavior is in the eyes of others. They both know and don't know what the alternatives would be to their behavior, and are usually terrified of risking and of freedom. Accordingly they are slow to risk any close relationship with the therapist.

The avoidance of risk is deadly serious business for them, and whatever humor the therapist introduces must not make light of the obsessive-compulsive syndrome. At best, the therapist may convey his or her understanding of the futility of the patient's attempts to suppress compulsive thoughts by means of a challenge such as, "I bet you that you cannot even count to 10 without thinking of a hippopotamus!" Obsessive-compulsive patients may sometimes make fun of themselves, which often is but a thin disguise of their fear of change.

Patients suffering from depressive, hysterical, and anxiety neuroses - often referred to in the past as "transference neuroses" - may be able to establish a trusting relationship with the therapist somewhat faster than obsessive-compulsive patients. With these patients, humor can be dealt with more casually, keeping in mind the aforementioned technical considerations. The same approach could apply to treating patients with psychosomatic disorders.

Here, taking notice of or replying with slightly witty expressions becomes a way of pointing at psychosomatic connections: (to a patient with neurodermatitis) "Name the people who are crawling under your skin!" and (to a patient with extreme difficulty in swallowing) "It seems that you can't swallow your mother-in-law!" A patient remarked, "The body is something nasty; it's just something you carry around dangling below your brains!" After appreciating the humorousness of this remark, its deeper implications for the patient's main psychosomatic symptom, impotence, were pursued.

Humor must be used with circumspection in the treatment of the alcoholic, the drug abuser, and the sociopath. Occasional warm humor in expressing acceptance may be valuable, but the use of jokes for interpretation or for showing options may sometimes be countertherapeutic if it strengthens these patients' tendency to deny, bagatellize, or make fun of the most serious problems.

More useful than diagnostic criteria in gauging the advisability of humor are some existential categories. In my own work I have found that Kierkegaard's three main polarities (finitude/infinitude; necessity/possibility; temporality/eternity) were quite useful. Kierkegaard showed most eloquently how human beings tend to evade the ambiguities of existence by becoming overly one-sided. The avoidance of ambiguity, of the paradoxes of human existence, can lead to narrowness, ineffectiveness, or inauthenticity. This is what Kierkegaard (1848/1954b) considers to be "despair."

With respect to the finitude/infinitude polarity, some persons never expect anything special of themselves, and are resigned to whatever finite achievement they gain, while some accept nothing but infinite perfection in their pursuits. On one pole are those satisfied with mediocrity, on the other those who desperately seek unblemished love, absolute virtue, or flawless achievements. A very fine student who well deserved an "A" demonstrated this search for infinitude when he asked me whether I would change his "A" to an "A+" because he was in the habit of collecting A+'s. Some such polarized persons may successfully hide their predicament from themselves, while others who are similarly afflicted may become dimly aware of being in trouble and seek help. These, according to Kierkegaard, are the individuals "aware of being in despair." For them the ambiguity of jokes may be helpful given the surprising message of jokes that things are rarely either/or in real life. With a few patients caught in "finitude," I have used the anecdote of the union leader who triumphantly announced at a strike meeting that from now on everyone had to work only on Wednesdays; whereupon one of the members stood up and asked, "You mean *every* Wednesday?" On the other hand, to some patients reaching for infinitude I have related the sadly humorous meeting I had with a nice-looking, pleasant, and brilliant mathematician. She had become depressed to the point of giving up after she statistically figured that there were 1,732 women in the United States who were smarter than she. "What's the use trying?" she concluded.

Regarding the necessity/possibility polarity, there are some people who aim for absolute security, never wanting to risk, never undertaking something new, accepting whatever situation they are in as necessary. There are others who never seem satisfied with the discovery of a new possibility, but aimlessly and desperately reach for something bigger and better. They never translate the discovered potentials into effective, enduring action. With both of these extremes, I sometimes use the delightfully humorous Grimm's tale of "The Fisherman and His Wife." In this tale, the fisherman represents the Kierkegaardian "despair of necessity," inasmuch as he would never risk anything, willing to live all his life in a pot. His wife, on the other hand, dramatically portrays the "despair of possibility." Never satisfied, she first acquires a cottage, then a castle, then a palace, and the greater her potentials become, the quicker she is dissatisfied with them. Thus she wants to become first King, then Emperor, then Pope, and finally "like the good Lord." The story ends abruptly, when both fisherman and wife are again back in their pot, permanently (Heuscher, 1981a)!

In considering the temporality/eternity polarity, one discovers that time is experienced as a sequence of unrelated instants for many individuals. For such persons, time is made up of a series of measurable, separate, seconds, minutes, or hours. They have no genuine appreciation of their own or of their world's continuity. At the other extreme, we find people who are so aware of their eternal soul, so aware that this world is but a vale of tears between birth and paradise, that they are incapable of relishing the present. Kierkegaard would see the first group as caught in the "aesthetic" mode. He would see them as childishly comical because of their utter inability to defer pleasure while willingly deferring anything unpleasant. They resemble the optimist who jumps from the Empire State Building and on passing the 40th floor happily says to himself, "so far so good."

The truly authentic person neither denies nor totally accepts this aesthetic side of life. Though aware of the temporal continuity of the Self's eternal aspect that transcends any momentary joys or sorrows, he or she is equally aware that this Self can meaningfully express itself only in each and every moment. Otherwise he or she may end up like the person meeting Saint Peter at the Pearly Gates. When asked about the good deeds performed during a lifetime on earth, the aspirant to heavenly admission replied: "I've scorned everything worldly and tried to be like Jesus Christ," to which Saint Peter harshly retorted: "Here we do not ask whether you have been like Jesus Christ; we ask whether you have been like yourself!"

What patients, as well as most "nonpatients," have forgotten with regard to the preceding existential polarities is that they must acknowledge both extremes, contradictory as these extremes may appear. By ignoring one of the two polarities, they try to avoid the kind of anxiety that normally belongs to human existence. This ignoring requires self-deception, or what Kierkegaard calls "double mindedness" and "unawareness of despair." This form of inauthenticity may be little noticed in the world. Though usually not labeled as "patient," persons in this inauthentic mode may hiddenly do more harm to their soul and to others than patients with clear-cut psychiatric symptoms who have been less successful in deceiving themselves. On the other hand, psychiatric patients may suffer from incapacitating guilt, phobias, and compulsions, as well as psychosomatic symptoms.

To be exact, it is not so much one of the poles in their polarities that individuals forget. What is forgotten is their very Self from whose vantage point alone the seemingly paradoxical pairs of opposites can be experienced as sources of ongoing energy. They become "outer-directed." But the person's Self cannot die and its claim manifests itself in redoubled defenses, in symptoms, or in the feeling that life has become meaningless. Jokes may overcome the forgetting, even if only for a fleeting moment, by tolerating existential ambiguities and furthering increased Self-awareness.

A unique method for dislodging patients from their polarized position and awakening their awareness of the creative-responsible Self is described by Corey (1966), who bases his approach upon the philosophy of J. P. Sartre. Corey's approach clearly includes a humorous dimension. Instead of encouraging change, Corey tends to affirm over and over again that he does not see any reason for change and that the patient, stuck in a particular position, feels or behaves the way he or she does for good reason. As a result of this technique, the patient begins to experience himself or herself as the chooser, as Self, who has chosen a polarized way of "being-in-the-world." This in turn makes the patient aware of alternatives, of the opposite poles. A fragment from Corey's delightful examples may illustrate this:

Patient: I don't have anything to talk about today.
Therapist: That's fine.
Patient: Why do you say that?
Therapist: Why not? You seem to be implying that talking is in some way superior to not talking. I take it, if you don't want to talk today, it must be *for a good reason.*
Patient: Actually there are things I thought of discussing with you, but . . . I don't know what you might think.
Therapist: Well, I can see why you have chosen to be silent today. *You are right;* it is frightening to confide in someone when you don't know how they are going to react. . . .
Patient: Yes, you might think I was stupid and childish, too.
Therapist: *You are quite right*; I might think that, and of course neither of us would know . . . until after you had told me whatever it was you had on your mind. There are no guarantees, living is risky business.

Here Corey clearly affirms normal existential anxiety and fully agrees with the patient that being withdrawn from others controls this anxiety. There are a number of additional exchanges until the end of the hour when the patient comments:

> Thank you, I have certainly enjoyed talking to you this hour. . . . Do you think it would do me any good to come more than once a week?

Now the patient, growing aware of choosing to avoid existential anxiety by silence, gains access to the opposite pole: openness and communication. Kierkegaard would view this approach as Socratically ironical, because it helps the patient discover how narrow a slice of life he or she is clinging to.

Every psychological problem, whether personal or interpersonal, no matter how serious, can be modified by tactful and properly timed humor that allows it to be viewed from new perspectives. The therapist, however, must most carefully avoid labeling as simply pathological that which may in fact be a genuine, existential problem for the individual. Empathy and experience are helpful in this regard. Nonetheless, in the final analysis, only the patient can attain some degree of conviction about his or her own authenticity. Kierkegaard drove this point home again and again. Indirect communications, including appropriate humor, are less likely to violate the patient's autonomy. Indirect communications in an atmosphere of unconditional acceptance allow patients maximal liberty to decide whether they adhere to a more or less extreme or one-sided viewpoint because they are attempting to avoid existential anxiety, or whether they are doing so for authentic reasons.

Though they most commonly tend to focus on problems of aggression and sex, jokes and other forms of humor can touch on each and every human concern: envy, feelings of inadequacy, inferiority or rejection, pride, fear of death, loneliness, and need for warmth and belonging. The following joke reassures men that they must not always and exclusively prove their potency, and that their wish for warmth from another human being is legitimate:

> A married executive on a business trip goes to a brothel and asks for "the worst lay in the house." When asked why he made this strange request, he replied, "I'm not horny, just homesick!"

In this joke, the masculine taboo against loneliness and neediness is broken. True, the images and wordings of such jokes may appear simple, instinctual, even coarse. Yet the wordings often cover up basic ultimate human concerns that would make for anxiety or embarrassment if given more direct expression.

By widening one's everyday world, humor makes thoughts, feelings, and actions with personally or socially taboo qualities available to the patient, and simultaneously activates the Self to become more accountable to its structured world. We must keep in mind that the joke not only provides a vicarious release of instinctual drives, risky ideas, or forbidden impulses, but also a relief from them. Being able to smile at the drives, longings, impulses, convictions, and fears that seem to enslave us awakens at least a transitory awareness of our freedom or of our Self. We may not get rid of these processes within us but, instead of feeling owned by them, we begin to own them and to employ them in continuing to create a world that is meaningful to us.

If the precautions mentioned previously in connection with technique and with particular psychiatric disorders are observed, there are no limits to the use of humor in psychotherapy. It is to be kept in mind, however, that humor has only a limited scope in psychotherapy. It can be tremendously effective in temporarily jarring patients away from ways of being-in-the-world (scripts, rigid presuppositions, narrow feelings) that they had hitherto experienced as immutable. However, this result is ephemeral unless it can be given permanence by any or all the various psychotherapeutic interactions that shed light upon the patient's existential mode. These interactions include not only serious reflections upon the implications of humorous episodes, but also other psychodynamic interpretations, explorations of dreams, amplification of the ongoing patient-therapist relationship, free association, guided daydreams, Gestalt procedures, and illustrations with themes taken from other patients' lives or from literature and folklore. In supervising a therapist or a psychiatric resident who is relatively unfamiliar with the usefulness of humor in psychotherapy, I would view my relationship with the supervisee as a prime opportunity for putting into practice and illustrating what I have been preaching. Supervision has the characteristics of a therapeutic relationship with a clearly circumscribed goal, namely to increase a supervisee's intellectual and emotional perceptiveness as well as his or her flexible use of various techniques. I would approach humor arising in this relationship exactly as I do when it arises in my relationship with patients. Additionally, I would reflect with the supervisee upon the effectiveness or ineffectiveness of any such approach. I would also explore with him or her the meaning or implications of humorous episodes that occurred in the treatment of patients presented to me. This can be done even more effectively if the supervisee has taped or videotaped the interviews, or if I have had the opportunity to be present at one of the sessions with the supervisee's patient.

Although I heavily rely on the preceding approach, I will not shy away from a more academic discussion about the use and misuse of humor in psychotherapy, or from recommending some reading materials such as this volume. Whether they intend to use them in therapeutic work or not, I would encourage therapists to learn by heart as many interesting jokes as possible. The purpose of this request is not so much to increase the therapist's popularity at parties (a secondary gain, to be sure), but because reflecting on and memorizing jokes increases a person's flexibility and tolerance, and widens his or her psychological horizon.

I would certainly not advocate that the introduction of humor in psychiatric treatment is a must. Some therapeutic orientations lend themselves much less than others to such use, and every individual therapist is likely to have his or her own ways and limitations in appreciating and expressing humor. Therapy, I would stress, can be done effectively without the introduction or expression of humor on the part of the therapist. However, I would also stress that to ignore humor, puns, laughter, or jokes expressed by the patient would be missing important therapeutic opportunities. Furthermore, I would underline that a therapist who is incapable of laughter, at least in the life he or she leads outside the office, is bound to be quite ineffective in affirming, expanding, deepening, and enriching either his or her own world or the world of others.

Furthermore, I would repeatedly caution myself or anyone to whom I speak of psychotherapy that, when wittily voicing an idea or telling a joke or responding to a patient's humor, a therapist must be genuine and capable of savoring the comical. At the same time, he or she must remain alert to the opportunities that humor offers for challenging and weakening unnecessary taboos, for evaluating unacknowledged feelings, and for recognizing unexpressed thoughts or neglected options. Each such opportunity can be explored in depth, so as to enable the patient to reconsider the feasibility of hidden feelings, thoughts, and options now unveiled by the humor. Furthermore, I would point out that whether dreams, psychodynamic interpretations, or humor are discussed, the same thing always attains: The gained insight must be so thoroughly authenticated by the patients that it begins to manifest itself in their actual life. And with changes in their actual being-in-the-world, the basic characteristics of their dreams and of their humor may in turn change.

I would also caution against expecting such changes to result from valuable intellectual or emotional insights alone, reiterating that presentations of dynamic interpretation, of dream explanations, or of serious reflections upon humor, are only effective when there is a relationship of trust and respect between patient and therapist. Only then will patients respond to the challenge of stepping back and recognizing to what degree they are the makers of their world. No matter how accurate the interpretations of their behavior or of their humor may have been, their trust of their therapist coupled with their stepping back are also needed to help them explore new options in relating to their inner and outer circumstances.

CLINICAL PRESENTATIONS

In order to illustrate some theoretical and technical aspects of humor, succinct clinical examples have been offered in the previous three sections. The range of humor and of responses to humor is as wide as life itself, so that the following vignettes can, at best, be only a very inadequate sampling of this abundance. Like dreams, humorous statements or situations are easily forgotten for various reasons. Among the ones I recollect, I have chosen the following vignettes because they may illustrate basic, often overlapping, features of humor in psychotherapy.

ESTABLISHING A TRUSTING RELATIONSHIP

Not unlike a witty "Captivation of the audience's benevolence" at the beginning of a talk, a humorous remark introducing a therapy session may further a trusting relationship. Witty remarks have the additional effect of weakening established presuppositions and subsequently rendering the audience, or the patient, susceptible to unfamiliar ideas and unthought-of options.

Vignette 1. After several visits, a likable and sensitive nun began to disclose her abysmal lack of self-esteem. At our next appointment, I addressed her in the waiting room with one of the self-derogatory expressions she had repeatedly used: "How is my 'withered-up cold virgin'?" Only because the timing, my feelings, and my tone of voice were right, was this question not taken as derision. Instead, I believe it may have conveyed several things: that I remembered her as a specific individual whom I trusted to trust me; that I would not have teased her were it not for my conviction that her derogatory self-definition was unfair and prejudicially narrow; that any self-definition obscures the unique Self; and that I wanted to relate to and affirm this undefinable, unique Self.

Vignette 2. A single-minded, successful, workaholic researcher had been seeing me irregularly and reluctantly for a couple of months because his wife was threatening him with divorce. To my surprise, he suddenly asked for an emergency appointment and came in with his wife. She was in a towering rage and about to leave him, because "meaning-no-harm" and without consulting her, he had sold their home which she had decorated with fine taste and infinite care. In the preceding session, he had related a "strange" dream in which cataclysmic thunder and lightning was followed by his wandering along through dark streets. Synchronicity or sheer good luck were with me when, feeling rather hopeless about their dilemma, I met the couple in the waiting room. The very moment I opened the door, there was heavy thunder - rare in our part of California. Smiling, I turned to the husband and said, "The thunder and lightning in your dream really seem to have hit home; and now you are bringing them to my office!" Everyone laughed, the session went well, and the couple was able to correct many of their mutual misperceptions.

The man suffered from what Kierkegaard called "despair of infinitude." His extraordinary success in his narrow field of research was achieved at the cost of genuine intimacy and other interests. He was extremely meticulous in organizing his time, and felt quite upset when, not long after the previous episode, he was late to his appointment because his car had run out of gas. I took the opportunity to reassure him with a sad smile that seemingly neither of us was quite perfect, because I had just dented my own car's fender. We had something in common, and this strengthened the relationship. But my humorous reassurance also led to a deeper exploration of the diffuse lack of satisfaction that accompanied his single-minded and fantastically perfectionistic orientation.

OPTIONS

Humorous replies or jokes can make patients aware of how rigidly they limit their options.

Vignette 3. I had been seeing a long-married and long-arguing couple. The wife, more than her husband, would send conflicting messages, on the one hand stressing how much she cared for him, and on the other hand voicing devastating or belittling criticisms. The husband usually retaliated with anger, silence, or walking away. After his wife had done this several times during a session, the husband became exasperated, but then turned to me with a smile of satisfaction and asked, "How do you deal with a wife who hits you over the head with a pan while telling you that she loves you?" I found myself calmly replying, "I guess you find yourself another pan, hit her over the head with it, and tell her that you love her too."

Quoted out of context, the ironic reply may seem quite offensive, inappropriate, or stupid. Yet timed properly, it broke the impasse and brought about a relaxed, hilarious response. Now the couple proceeded to discuss various issues more congenially and without trapping each other with double-binds. My message, taken overtly, did not seem to convey any new options; but covertly it offered the one option neither had been willing to acknowledge: that human beings indeed do have ambivalent feelings, that there are interpersonal problems without clear-cut solutions, and that the very acceptance of this fact may paradoxically improve communications.

Vignette 4. Many jokes focus upon a person's inability to see options, and show that seemingly difficult problems allow for several solutions. I would like to mention one example of a joke I occasionally use to confront a patient with the one-sidedness of his or her position: A young patient kept on protesting that he could not help getting repeatedly involved in fights. I finally told him the story of the witness whom the judge asks, "Why didn't you try to stop your two friends from hitting each other over the head with bar stools?" "I'm sorry, your Honor," answers the witness, "but there wasn't another bar stool available." This helped the young man to see how the witness, in this case himself, was unable or unwilling to consider other available options.

Vignette 5. Sometimes I have the opportunity to point out the rigidity of a person's position by means of amusing incidents that occurred with other patients. A frustrated and unhappy wife protested to me at length that she had not been sexually intimate with her husband for months because there were frequent arguments between them that forced her to reject him in bed. As she seemed to trust me, I told her of an incident with a couple who consulted me some years ago. They had gradually grown so angry at each other that they had not exchanged a single word for 3 months. They kept enumerating their grievances to me until I finally could no longer hold my tongue. As tactfully as I knew, I asked about the status of their sexual relationship. They immediately blurted out, joyfully and in unison, "Oh, we never let anything interfere with *that*!"

Vignette 6. Some options sound funny simply because they are unexpected. A phobic sales engineer felt afraid and lost whenever he had to travel. As he complained about this, I responded without thinking, "Regardless of where you are, you're never lost; you're always *here*!" This struck him as a very amusing truth to which he frequently referred in later sessions, and which offered him comforting solace on trips. Only in hindsight did I realize that I had suggested to him the option of experiencing himself as Self rather than as an object that can get lost.

Vignette 7. Though aware of an option, a patient may feel too "guilty" to exercise it. At times a joke portraying a similar option in a grotesquely exaggerated way can be helpful. A hardworking patient was driven to distraction by her "friend" who kept making exorbitant demands upon her time, her help, and her household supplies. The patient was unable to refuse her friend anything: "Jane would be hurt," she kept saying. One day I told her the story of the beggar visiting his millionaire cousin living in a big mansion. He showed him his tattered clothes, told him that his sick wife needed medicines, that his six children were starving, and that they were being evicted. The millionaire listened attentively for awhile, then rang for the butler, ordering, "Throw the bum out, he is breaking my heart." This inhumane joke helped to reveal to this patient our inalienable right and concomitant inescapable freedom in weighing our own needs, convictions, and feelings when we make a decision that may, in fact, unavoidably hurt someone else.

INSIGHT

Jokes may strengthen insights, or a patient's joke may reveal his or her insight.

Vignette 8. A pleasant, fortyish man felt a great deal of resentment toward his wife who hated his mother. The mother returned the favor by cunningly and desperately fostering the son's dependence, which he was loath to acknowledge. He gained some insight by talking about his childhood background and about current incidents in which he felt forced to side with his mother against his wife. At one point I mentioned a joke that seemed to strengthen his growing understanding. In this well-known joke a highly upset, fortyish man comes from his analytic session to his mother who inquires with great concern, "What in the world has that man told you this time?" "Mother," sighs the son, "he told me I have an Oedipus Complex!" "Ah, Oedipus, Shmoedipus," reassures the mother, "you have nothing to worry about as long as you keep loving your mother!"

Vignette 9. A good example of how humor can reveal a patient's growing insight is the following: A man working for the Post Office came to see me quite depressed. He felt that the entire world was stacked against him. As he gradually began to trust me, he shared his bitter criticisms of everyone he knew or had known. On a few occasions he became so self-righteous that I teasingly asked him, "Who do you think you are, Jesus Christ?" He seemed to ignore this remark. However, when Christmas came around he sent me a very lovely card on which he added, "I hope you'll enjoy my birthday."

AFFIRMATION

The aim of psychotherapy is not so much to change a patient's thoughts, feelings, or behavior, but to restore his or her sense of freedom, experience of Self, or awareness of having an active role in his or her world. Such affirmation, be it in a serious or humorous vein, is an important aspect of therapy. Affirmation of qualities which the patient has genuine doubts about, such as intelligence, performance, looks, and so forth, is sometimes helpful. Repeated affirmations of obviously positive qualities may lead *away* from the Self, as often happens with lovable, bright, "strokes-addicted" people. On the other hand, the affirmation of seemingly negative qualities can lead *toward* the Self, as we saw in the preceding example of Corey's patient who had "nothing to say."

The following example shows another such affirmation in a humorous vein.

Vignette 10. A school teacher came to see me from a town 50 miles away and managed to be 10 minutes late each time she came in. As the exploration of her tardiness yielded little but hurt apologies, rationalizations, and occasional meaningless psycho-dynamic clichés, and as she continued to be tardy, I said to her one day, "I must commend you for your exceptional ability to always be exactly 10 minutes late. Were you living across the street, it wouldn't be a great feat, but to always be 10 minutes late at a 50-mile distance, with changing weather and traffic conditions, that really takes careful planning." She responded to this by arriving well in time for the following session. But for the next visit she was 20 minutes late, regarding which I casually commented, "I see you made up for last time's punctuality!" She appreciated the serious implications of an interpretation with a witty exterior and began to recognize that her choice of being late was related to maintaining her sense of autonomy. Clearly, affirmation must not focus on the symptoms, which may be psychogenic or somatogenic, but on basic stances in life to which the patient clings while denying authorship.

PUNS IN DREAMS

Puns are fairly common in dreams. They thinly disguise weaknesses, wishes, or character traits that the dreamer is reluctant to acknowledge. Sometimes the dreamer becomes aware of the pun's humorous message upon awakening. However, at other times the pun's meaning only discloses itself in the psychotherapist's office.

Vignette 11. A patient whose marital difficulties were largely due to his persistent avoidance of closeness had a revealing dream at a time when his wife was undergoing various tests for a possibly malignant tumor. She was hurt and depressed at his inability to offer genuine empathy and support. He dreamt that he was desperately trying to put together various parts of a machine (he commented that it seemed to have been a "kidney machine") that would cure his wife. Unable to do so, and increasingly frustrated, he left home to look for assistance from the "Wells Company." The dream increased the patient's awareness of how he related to his wife in a rational and businesslike manner and how he had always unsuccessfully tried to "fix" their problems. He recognized his hidden hope to deal with her severe illness by going to the "Wells Company" just as he would deal with a defective bike by taking it to a "Fix-It Shop."

HUMOROUS DETACHMENT

The tendency to laugh at ourselves and our foibles or symptoms is a form of defense and inauthenticity whenever its aim is to belittle or avoid the problem. Yet, in other instances, the ability to laugh at oneself is the very beginning of dealing responsibly with what was previously viewed as hopeless or unmanageable. The ability of phobic, obsessed, or depressed persons to smile at the outward absurdity of their ideas may accordingly indicate a willingness to explore the reasons for clinging to their symptoms.

Vignette 12. A humorous detachment from symptoms can occur even in patients with psychotic symptoms when they begin to trust their therapist. I have treated, often at intervals of more than 1 year, a lady with recurring yet bizarre delusions that usually manifested themselves during periods of increased stress. As soon as she sensed that she could unconditionally rely upon me, she would call me at the beginning of any such schizophrenic episode. Half laughing, half concerned, she would explain that "someone" must have been attaching blossoms to her bushes at a time when they shouldn't bloom. And almost in the same breath, she would ask whether I thought she should resume taking pills for awhile.

Vignette 13. Similarly, a nun suffering from a longstanding schizoaffective disorder began to detach herself from her psychotic experiences when she laughingly stated, "My brain is like flickering neon lights and like Mexican jumping beans." This ability to detach herself from her symptoms, as well as her humorous sharing of this experience with me, carried over into our looking more dispassionately and with some humor at her innumerable angry and suspicious feelings toward her fellow sisters. Though such ability to detach oneself, to experience some autonomy of the Self, falls very short of a "cure," it is nevertheless a crucial step toward participating in therapy and functioning in society. For instance, the aforecited lady with the mysterious flowers never required hospitalization. She successfully raised two well-adjusted sons during the many years I had the opportunity to work with her.

HUMOROUS AVOIDANCE
OF DIRECT CONFRONTATIONS

I mentioned earlier that either member of the treatment dyad may use humor, wit, and sarcasm for the sake of avoidance. They may be unwilling to take themselves or the relationship seriously, or may use humor in order to carefully test or probe feelings. Both motivations are often simultaneously present.

Vignette 14.   An example of the first motivation is the man I've seen who told me with great and seductive wit about his latest drinking sprees.   In such an instance I always focus in upon the witty attitude, asking the patient why he is laughing or joking about something that he probably experiences as quite tragic.

Vignette 15.   An example of the second motivation was provided by a brilliant college student suffering from many paralyzing phobias.   He usually expressed his genuine feelings under the guise of skillful humor.   In such instances, I would usually focus upon the content of the humor.   This patient had been unable to voice any negative feelings toward me, even though there had been no improvement in his condition over several months.   Then, one day as he entered my office he asked whether I had personalized license plates.   Slightly puzzled I said, "No, why do you ask?"   "Well," he said with barely a smile, "I saw your car in the parking lot and wondered whether the BBS on your plates stood for "Big Bull-Shitter."   This prompted the exploration of his ability to express or share most feelings only in a sarcastic disguise. Humor offered him a safety valve.   It allowed him to "test" feelings safely, inasmuch as they could be denied in case of an unwanted response, by stating, "I was just joking."

ACCEPTANCE OF AMBIGUITY

This is frequently implied in humor, and especially in jokes. Life itself is pervaded by ambiguities; and the more perceptive a person is, the more he or she becomes aware of them.   Is it better to be red or dead?   A husband may see both his wife's and his daughter's viewpoints as valid, irreconcilable as they may be. Persons may waver between seeing life as senseless and seeing it as profoundly meaningful.   When trapped by such ambiguities, we usually try hard to resolve them.

Let me mention two humorous anecdotes I have used to convey that trying to resolve such ambiguities sometimes wastes energies available for fuller living.

Vignette 16. A seminarian experiencing a desire for religious life as well as a desire for marriage and family had postponed his ordination for priesthood twice without resolving his extremely painful ambivalence. He insisted that there must be a "right" answer. At a seemingly appropriate moment I told him the story of the dying rabbi: A long file of admiring students waited to hear his last wise words. The brightest among them stood nearest to the rabbi, asking, "What is life?" Weakly, the rabbi replied, "Life is a river!" Impressed, the brightest student passed on the words to the bright student behind him, and he to the next, all the way until they reached the dumbest student at the end of the line. The latter shook his head, asking, "What does the rabbi mean by 'Life is a river'?" And now this question traveled back from student to student to the brightest one who posed the question to the rabbi, "What does the master mean by 'Life is a river'?" And the rabbi, with his last breath, mumbled "So it isn't a river!"

This example charmingly conveys that the overcoming of ambiguity creates a sense of freedom. Lack of such transcendence implies lack of authenticity, fear of freedom, avoidance of active commitment and, finally, despair. In the above joke - as in many fairy tales - the "dumbbell" is the most liberated from the servitude of certainty by refusing blind dependence on authority and initiating the insight that life itself is ambiguous.

Vignette 17. A most conscientious and likable young lady had quit several jobs because of despair over ambiguity. Whenever she was criticized, she simultaneously experienced that 90% of the criticism was her error and 90% was the accuser's fault. Her hopelessness over this dilemma was crippling. At one point, I jokingly suggested that being a consistent paranoid might be preferable, as this at least allows a person to feel worthwhile. This quip led into her discussing how she had developed a deep hatred for life in her early years, because she could only gain security by self-effacement and self-blame. This choice made sense in view of her parents training her to always ask, "Have I been a good girl," whereupon they would point out instances of her shortcomings. As soon as she sat down at her next visit, I smiled, asking, "Have you been a good girl?" She immediately crossed her legs then burst out laughing, remembering how her parents had repeatedly scolded her for not sitting like a decent young lady.

SARCASM OR CYNICISM

Sarcasm or cynicism can be pseudo-humorous expressions of resignation in the face of ambiguity. While offering a momentary illusion of freedom, sarcasm or cynicism only intensify and consolidate the continuing ambiguity of the situation.

Vignette 18. I saw a couple where the wife voiced the common complaint that her husband only saw her as a sexual object and reluctantly let her spend money for her self-improvement courses. The husband seethed because he viewed these "far out" interests as a slap at his scientific orientation; he felt financially exploited and sexually rejected. Yet, trying to make light of the matter, he asked me in front of his wife, "Do you know what marital incompatibility is?" As I hesitated, he answered his own question: "Incompatibility occurs when the husband hasn't enough income and the wife isn't pattable." In another session, when his wife complained that she couldn't hear well because of a "cold," he joked, "Now I can speak freely to Dr. H without your being able to cut me down!" Such cynical comments were part of their everyday deadly cycle in which the desperately dependent husband achieved short-lived distance and superiority, followed by guilt, followed by atonement by acceding to the wife's wishes, followed by stirrings of anger and desire for independence, then followed by cynical remarks.

HUMOROUS ILLUSTRATIONS

Jokes can be helpful in providing concrete, though grotesquely exaggerated, illustrations of psychodynamic processes.

Vignette 19. A lady consulted me because her marriage was severely jeopardized each time her husband visited his "domineering, scheming, evil" mother. She was loath to recognize that her intense feelings against her mother-in-law might be quite similar to those which she hiddenly harbored against her own mother. She could only gradually recognize and tolerate these feelings after we talked about mother-in-laws and stepmothers in fairy tales, who also take the brunt of the negative feelings originally directed toward mother. Jokes about mothers-in-law allow the vicarious expression of these same taboo feelings. I illustrated this by telling her the story of the lady who asked her friend how one could tell "good" from "bad" mushrooms. "It's easy," her friend responded, "you serve them to your mother-in-law; if she dies they're good, if she doesn't, they're bad!" My patient recognized how this joke, though a bit morbid, would be truly "sick" if applied to mothers. And yet, every mother-in-law, by necessity, *is* a mother!

HUMOROUS INSTRUCTIONS

I have already discussed treatment by paradoxical intention. I would like to add a related example of instructions containing gentle humor, which I have used in many variations.

Vignette 20. "How can I stop running myself down?" asked a fine, young school teacher. "I'm just a neurotic, no good! I feel like hitting myself each time I do it; I should have will power, but I'm weak, I don't try!" "Feel free to run yourself down, Jane," I replied, "it will happen anyhow, even before you think of stopping it; but each time you become aware of doing it, please smile at yourself as kindly and warmly as you can, and simply say, 'Here I go again, it's perfectly alright.' "

It is important to note that the previous vignettes cannot do justice to the infinite variety of humor that occurs in the therapeutic relationship or to the innumerable modes of expressing or responding to humor used by *different* therapists. Neither do these vignettes enumerate all the benefits of humor or convey all the situations in which a patient will not respond to humor. But I will take a dose of my own medicine and say, "Julius, you feel maybe you are inadequate, but it's perfectly alright!"

SYNTHESIS

Xingu, once a prince and now but a ragged minstrel, "a thing of shreds and patches," had grown weary of all his possessions. Armed only with a lute, he confronts the ruler of another land, the Cold Duke of Coffin Castle.

Xingu's *irony* reflects the boredom that awaits mere esthetic existence. Having deconstituted his own world, he proceeds to undermine, with his delightfully ironic ballads, the nihilistic power of the Cold Duke.

The Cold Duke's *cynicism* has killed time, and has imprisoned what could revive life's meaning, the beautiful Princess Saralinda: The 13 clocks whose seconds, minutes, and hours he has slain with his sharp sword - and tongue - are standing still. His hidden power resides in his monster, Todal, a "blob of glup" whose presence would "frighten Octopi to death." At the mere mention of Todal's name the guard's hair turns white and the mask of the Duke's spy pales.

Yet the most baffling figure in James Thurber's (1950) charming tale *The 13 Clocks* is Golux, a dwarf-like creature who constantly forgets things, who keeps making mistakes, and who is on the side of the good solely "by accident and happenchance." Half of the places that Golux says he has been to never were, and "half the things he says are there cannot be found." Though aged, his eyes are "wide and astonished, as if everything were happening for the first time." Almost beyond good and evil, his ever-new openness to everything renders him somewhat oblivious to the past. Yet Xingu must place his full trust in this seemingly fumbling and unreliable being who comes up with some of the most brain-twisting suggestions and statements. Needing a thousand precious jewels, they journey together to Hagga, the woman whose tears are reputed to turn into gems. Golux's skill at transcending the most dire problems, and at seeing ever-new options, is most poignantly manifested by his *humor* and laughter. Posing as a humorist, much like Kierkegaard's Johannes Climacus, joyfully humble, often equivocating himself, never compelling, never exploiting, never focusing upon his own needs, Golux turns out to be an ideal guide, therapist, and indirect communicator. He never lessens Xingu's freedom or responsibility to make his own decisions. And once the Prince has found his deepest meaning by freeing Saralinda, Golux steps aside, like any caring therapist, and bids the couple goodbye, wishing them well with a warm admonition: "Remember laughter; you'll need it even in the isles of ever-after!"

Maybe the main difference between a "patient" and a "nonpatient" is contained in this leave-taking. The "patient" needs a guide, a therapist who promotes within him or her the progressive revelation, acceptance, and exercise of freedom (Heuscher, 1980).

Once individuals have found the meaning (Saralinda) of their life, they will journey on by themselves, provided that they "remember laughter" and the need to question their current existence. If they forget, they are in danger of again losing their meaning. Then, hopefully, they will find a new Golux in order to escape from the new Coffin Castle, from the Cold Duke, and from Todal. The essence of this chapter might be condensed into two letters - "Be!" (if it is addressed to the readers) or into three letters - "I am!" (if it is addressed to the writer). This essence does not portray a final, fixed, immutable, or even attainable goal - at least not as long as we play and toil on this our earth. Yet it nourishes the inexhaustible and variegated ideas that shape poetry, novels, or even books like the present one. This essence pervades any effective psychotherapy that carefully, patiently, and perceptively deals with the manifold and protean defenses behind which authenticity is hidden. Though the essence may be condensed in two or three letters, it will never be exhausted by what we can experience, live, and create in our everyday lives. Publishers will not run out of books, therapists will not run out of patients, and everyone else will never be overwhelmed by the bored recognition that there's nothing new to strive for.

The vagaries of life, the rich and changing designs of artistic creation, as well as the therapist's and patient's experiences in psychotherapy keep teaching us about modesty. It is the modesty of recognizing what was Faust's ultimate insight: "Only he who must conquer them daily anew deserves freedom and life." In fact, it is the awareness of the *potential* for freedom and change, the awareness of *I am,* of Self, that counts, rather than some structureless freedom.

In his First Elegie, Rilke (1963) proposes that the limits we set to our world are necessary. These limits become a "Coffin-Castle" only if we stop challenging them while refusing to accept that there are numerous hidden "spheres" beyond our conventional world. Beauty and joy await us as we dare, carefully, to transgress the limits. Yet terror would strike us, says Rilke, if the "angels" in these spheres did not allow us to linger near the limits but forcefully pulled us into their arms. Even a modest detachment from our world is usually experienced as frightfully beautiful, as terrifying, or as radically affecting all our views.

In *The 13 Clocks,* Hagga's tears of laughter become the required precious stones that overcome the Cold Duke. Just as the tears liquefy after a week, so humor is an initially fleeting yet ultimately essential factor in overcoming a world that would otherwise become drearier and drearier.

Humor removes constraining, prejudicial, or growth-stifling barriers only in a loving context. However, in a cold, cynical, or sarcastic context the selfsame humor may lead to progressive rigidity and regression to a more primitive, nonhuman level. Mindess (1971) beautifully summarizes what I have tried to say:

> You can never be sure your humor won't be interpreted as derision, or callous indifference, if not as calculated cruelty. In fact, you can be sure it will unless, and this is the crux of the matter, the person you are trying to help unequivocally perceives you as his true ally. If he knows that basically you respect him and wish him well, he may get the point that what you are trying to do is encourage him to train his own sense of humor on himself. The safest course, I think, is to watch for any sign that the sufferer himself has an inkling of the ridiculousness of his behavior or the irony of his predicament and then jump in and reinforce it. (p. 10)

I will end with an additional quote from Mindess (1971): "The extent to which our sense of humor can help us to maintain our sanity is the extent to which it moves beyond jokes, beyond wit, beyond laughter itself. It must constitute a frame of mind, a point of view, a deep-going, far-reaching attitude to life" (p. 10).

I think Golux would agree.

REFERENCES

Buber, M. (1949). *Die Erzaehlungen der Chassidim.* Zurich: Manesse Verlag.

Corey, D. Q. (1966). The use of a reverse format in now psychotherapy. *The Psychoanalytic Review, 53,* 107-125.

Fromm, E. (1971). *Escape from Freedom.* New York: Avon Books.

Fry, W. F., Jr. (1963). *Sweet Madness.* Palo Alto: Pacific Books.

Heidegger, M. (1961). *An Introduction to Metaphysics.* New York: Doubleday Anchor Books.

Hershkowitz, A. (1977). The essential ambiguity of, and in, humor. In A. J. Chapman & H. C. Foot (Eds.), *It's a Funny Thing, Humour* (pp. 139-142). Oxford, England: Pergamon.

Heuscher, J. E. (1964). What is existential psychotherapy? *Review of Existential Psychology and Psychiatry, 10,* 158-167.

Heuscher, J. E (1974). *A Psychiatric Study of Myths and Fairy Tales.* Springfield, IL: C. C. Thomas.

Heuscher, J. E. (1980). Psychotherapy as uncovering of freedom. *Psychotherapy, 17,* 467-471.

Heuscher, J. E. (1981a). *Existentialism and Folklore.* San Jose, CA: Institute for Clinical Philosophy Press.

Heuscher, J. E. (1981b). The role of humor and folklore themes in psychotherapy. *American Journal of Psychiatry, 131,* 1546-1549.

Husserl, E. (1953). *Ideas.* New York: Macmillan.

Kierkegaard, S. (1941). *Concluding Unscientific Postscript to the Philosophical Fragments* (D. F. Swenson, Trans.). Princeton, NJ: Princeton University Press. (Original work published 1846)

Kierkegaard, S. (1954a). *Fear and Trembling* (W. Lowrie, Trans.). Garden City, NY: Doubleday. (Original work published 1842)

Kierkegaard, S. (1954b). *Sickness Unto Death* (W. Lowrie, Trans.). Garden City, NY: Doubleday. (Original work published 1848)

Kierkegaard, S. (1959). *Either/Or* (Volumes I and II) (D. F. Swenson, Trans.). New York: Doubleday Anchor Books. (Original work published 1841)

Kierkegaard, S. (1965). *The Concept of Irony* (L. M. Capel, Trans.). Bloomington, IN: Indiana University Press. (Original work published 1841)

Kubie, L. S. (1971). The destructive potential of humor in psychotherapy. *American Journal of Psychiatry, 127,* 861-866.

Levine, J. (1977). Humor as a form of therapy. In A. J. Chapman & H. C. Foot (Eds.), *It's a Funny Thing, Humour* (pp. 127-137). Oxford, England: Pergamon.

Mindess, H. (1971, August 21). The sense in humor. *Saturday Review,* p. 10.

Reik, T. (1962). *Jewish Wit.* New York: Gamut Press.

Rilke, R. M. (1963). *Duino Elegies.* New York: Norton.

Schreiber, F. R. (1974). *Sybil.* New York: Warner Books.

Thurber, J. (1950). *The 13 Clocks.* New York: Simon and Schuster.

Yalom, I. (1980). *Existential Psychotherapy.* New York: Basic Books.

Postscript:

My Grandmother Tamem's Chicken

Having completed my umpteenth reading of all the chapters comprising this volume, having driven my pen through each sentence, and having weaved my thoughts with the thoughts of each contributor as I read on and on, I finally stopped. Pausing for a few moments of reflection at this cliff of awareness I had reached, I tried to make sense of what I had read. I searched for the gestalt of it all, for an encompassing structure, for a recognizable shape. Then, in the twinkling of an eye, the fit of it all struck me. It struck me that all the writers in this volume belonged to the same intellectual and emotional family, the same tribe. In their own ways and styles, they had each reached for the essence of the same truth. They were consensual, in unison, regarding the need for change in the therapist's persona. Yorukoglu shared his residency struggles with the sacred rules of therapy. Surkis questioned the traditional therapist's conservative approach to self-expression. Heuscher noted the limitations of the blank screen therapist. Furthermore, in moving beyond the original territory within which we were all intellectually raised, each author came to a new meeting place and brought along some favorite companions. The new meeting place was, in my heart and imagination, a place of laughter, joy, contentment, mutual respect, detachment, transcendence, and play. There they stood, the Magi, the wise men of humor. Mosak came with Adler and Maniacci. Kuhlman came with Popeye and a cow called "MU." Yorukoglu came with Nasreddin Hodja and three bright-eyed children, two boys and a girl. Schimel came with Victor. Maher was there with his duck.

Surkis was there with his "nice gool." Eberhart brought along his clown, and Amada was there with his amoeba. Heuscher came with Kierkegaard and Golux, while McKiernan stood under a blossoming almond tree with his daughter Laura. I stood close by with my friends William Fry, Dr. Shamrock, Tiara, Sisyphus, Joha, and Candide. And in the midst of all the words, in the bosom of all the translations, was a message about contentment with the moment, pleasure in what was given to us, and acceptance of our imperfect world. Technically untechnical, we all reached for a meaningfulness beyond ordinary meanings, meeting symbolically at a felicitous point in time as concretely incarnated in this book. We asked for a new way of looking at the world, for an alternative point of view, and for the type of psychological victory that occurs when therapists and patients become in reality who they are in the eyes of their healthy imagination. On the stage of this allegorical theater where uncirculated psychological history was unfolding, I saw resplendent interpersonal mosaics and witnessed the overcoming of fear and rejection. I further dared to imagine a humor hall of fame where the superb efforts manifested by the contributors to this book and many others would be continuously recognized, a sort of comical counterpart of the baseball and rock and roll halls of fame. At that moment of magical reality, I could see my Grandmother Tamem with us, smiling serenely to everyone, her red cheeks radiating health and vibrancy, her beautiful silver-white hair wrapped in a graceful bun. She was wearing her special occasions dress with the blue and white flowers. I thought that she, too, would deserve to be in a humor hall of fame. She was, after all, an exceptionally humorous person despite having endured more than her share of life's swinging hatchets. She naturally belonged with our group, and I welcomed her to our symbolic get-together with eagerness and love.

Grandmother Tamem was a blessed soul. My grandmother had no substantial formal education, yet she was a highly educated individual in her expansive love for people and her sensitivity to the feelings of others. She had not been trained in any psychotherapeutic program, yet she had what I would call a therapeutic presence. She was an organic therapist, a natural healer. Her healing was expressed in her way of being with others, in her soothing yet humorous commentaries, and in the way she took care of others by offering them her food. My grandmother was, among other things, an expert at making barbecue grilled chicken, a topic I will return to later. My brother and I spent some of our childhood summer vacations with her when we were off from school. For me, these summers were a special time that I relished and looked forward to every year because I felt close to my grandmother and enjoyed being around her. In honor of the contributors and the readers, and in honor of my grandmother's memory, I would like to share some of the special humorous moments I experienced with Grandmother that somewhat encapsulated her therapeutic philosophy of life. Her therapeutic messages have been encoded in my soul and my way of being with others, and I believe they hold important values and understandings about life, therapy, and humor. I shall call these learning experiences Grandmother Tamem's Therapeutic Principles. Each of my experiences with my grandmother will be described, then followed by an axiom stemming from the learning experience:

1. When I was about 11 years old, I was rather inquisitive about the outside world and had a bunch of childhood friends that were of similar ilk. Together with my friends and my brother, we formed a group of roving Jacques Cousteaus, brimming with curiosity, always looking for new worlds to explore. On a hot summer day, we were engaged in one of our exploratory safaris when we discovered a main fire hydrant. We started playing with the fire hydrant, trying to unscrew it or drink water from it. All of a sudden, the protective mechanism fell apart and a gigantic torrent of water gushed out of the fire hydrant, uncontrollable, like an unceasing eruption of white lava. My brother and I felt so scared, and I started thinking about the consequences. In my child's mind, I imagined that the fire hydrant would keep overflowing, that no one would be able to shut it off, and that it would drown the entire town.

    Full of gloomy apprehension, and feeling burdened with a thousand fears, my brother and I ran back to my grandmother's house and I told her what had happened. In my pang of contrition and repentance, I also told my grandmother about my fear that the evil waters of the fire hydrant would drown the town. What provisions could be made to prepare for the deluge? To my surprise, Grandmother smiled when I shared my apocalyptic vision with her. She first contacted the authorities and told them about the fire hydrant. She then looked at me and my brother, tried to contain her laughter, and proceeded to give each of us a perfunctory spanking for our misdeed. I had the feeling that, for her, the spanking was just part of carrying out her parental duties, yet I noticed her winking at me as she spanked me. At that instant, I realized that she appreciated the absurdity inherent to this whole incident. Her winking represented a signal for me not to worry. As I understood it, the message in her reaction to my adventure was that I was not to play with fire hydrants in the future but also that it was not the end of the world if I made a mistake. Her love for me would not cease just because I was a bit mischievous.

Grandmother Tamem's first therapeutic axiom is: "Try to have fun in life. If you make a mistake, do not condemn yourself for it but see what you can learn for next time. Mistakes are the vehicles of discovery. It is okay to make mistakes because we are all human."

2. During our early childhood years, my grandmother used to put me and my brother to bed every night by telling us stories before we slept. On one occasion, she had tucked us in bed and was telling us a story when my brother asked if he could have something to eat before going to sleep. She did not answer him and continued with her story. My brother repeated his request for food with some insistence. However, it became apparent to me that Grandmother did not want my brother to eat right before he slept, especially since each of us had gobbled up a hearty meal earlier that evening. Suddenly, my brother let out some gas with a rather high-pitched rumbling sound. Seizing the golden opportunity offered by this occurrence, and with good timing, my grandmother put together a message that utilized the leaven offered by the moment. Imitating the sound of the expelled gas, she said to my brother, "You see, this is telling you that eating before you go to sleep is b-b-b-b-b-b-b-b-b-b-a-a-a-a-a-a-a-d for you!" At that point the three of us exploded in laughter, and my brother stopped asking for food. Shortly thereafter, my brother and I were fast asleep.

My grandmother's therapeutic axiom on this is: "Use what you have at hand to resolve the problems you encounter, and use humor to resolve these problems whenever possible. The solution to the problem is usually in the present, right around the corner."

3. When I was 15 and my brother was 13, he started socializing with a group of other children whose behavior was not approved of by Grandmother. These children had started a so-

cial club, and my brother became engrossed in the workings and activities of the social club. He spent much time with this group of children and wanted to join their club. Grandmother did not like that. Nonetheless, she appreciated that my brother needed some form of affiliation and that his involvement with this group of children was important to him. On one occasion when the three of us were together, Grandmother told my brother, "You know, about your club, you can talk to them and be with them, but you know, honey, you don't need to register your name in their book." This comment struck both me and my brother as very funny, and we still reminisce about it to this day. It was a lighthearted way of telling my brother to see the relativity of the situation, to keep his own perspective, and not to get overly immersed in one way of looking at things to the exclusion of other vantage points.

Grandmother Tamem's third psychotherapy axiom relating to this is: "Stay away from polarization. Do not show blind adherence to any particular theory or person. Keep your freedom of thought and judgment. Everything is relative."

4. As I mentioned, my grandmother was an outstanding cook. Her artistic talents with respect to cooking were particularly highlighted in the way she fixed chicken grilled on a charcoal barbecue. The process of preparing the chicken for cooking consumed most of her typical summer weekend. On Saturday, my grandmother would salt the chicken pieces and marinate them overnight in her special crushed garlic and olive oil marinade. She would then cook the chicken on Sunday for our family's Sunday lunch. The grilled chicken Sunday lunch at my grandmother's home was an event for which she was renowned. The heavenly aroma of the chickens as they grilled was enough to bring an ailing person back to health. Any friends or even acquaintances that happened to be in the neighborhood were welcome to come by and have some chicken, because my grandmother always prepared extra chicken to cover unannounced visitors. In fact, the Sunday lunch represented a special occasion for a healing get-together. My mother and father would come, my brother and I were always there, my aunt and her children would come, and some of our relatives and neighbors would also show up. On certain Sundays, my brother and I would invite our friends or favorite schoolteachers to join us for Grandmother's Sunday lunch. On other occasions, family friends from out of town would

join us and bring their children with them. The ceremony of preparing the chicken would actually become a big and lovely party to which anyone that cared to come was invited. We would all be bantering, exchanging jokes, enjoying each other's presence, and just having a plain old good time. My grandmother ceremoniously presided over the whole affair, sitting on a low chair next to the barbecue, fanning the chickens so that they would get evenly done, turning them over from one side to the other, and all the while joking and conversing with her family and guests. During this process, my brother and I would sneak around and steal small pieces of chicken when they were done, or Grandmother would ask my mother for us and give us some pieces to munch on before lunch was ready. I remember the good feelings generated by these get-togethers, and I am struck by how everyone that participated in our Sunday celebrations still recalls them with great fondness, although my grandmother has now passed away. I remember standing by her grave 2 years ago in a Detroit, Michigan cemetery, my mother next to me, my heart heavy with sadness and nostalgia. As I was digging the soil around the grave to plant some flowers, I turned to my mother. We both had tears in our eyes, and the image of those lovely Sundays suddenly returned to me. My grandmother's generosity, her sense of humor, and her relentless giving of herself was very touching to me and to anyone who knew her. I mentioned the Sunday get-togethers and Grandmother's chicken to my mother and suddenly our sadness was imbued with laughter and appreciation. I am sure that Grandmother Tamem was with us at that moment.

My grandmother's existence has taught me that death is not synonymous with presence. Her humor and her love, invincible, have transcended and even outgrown death. Wherever and whenever along the continuum of time, dead or alive, real partners come together.

Grandmother's fourth therapeutic axiom on this is: "Be generous with what you have, and always give the best of you."

Four is enough. There is something ineffable in love, just like there is something ineffable in humor. The Zen master said that four parts out of five is fine, leaving some space for the wondrous.

And now Grandmother Tamem was back here with me at this imaginary meeting place, incarnated by this book, with all the wizards of humor and their companions. I saw her preparing her chicken and asking everyone what part of the chicken they preferred. It was very important to my grandmother that each person got the piece of chicken he or she liked. I saw her at our humor get-together, asking each person present what part of the chicken he or she preferred. Would they want wings, breast, the neck, thighs, or what else was their preference? Everyone got a delicious piece of chicken. And in a fleeting fantasy I imagined my grandmother serving each of our readers a piece of her chicken, the piece that each one preferred, as they joined us and our companions in creating another lovely symbolic get-together full of appreciation, lightheartedness, and laughter. We all shared nourishment from the body of love, basking in the plenitude of her caring.

In Chapter 11 of this volume, Dr. Julius Heuscher mentions James Thurber's *The 13 Clocks,* wherein Prince Xingu seeks to restore meaningfulness in his life by finding and liberating the beautiful Princess Saralinda from the clutches of the Cold Duke of Coffin Castle. Thus, Princess Saralinda becomes the focused symbol of Xingu's or any other human being's yearning for fulfillment.

We are all looking for our Saralindas, and my sincere hope is that Saralinda will materialize in some form in the life and endeavors of each human being. In my ear a white-coated Muse whispered that humor may be the Saralinda of psychotherapy. And I know that Grandmother Tamem would have agreed.

Waleed A. Salameh
San Diego
April, 1993

Appendix*

Comprehensive Research and Clinical Bibliography on Humor and Psychotherapy (1964-1991)

Asch, S. S. (1985). Depression and demonic possession: The analyst as an exorcist. *Hillside Journal of Clinical Psychiatry, 7,* 149-164. Notes that attempts to understand mental illness, and especially depression, have historically alternated between 2 general concepts--a belief in some form of evil spirits that have invaded the body or impressions of an internal black toxic substance, melancholia. Each age and culture has devised its own appropriate treatment for depression, which involves removing the biochemical cause of the disease process by means of prayer, exorcism, or fire or eliminating the evil spirit. Psychoanalysis has evolved a concept of depression that deals with ideas about introjects, rather than conceiving of them as concrete toxins or demons. Psychoanalytic treatment is a cognitive technique for exorcising depressive identifications by delineating them and then neutralizing them through understanding. The superficial similarity of historical and psychoanalytic concepts of depression, and their substitution of a tangible substance by an ideational one, helps to explain why it has been so difficult to avoid the temptation to reify psychoanalytic concepts. The Greeks' black humor, the demon, and the mental construct of an ambivalent introject can be understood as different metaphors of a similar universal concept. Clinical material is presented. (19 ref)

Assagioli, R. (1973). Cheerfulness: A psychosynthetic technique. *Psychosynthesis Research Foundation, 33,* 12-21. Discusses psychosynthetic techniques which can be used to cultivate cheerfulness. Cheerfulness is closely related to humor, joy, and play, and is blocked by criticism, hostility, anger, self-pity, impatience, and worry. Cheerfulness can be achieved by cultivating beneficial states of mind through intentional self-exposure to psychologically healthy influences. Techniques which help to develop cheerfulness include using positive evocative words, reflecting on the values of cheerfulness, and neutralizing moods of depression and irritation by acting as if they are nonexistent. It is suggested that cheerfulness has valuable applications in psychotherapy, in family life, and in general social relations.

Banmen, J. (1982). The use of humour in psychotherapy. *International Journal for the Advancement of Counselling, 5,* 81-86. Reviews the literature on humor and offers suggestions about the use and further study of humor in therapy. Research has been in accord with Freud's theory of humor (i.e., humor releases aggression). At the same time, an implicit association between humor and mental health has persisted. It appears that humor allows one to purge oneself of hidden thoughts in a socially acceptable form. Psychiatric patients have been observed to possess a lower appreciation level of humor than normal Ss. Humor responses have been found to be a good indicator of patient change. Much of the research in the area has been anecdotal in nature. Nevertheless, there is support for the use of therapeutic humor that is exclusively positive and always meant to be constructive. Humor breaks the ice, gives clients greater insight, and is an avenue of simple understanding. It is suggested that training programs on the use of humor as a therapy must stress its spontaneous nature and the discretion necessary to ensure that its use is not counterproductive. (54 ref)

Baptiste, D. A. (1989). Using masks as therapeutic aids in family therapy. *Journal of Family Therapy, 11,* 45-58. Describes a treatment for families in conflict, which uses play, humor, and the power and "magic" of masks to paradoxically "unmask" family members. This treatment facilitates reality-testing of perceptions distorted by the emotional masks people create and project onto each other. Mask usage is suggested as an adjunct to other therapeutic approaches. The technique is illustrated in the case example of a reconstituted family, consisting of a divorced couple and their 3-15 yr old biological and adopted children. The therapeutic use of masks is recommended for families who are at an impasse, are rigid in their communications, resistant to other approaches, yet highly engaged and motivated to try something different.

Benningfield, M. F. (1990). Addressing resistance stage by stage. *Journal of Family Psychology, 3,* 251-253. Comments on the 4-stage intervention model for family therapy described by J. M. Coche (see PA, Vol. 77:20439) and suggests that treatment of despair is exaggerated. Resources such as boredom and humor may also be used to reactivate a couple's growth process.

Bloch, S., Browning, S., & McGrath, G. (1983). Humour in group psychotherapy. *British Journal of Medical Psychology, 56,* 89-97. Humor has an important role in a therapy group, can be a valuable therapeutic mode, and may be fostered by certain attitudes and techniques on the part of group leaders. Inappropriately applied humor is antitherapeutic and potentially destructive. The therapist's use of humor can serve as a valuable model for group members, allow the therapist to evidence aspects of his/her own personality to patients, and aid in overcoming group resistance. Humor affords patients a sense of proportion of their problems and aids them in overcoming earnestness, promoting development of social skills, and easing problems of self-disclosure. Humor facilitates group cohesiveness, insight into group dynamics, and tension reduction. Humor is misused when it is wielded as a defense against anxiety, as a mask for aggression against another group member, as a tool for self-display and ingratiation, or as a device for frivolous avoidance of important issues. It is the therapist's responsibility to ensure that humor is not misused in group therapy. (16 ref)

Bloomfield, I. (1980). Humour in psychotherapy and analysis. *International Journal of Social Psychiatry, 26,* 135-141. Discusses reasons for the scarcity of work on humor in therapy and presents illustrative case examples of the therapeutic use of humor. Humor in different cultures and the development of a sense of humor are also discussed. Humor is a direct expression of unconscious processes. It brings together opposites, highlights contradictions, and shows up the absurdity of irreconcilable wishes. It is the paradox and the absurdity that makes one laugh. In humorous laughter an aggressive thought or feeling is successfully disguised and given a socially acceptable form. It is concluded that the ability to laugh at oneself requires a recognition of one's own contradictions and mastery of the relationship with the self and presupposes a high degree of maturity and an ability to stand apart from oneself, to observe one's own antics, and to understand oneself better.

Bolk-Weischedel, D. (1978). Alterations in the untreated partner of the patient during analytic psychotherapy. *Zeitschrift fur Psychosomatische Medizin und Psychoanalyse, 24,* 116-128. Conducted a follow-up study of 50 married patients who had received psychoanalytic treatment. Symptomatic and structural changes in the patients and especially in their spouses were determined. 35 spouses had symptoms before, during, and after treatment. During therapy, spouses primarily showed the psychogenous symptoms of anxiety, depressive variation of humor, temporary impotence, and gastrointestinal disorder; after therapy, they complained primarily of backaches. 32 spouses came to a partial or satisfactory structurally progressive development, while 3 regressed. 16 pairs succeeded in improving their professional positions. There was generally no change in spouses of patients with poor results from treatment. There were also alterations in the internal and external references of the pairs: 10 divorced, but 24 judged their marriages as satisfactory or good. (18 ref)

Brody, M. (1976). The wonderful world of Disney: Its psychological appeal. *American Imago, 33,* 350-360. Analyzes the influence of Walt Disney and his creations--Silly Symphony, Mickey Mouse, Donald Duck, Disneyland, and Disney World, and his important feature-length movies, especially Pinocchio, Snow White, and Cinderella--and their value in shaping American culture. Disney's works are seen as essentially positive social influences in which "anal themes are used to lessen the anxiety of oral aggression," fears and anxieties are time limited, and castration anxiety is mastered as Disney's ingenious works plug into our unconscious.

Brown, J. R. (1978). Ritual and Gestalt: The Gestalt group in high relief. *Gestalt Journal, 1,* 68-74. When group process is considered in terms of society, the Gestalt therapy group fulfills an important function equivalent to the role ritual in primitive societies: (a) evoking strong emotions, (b) distancing these emotions sufficiently to make them bearable, and (c) discharging the emotion. Contributing to the evocation of emotions are the setting, interventions, philosophy, goals, and the power of suggestion in the group. Distancing is facilitated by the presence of the group, the voice of the therapist, some therapeutic interventions, and humor. The discharge of emotions is an expected activity in a Gestalt therapy group and is aided by all the aforementioned factors. These functions appear to fill a gap which exists in many of today's mass technological societies. (5 ref)

Brown, P. E. (1981). Effectiveness of humorous confrontation in facilitating positive self-exploration by clients in an analogue study of therapy (Doctoral dissertation, University of Kentucky). *Dissertation Abstracts International, 42,* 363-364.

Buckman, E. S. (1980). The use of humor in psychotherapy (Doctoral dissertation, Boston University School of Education). *Dissertation Abstracts International, 41,* 1715.

Burbridge, R. T. (1978). The nature and potential of therapeutic humor (Doctoral dissertation, California Institute of Asian Studies, San Francisco). *Dissertation Abstracts International, 39,* 2974.

Cade, B. (1986). The uses of humour in therapy. *Family Therapy Collections, 19,* 64-76. Discusses the use of humor in therapeutic situations. Therapists need feel no obligation to be funny, but should be open to using amusing or absurd ideas as they occur during therapy to facilitate relationships or reduce tensions. Humor is most therapeutic when inclusive rather than exclusive. It must be employed in a caring, loving way. Humor can be used with cues as a preface or it can be inserted without prior buildup as a surprise for the client. Sarcasm is rarely appropriate, and it must always be remembered that the butt of the humor is the person's ideas, behaviors, or responses, and not the person him- or herself. Forced or clumsy humor can result in embarrassment.

Carozza, P. (1986). Humor in psychotherapy: A phenomenological study of the experience of humor in therapy for the therapist (Doctoral dissertation, Union for Experimenting Colleges & Universities). *Dissertation Abstracts International, 47,* 2152.

Cassell, J. L. (1974). The function of humor in the counseling process. *Rehabilitation Counseling Bulletin, 14,* 240-245. Considers that the humor response has been ignored as a communication tool for individuals in therapeutic settings. A review of the literature reveals the significance given to humor-response variables as relevant indices in intraindividual and group interactional processes. Counselors using various methods to focus on the client's problem areas should be aware of the potentially rich responses offered by the humor process. From a review of studies primarily concerned with persons with disabilities, it is concluded that for the counselor the humor response can be an important and useful tool for monitoring and diagnostic purposes and for evaluation of change, and that for persons with disabilities it can be a general coping device. (23 ref)

Childs, A. W. (1976). A tale of two groups: An observational study of targeted humor (Doctoral dissertation, University of Tennessee). *Dissertation Abstracts International, 36,* 5860.

Christiansen, N. H. (1985). A preliminary contribution to an understanding of the use of playfulness in family therapy (Doctoral dissertation, University of Massachusetts). *Dissertation Abstracts International, 46,* 1517.

Cox, J. L. (1986). Long term psychotherapy of schizophrenia: Personal insights from the experience of long term psychotherapy of schizophrenia: Crises and countertransferences. *Psychiatria Fennica, 17,* 111-126. Discusses therapists' feelings in the process of long-term psychotherapy of schizophrenia, using examples from the experiences of the author as a therapist. Initially, the author expected that if he was a good enough therapist, the patient could be cured. Upon maturing, the author saw that helping people regain stability or satisfactory adjustment meant more than "curing." Specific characteristics needed by therapists include flexibility, humor, and honesty. Therapists must not expect to feel good about what occurs in therapy with the psychotic patient, and they must avoid traps of countertransference. It is concluded that it is essential for therapists to know themselves in order to be able to function in the world of the psychotic.

Daniels, E. B. (1974). Some notes on clowns, madness, and psychotherapy. *Psychotherapy & Psychosomatics, 24*, 465-470. Discusses the relation of clowning behavior and madness to illustrate the nature of the therapeutic relationship.

Dimmer, S. A., Carroll, J. L., & Wyatt, G. K. (1990). Uses of humor in psychotherapy. *Psychological Reports, 66*, 795-801. Reviews recent literature and research on therapeutic humor. Uses of humor in psychotherapy include alleviating anxiety and tension, encouraging insight, increasing motivation, and creating an atmosphere of closeness and equality between therapist and client. Humor should not be used to avoid uncomfortable feelings by patients or therapists, to defend against accepting the importance of patients' illness, or to mask therapists' hostilities toward the patient. Humorous interventions can be applied constructively if therapists do not use humor to serve their own interests to the disadvantage of the patient.

DiNicola, V. F. (1985). The acoustic mask: A review of "Behind the Family Mask" family therapy workshop with Maurizio Andolfi. *Journal of Strategic & Systemic Therapies, 4*, 74-80. Reviews "Behind the Family Mask," the family therapy workshop presented by M. Andolfi in Montreal in April 1984. Andolfi described his relational approach to therapy, using provocation, metaphor, and humor as therapeutic tools. Rigid family systems and their defensive masks are defined, and a masterful approach for entering the family system and getting behind the family mask without provoking insurmountable resistance is described. The origins of this active, creative, and sometime theatrical style in Italian schools of family therapy are traced to cultural traditions. A case example of an Italian immigrant family with an elective mute child is presented to illustrate the image of an acoustic mask. This case highlights the symptoms of mutism as a response to the family's "stuckness" and ambivalent status as cultural outsiders. Problems of immigrant families and therapy with bilingual families and therapists are also addressed. (18 ref)

Domash, L. (1975). The use of wit and the comic by a borderline psychotic child in psychotherapy. *American Journal of Psychotherapy, 29*, 261-270. Presents a case report of a borderline psychotic 9-12 yr old treated in psychotherapy. The report is used to illustrate the defensive function of wit. Specific techniques for the therapeutic reinforcement of wit are suggested. (15 ref)

Ellis, A. (1983). Rational-emotive therapy (RET) approaches to overcoming resistance: II. How RET disputes clients' irrational, resistance-creating beliefs. *British Journal of Cognitive Psychotherapy, 1(2)*, 1-16. RET employs a variety of cognitive methods to interrupt, challenge, and alter the irrational beliefs that underlie client's self-sabotaging resistances to therapeutic procedures. The primary method of overcoming resistance consists of showing clients that they choose to subscribe to a philosophy of low frustration tolerance and/or of self-deprecation that in turn largely causes their resistance. RET also involves the replacement of these irrational beliefs with positive coping statements, the examination of the disadvantages of resisting and the advantages of working at therapy, and the challenge of self-change. Cognitive distraction, through methods such as meditation and relaxation exercises, is used in RET to divert clients from anxiety and depression. Humor and paradoxical intention sometimes work with highly resistant and negativistic clients, and biblio- and audiotherapy can be effective. RET also focuses on clients' capacity for self-actualization, expectancies, irrational beliefs underlying the avoidance of responsibility, and the acquisition of emotional insight. (67 ref)

Ellis, A. (1977). Fun as psychotherapy. *Rational Living, 12*, 2-6. Rational Emotive Therapy contends that emotional disturbance consists largely of taking life too seriously and "exaggerating the significance of things." Psychotherapy would then be defined as helping people to combat their over-seriousness. To this end humor can be employed in various ways, and examples of its powerful, therapeutic force are given.

Erickson, M. O. (1984). A serious case for silliness. *Psychotherapy in Private Practice, 2,* 49-55. Presents an alternative approach to therapy that stresses an appropriate lack of seriousness, including the use of stories, anecdotes, and cartoons that illustrate the double bind, the paradox, the issue of responsibility, and the power of language. It is suggested that silliness in therapy helps prevent burnout and promotes positive change in the clients.

Finney, B. C. (1968). Some techniques for teaching psychotherapy. *Psychotherapy: Theory, Research & Practice, 5,* 115-119. The collection of techniques for teaching graduate students in therapy includes having each serve as a therapist to 1 fellow student and as a client to another. A collection of rubber stamps (begun in humor) saves time by stamping commonly given abbreviated reactions to students' case reports, e.g., zip for zip the lip "used when the counselor is talking and not listening."

Fisher, H. (1976). A credo for responsible group therapy with hospitalized adolescents. *Clinical Social Work Journal, 4,* 121-126. This humorous essay presents the author's thoughts on conducting group therapy with adolescent psychiatric patients. Beneath the humor is a philosophy of common sense developed from the author's personal experience.

Foster, J. A., & Reid, J. (1983). Humor and its relationship to students' assessments of the counsellor. *Canadian Counsellor, 17,* 124-129. 93 college students viewed a videotaped simulated counseling session containing either facilitative counselor humor, nonfacilitative humor, or no humor and then rated the counselor on likableness, approachability, ability to create a positive relationship, and ability to lead the client to a better understanding of the problem. Results indicate that nonfacilitative humor is less desirable than facilitative humor or no humor at all in terms of counselor likableness, approachability, or ability to create rapport but not in terms of client understanding. Ratings were unaffected by sex of the rater. (20 ref)

Fry, W. F., Jr., & Salameh, W. A. (Eds.). (1987). *Handbook of Humor and Psychotherapy: Advances in the Clinical Use of Humor.* Sarasota, FL: Professional Resource Exchange. Includes 14 chapters that clarify the clinical applications of humor in psychotherapy. Elucidates the theoretical and clinical underpinnings for utilizing humor within diverse clinical approaches and with different patient populations.

Furman, B., & Ahola, T. (1988). The use of humour in brief therapy. *Journal of Strategic & Systemic Therapies, 7,* 3-20. Asserts that the use of humor in therapy creates a context for treatment where new ideas and alternative perspectives may emerge. It is suggested that humor can be promoted through the use of anecdotes and jokes, humorous comments, humorous deframing and reframing, and humorous fantasies and task assignments. It is argued that humor is not an inborn talent but a natural product of the constructivist therapeutic philosophy that encourages therapists to keep on challenging any one true way of seeing things.

Gervaize, P. A., Mahrer, A. R., & Markow, R. (1985). Therapeutic laughter: What therapists do to promote strong laughter in patients. *Psychotherapy in Private Practice, 3,* 65-74. Attempted to classify therapist statements into 8 categories proposed by A. R. Mahrer and P. A. Gervaize (in press). Categories include directed interpersonal risk behavior, defined risk behavior by patient or other, ridiculous explanation/description of patient, and excited pleasure over risk behavior. Therapist statements preceding 60 instances of strong laughter, 30 instances of nonlaughter, and 30 instances of mild/moderate laughter were drawn from a pool of 280 hrs of audiotaped sessions conducted by 15 professional therapists with 75 adult patients and were examined. Results confirm the use of defined categories of therapist statements antecedent to the strong laughter event. Therapeutic conditions and sequencing of therapist statements leading to strong laughter are discussed, with reference for those therapies that value the occurrence of strong patient laughter. (21 ref)

Gitterman, A. (1989). Building mutual support in groups. *Social Work with Groups, 12,* 5-21. Explores professional tasks and skills associated with building mutual support (MS) in groups. To build an MS system, the worker helps group members to develop a sense of commonality and integration. The direct and indirect professional skills of the worker are discussed in terms of their ability to mitigate maladaptive patterns, which may become obstacles to MS. Illustrations are offered for the problems-in-living formulation, which provides a framework that encourages greater focus and direction to practice interventions. The role of humor in intervention is noted.

Golan, G., Rosenhein, E., & Jaffe, Y. (1988). Humour in psychotherapy. *British Journal of Psychotherapy, 4,* 393-400. Explored the reactions of 60 female obsessive, hysterical, or depressive patients (aged 21-49 yrs) to therapist interventions that used humorous or nonhumorous control reactions. Ss' reactions to humorous vs nonhumorous interventions were measured by having them respond to 12 recorded simulations of psychotherapeutic interactions. Results show that (1) nonhumorous interventions were consistently favored over humorous interventions, and (2) the extent of preference for nonhumorous interventions depended on the interaction between personality and kind of humor.

Gold, M. (1985). Sexual jokes. *Medical Aspects of Human Sexuality, 19,* 210-214. Discusses the psychodynamics of sexual humor, focusing on what it means in terms of anxieties when patients tell such jokes and how physicians can respond to them appropriately. (0 ref)

Golub, R. R. (1979). An investigation of the effect of use of humor in counseling (Doctoral dissertation, Purdue University). *Dissertation Abstracts International, 40,* 2837.

Gomez, E. A., & O'Connell, W. E. (1987). Re-viewing the initial interview. *Journal of Integrative & Eclectic Psychotherapy, 6,* 37-45. Suggests that the initial interview between patient and client is an artful, creative, and unique therapeutic interaction that should be periodically reassessed to increase its usefulness to psychotherapeutic strategies. The resolution of apparent dualisms and the processes (psychotherapeutic, imaginative, and creative) are emphasized. It is suggested that imaginative and creative empathy, human connectedness, and sense of humor are important in that they add new dimensions to the diagnostic and therapeutic purposes of the initial interview.

Greenwald, H. (1975). Humor in psychotherapy. *Journal of Contemporary Psychotherapy, 7,* 113-116. Describes the author's experiences as a psychotherapist, emphasizing the importance of humor as a tool for achieving therapeutic insight. Humor as a mirroring technique is also exemplified, and the ways it assists in the process of splitting the observation ego from the active ego, especially important for persons who feel helpless, are noted.

Grotjahn, M. (1972). The qualities of the group therapist. In H. I. Kaplan & B. J. Sadock (Eds.), *New Models for Group Therapy.* New York: E. P. Dutton. Contends that the group therapist's awareness of himself and of his impact on people is of central and decisive importance in the dynamics and outcome of his group's interaction. Qualifications of the group psychotherapist are discussed, including spontaneity, trust, performance, humor, transferences, fallibility, mental health, and attitudes toward his marriage, wife, and children. (22 ref)

Grotjahn, M. (1971). Laughter in group psychotherapy. *International Journal of Group Psychotherapy, 21,* 234-238. Suggests that while a therapist does not cry with or rage at his patients, he should feel free to laugh with them. By showing reaction to the group emotional freedom is demonstrated, and laughter is considered to be a sign of freedom. However, laughter in group or individual therapy should be sincere. Jokes are considered a good method of making an interpretation. Also, discussed is (a) the joke as resistance, (b) the laughter of mastery, and (c) laughter at the unmasking of the unconscious. It is concluded that laughter "in therapy is as welcome as any other sign of spontaneity, strength, mastery, and freedom."

Haig, R. A. (1986). Therapeutic uses of humor. *American Journal of Psychotherapy, 40,* 543-553. Examines psychological aspects of humor from a Freudian perspective and explores the relationship between humor and childhood development. The role of humor in psychotherapy is reviewed. 15 constructive and 5 destructive aspects of humor are noted. Brief clinical examples from a case are given.

Hammer, E. F. (1975). Imagery: The artistic style in the therapist's communications. *Art Psychotherapy, 2,* 225-231. Discusses the "special affinity" between the psychoanalyst and the artist. Both have a common dedication to unify life, enhance the self, and deliver the truth so as to experience richly, feel genuinely, and assist in personal growth. Other similarities and some differences are suggested. The artist communicates himself; the analyst communicates with the patient. The analyst can learn much from the artist about imagery. A method of interpretation is presented which employs imagery to achieve insight. Metaphors are first cousins to images, and both bring feelings to felt awareness. It is noted that humor, poetry, parables, and literature have similar functions of cutting through cliches and facilitating insight. Examples are given of interpretations to a masochist, an intellectualized obsessive compulsive, a hysteric, and others. (32 ref)

Hand, I., & Lamontagne, Y. (1974). Paradoxical intention and behavioral techniques in short-term psychotherapy. *Canadian Psychiatric Association Journal, 19,* 501-507. Notes that the logotherapeutic technique of paradoxical intention, and several behavior therapy techniques use almost identical ways of treating patients with phobias, obsessions, and anxiety states. The techniques involve confronting the patient with stimuli that elicit anxiety or avoidance, discouraging overreaction to symptoms, and encouraging alternative responses. Patients learn various ways of coping during the confrontation trials, and therapists use a variety of ways to motivate the patients. V. Frankl asserts that humor is useful for motivating patients to cooperate in treatment. The present authors, using group behavior therapy for agoraphobics, have observed that the patients use humor spontaneously as a main coping mechanism. (36 ref)

Harper, R. A. (1984). The goal is the process: To enjoy. *Psychotherapy in Private Practice, 2,* 21-26. Discusses the importance of enjoyment, both as a philosophical tenet of life and a creed for psychotherapeutic practice. The author's attitudes toward long-term hedonism as an approach to life and practice are discussed with reference to 3 influential colleagues. It is suggested that the lack of a sense of humor and lightness about oneself and life is a hazard for both the psychotherapist and his/her clients. In both cases, the emphasis is on process and the process is to enjoy.

Heuscher, J. E. (1980). The role of humor and folklore themes in psychotherapy. *American Journal of Psychiatry, 127,* 1546-1549. Humor has a useful role, mainly as a deconstituting force, whereas folklore emphasizes the revitalization of existence. Yet humor can be harmful in situations where there is a lack of mutual respect, and it can be growth-retarding if it becomes a substitute for needed change. The effectiveness of humor and folklore themes is proportional to the genuineness of the interpersonal relationship. In folklore, humor reinforces the injunction to seek wider worlds beyond the one that has become monotonous and stifling. Humor and folklore themes can, therefore, prove helpful when used judiciously in psychotherapy. Clinical examples are presented. (13 ref)

Hickson, J. (1977). Humor as an element in the counseling relationship. *Psychology, 14,* 60-68. Considers the role of humor in the therapeutic process. Psychoanalytic, drive-reduction, and cognitive-perceptual models of humor have been proposed by counseling theorists. Humor can be used to evaluate the client's dynamic state: An inhibition of responses to humorous stimuli indicates psychological disturbance. Production and appreciation of humor by the therapist can facilitate interpersonal exchanges through their expression of empathy, positive regard, genuineness, and concreteness. Production and appreciation of humor by the client provide clues to repressions and anxieties, show a readiness to disclose previously disguised thoughts and feelings, and help the client put psychic distance between the neurotic symptom and the self. Humor becomes a negative factor if the therapist uses it to exploit the patient, allows it to trivialize serious subjects or jeopardize therapeutic authority, or permits it to be used by the client as a defensive strategy. Introduction of appropriate humor after trust in the therapeutic relationship has been established increases the likelihood of positive results. (43 ref)

Hinton, W. L. (1981). Buffoni, buffoneria e senso del ridicolo (Fools, fooling, and the sense of the ridiculous). *Rivista di Psicologia Analitica, 12,* 129-141. Analyzes the archetypal, magical, ritual, and dynamic functions of laughter and the laughable, linking them with creative psychotherapy. The roles of court jesters, Shakespearean fools, and "holy fools" are discussed in relation to their flexibility in adapting their seemingly absurd roles to all situations and to their metaphysical existence outside the structures of reality and society. The symbolism of "the Fool" in the Greater Arcana of the Tarot cards and the role of the ritual fool as shaman in different cultures are also discussed, and the author calls for the symbolic assumption of the fool's creative simplicity on the part of Jungian psychotherapists. It is suggested that defensive attitudes and the inability to visualize oneself in humorous situations characterize untreatable psychiatric patients.

Hirdes, S. C. (1988). The use of humor and guided imagery in the enhancement of self-disclosure (Doctoral dissertation, University of Northern Arizona). *Dissertation Abstracts International, 48,* 1709.

Huber, A. T. (1974). The effect of humor on client discomfort in the counseling interview (Doctoral dissertation, Lehigh University). *Dissertation Abstracts International, 35,* 1980.

Humberger, F. E. (1985). Logotherapy's impact on counseling the executive. Special Issue: Viktor E. Frankl--80 years. *International Forum for Logotherapy, 8,* 47-53. The author describes his efforts as a business executive turned logotherapist who spends his professional life assisting others who are in the business world. Examples are presented to show how self-distancing and attitude modulation have made an impact on his own life and the lives of other executives he has counseled over the past 22 yrs. The logotherapy methods that were applied to an alcoholic executive are described: attitude modification, dereflection, and paradoxical intention and humor. (1 ref)

Ietswaart, W. L. (1988). Humor and the psychoanalyst. *Zeitschrift fur Psychoanalytische Theorie und Praxis, 3,* 187-198. Defines humor as the capacity to consciously and simultaneously make essential contradictions, often resulting from the different impact that a word/statement can have on secondary and primary thought processes. A resemblance to the psychoanalyst's work is noted, in which the defenses against primary process diminish and words obtain a conscious meaning in both the secondary process and primary process. Humor and psychoanalysis reveal the split between rational and irrational ego aspects. When applied at the right moment, humor can be useful in psychoanalysis and can help in analyzing one's own countertransference; however, its use may be contraindicated in cases of severe neurotic suffering. (German abstract)

Isohanni, M. (1986). Humor in the therapeutic community. *Psychiatria Fennica, 17,* 137-144. Discusses the role of humor in psychotherapy as a component of the therapeutic community principle and practice. Humor, an integral part of human interaction and the psychotherapeutic process, can be misused. In insight-oriented individual psychotherapy, humor has a very limited role. In mainly supportive-oriented psychotherapy, it can be used as a component of an adaptive defense organization. In the therapeutic setting, it is essential that the therapist laugh and smile with, not at, the patient. Staff members of the therapeutic community must be able to be serious or humorous according to the situation, as mature humor can strengthen group spirit and ward atmosphere, and immature humor can have detrimental effects on the same.

Jablonski, B., & Range, B. (1984). O humor e so-riso? Algumas consideracoes sobre os estudos em humor (On humor and laughter: Various considerations of studies of humor). *Arquivos Brasileiros de Psicologia, 36,* 133-140. Reviews the roles of such factors as incongruency, surprise, superiority, and tension relief in the humor process. New methods for carrying out research, including the use of psychotherapy, are discussed. (English abstract) (17 ref)

Jackson, S., & Chable, D. G. (1985). Engagement: A critical aspect of family therapy practice. *Australian & New Zealand Journal of Family Therapy, 6,* 65-69. Discusses the importance of client engagement in the therapeutic process. Engagement is described as a complex, reciprocal process in the client-therapist relationship, referring to the specific adjustments that the therapist makes to him/herself over time to accommodate to the family under therapy. Engagement is discussed in relation to its use as a source of information and as the basis of treatment. Several strategies for facilitating engagement are described, including circular questioning and neutrality, joining, problem clarification, linking affect and behavior, expressing warmth and empathy, and using humor and spontaneity. (13 ref)

Johnson, D. R., Agresti, A., Jacob, M. C., & Nies, K. (1990). Building a therapeutic community through specialized groups in a nursing home. Special Issue: Mental health in the nursing home. *Clinical Gerontologist, 9,* 203-217. Describes the development and implementation in a nursing home care unit of a group program in which a therapeutic persona was used to create community feeling. The staff created a playful interpersonal environment through humor, mild self-disclosure, and provocation that encouraged community members to experience the suppressed negative aspects of their own experience. The success of these techniques appeared to be due to the outlet they provided for residents' aggression. A transcript of a group discussion is included.

Johnston, R. A. (1990). Humor: A preventive health strategy. XIIIth International Round Table for the Advancement of Counselling Conference (1988, Calgary, Canada). *International Journal for the Advancement of Counselling, 13,* 257-265. The literature suggests that humor can foster the counseling relationship, can help in understanding clients, and can be used to overcome client resistance. The role of humor in helping the client cope and build social supports is discussed, and the capacity of humor to function as a proactive, preventive health strategy is explored. It is asserted that the profession has only begun to appreciate the benefits of humor to both sides of the counseling relationship.

Kahn, E. M. (1984). Group treatment interventions for schizophrenics. *International Journal of Group Psychotherapy, 34,* 149-153. Reports a set of techniques developed by the present author and his colleagues that facilitate group treatment of schizophrenics, based on an 8-yr group therapy effort with outpatient chronic schizophrenics. Techniques include the use of structured exercises, style of interpretation, paradox, and humor. Through this interpersonally focused treatment, patients may develop a greater capacity to achieve and tolerate closeness and may begin to overcome the isolation, depression, and meaninglessness that have pervaded their lives. (11 ref)

Kaneko, S. Y. (1972). The role of humor in psychotherapy (Doctoral dissertation, Smith College, School for Social Work). *Dissertation Abstracts International, 32,* 5344.

Kazrin, A., Durac, J., & Agteros, T. (1979). Meta-meta analysis: A new method for evaluating therapy outcome. *Behaviour Research & Therapy, 17,* 397-399. Humorously evaluates the efficacy of psychotherapy and the effect of independent variables on dependent variables. It is concluded that psychotherapy is of definite tentative value for people in need of help, excepting those who have psychological problems. (5 ref)

Kerrigan, J. F. (1983). The perceived effect of humor on six facilitative therapeutic conditions (Doctoral dissertation, University of Arizona). *Dissertation Abstracts International, 44,* 1694.

Killinger, B. E. (1978). The place of humour in adult psychotherapy (Doctoral dissertation, York University, Toronto, Canada). *Dissertation Abstracts International, 38,* 3400.

Klauber, J. (1967). The psychoanalyst as a person. *Psyche, Stuttgart, 21,* 745-757. Despite the necessary emphasis on developing psychoanalysis as an objective method, "it is a fact that when psychoanalysts discuss a case, almost each one attributes importance to a different part of the treatment." This, along with the experience that some patients cannot be treated by some analysts, suggests participation of the therapist's ego structure (not to be understood as "countertransference") in the treatment process. "Each analyst must modify the method to fit his own personality needs, say his need for clarification, communication, expression of humor, his passivity, or tendency to rationalization. . . ."

Klein, J. P. (1976). Rationality and humour in counselling. *Canadian Counsellor, 11,* 28-32. Suggests that although humor is frequently employed by counselors on a nonsystematic basis, it is a relevant therapeutic variable in need of theoretical explication. The role of humor is demonstrated by contrasting it with the function of reason, and some of the psychological mechanisms of humor are explained. Drawing on examples from his own counseling experience, the author discusses such related topics as the new diagnostic category of "identity crisis," the understanding of counselor training as a form of operant conditioning, and the role of theory in counseling. (French abstract)

Klein, J. P. (1974). On the use of humour in counseling. *Canadian Counsellor, 8,* 233-237. Describes the techniques of famous comic playwrights in an attempt to establish prominent parallelisms between the literary and therapeutic use of humor. On the first level of comparison, the sources of human belief in what is true and real are explained. It is shown that they rest on certain subjective but rarely questioned assumptions about human nature. Using the well-developed literary devices as a model for illustrating the manifold ways in which reality can be interpreted, the ways in which the counselor can profitably employ similar strategies with his clients are discussed. On a deeper level of comparison, it is suggested that the miniature world of the theater and the phenomenological universe of the client both emerge from an arbitrary verbal syntax which circumscribes the number and nature of the possible alternative explanations of reality. The author's assumption about truth is that by using the model as a form of intellectual inquiry, results of psychological investigation can be confirmed and advanced by external disciplines. (French summary)

Koelin, J. M. (1988). A phenomenological investigation of humor in psychotherapy (Doctoral dissertation, University of Tennessee). *Dissertation Abstracts International, 49,* 1391.

Korb, L. J. (1988). Humor: A tool for the psychoanalyst. *Issues in Ego Psychology, 11,* 45-54. Presents a case for the use of humor in psychoanalysis and suggests that the use of humor intervention affords the analyst a methodology to augment the psychoanalytic process and facilitate structural changes but, not as a means of either replacement or reconstruction thereof. Humor may be used as a triggering device, as a bridge. Case material is provided to offer additional insight into the use of humor in psychotherapy. Humor intervention is not intended either to circumvent or bypass resistances, rather it seeks to bridge gaps not transversed by other aspects of the psychoanalytic approach.

Korb, L. J. (1988). The psychoanalyst's use of humor as a tool for augmenting the psychoanalytic process and for facilitating structural changes (Doctoral dissertation, Union for Experimenting Colleges & Universities, Ohio). *Dissertation Abstracts International, 49,* 1945.

Kraiker, C. (1986). Quarks und superquarks: Grundprinzipien der Neuen Psychotherapie (Nonsense and supernonsense: Basic principles of the new psychotherapy). *Hypnose und Kognition, 3,* 60-63. Presents a tongue-in-cheek review of the basic principles of the "new psychotherapy" (NP) (i.e., current fads and fashions in psychotherapy). The NP's emphasis on a holistic approach, circular processes, trust in the constructive powers of the unconscious, process orientation, and Oriental wisdom is described and contrasted with the treatment of comparable concepts in the "old psychotherapy."

Kridler, K. L. (1987). The relationship of sense of humor presence and use to stress, adaptivity, pathology, and prognosis for treatment in a combined substance abuse/psychiatric hospitalized sample (Doctoral dissertation, University of Akron, Ohio). *Dissertation Abstracts International, 48,* 1801.

Kropiunigg, U. (1985). Warum wirkt Psychotherapie? (Why does psychotherapy work?) *Zeitschrift fur Individualpsychologie, 10,* 57-71. Describes various mechanisms and processes that explain the effectiveness of psychotherapy, and suggests 4 factors that deserve greater attention with regard to their role in enhancing therapeutic efforts. These factors are (1) using the integrative power of humor, (2) developing a relaxed attitude on the part of the therapist, (3) encouraging the patient to tell the whole story, and (4) developing an adequate theoretical framework. Individual psychology practitioners are urged to develop a theoretical analysis of the will to power. (English abstract) (17 ref)

Kubie, L. S. (1970). The destructive potential of humor in psychotherapy. *American Journal of Psychiatry, 127,* 861-866. Asserts that the use of humor by the psychiatrist is potentially destructive to the psychotherapeutic relationship. Sometimes experienced therapists can use humor without doing harm, but beginning therapists who imitate them may do irremediable damage. Too often the patient's stream of feeling and thought is diverted from spontaneous channels by the therapist's humor; it may even be arrested and blocked. Toward the end of successful therapy, as a patient gradually achieves a progressively deeper self-understanding, gentle and sympathetic humor can sometimes help him to mobilize a determination to utilize his new insights so that he can limit, control, and guide the symptomatic expression of what remains of the neurotic process.

Labrentz, H. L. (1974). The effects of humor on the initial client-counselor relationship (Doctoral dissertation, University of Southern Mississippi). *Dissertation Abstracts International, 34,* 3875.

Lacroix, M. (1974). Humorous drawings and directed-reverie therapy of children. *Etudes Psychotherapiques, 15,* 17-27. Presents the case of a boy 12 yrs old, with high intelligence but failing in his school work. 23 of his 46 therapy sessions were devoted to his making humorous drawings of his own devising. Interpretations of 19 of these drawings show his progress in the therapy.

Lederman, S. (1988). "Humor: A tool for the psychoanalyst": Comment. *Issues in Ego Psychology, 11,* 55-59. Comments on L. J. Korb's (see PA, Vol 77:5333) article concerning the use of humor in psychoanalysis. The author concurs that humor can be a useful tool in encouraging the productive use of pleasure; the healthy expression of pleasure is one of the original therapeutic goals of psychoanalysis. The author elaborates on how dreams and jokes are similar in several respects (e.g., they arise from the unconscious and their use of displacement). The study of jokes and humor may allow penetration of the fascinating world of the unconscious.

Loewald, E. (1976). The development and uses of humour in a four-year-old's treatment. *International Review of Psycho-Analysis, 3,* 209-221. Discusses the uses of humor as a therapeutic tool, a diagnostic and prognostic indicator, and an outcome criterion in the psychoanalytic treatment of a 4-yr-old. Humor functioned as a "transitional point of view," facilitating integrative process much as a transitional object smooths the process of separation-individuation. Humor also functioned as an ego channel for libidinal and aggressive drives, thereby fostering integration and sublimation, rather than repression. The role of humor in negotiating 3 developmental hurdles involving anal and phallic conflicts, and termination are examined. The literature on humor, wit, and the comic is briefly reviewed.

Lukas, E. (1982). The "birthmarks" of paradoxical intention. *International Forum for Logotherapy, 5,* 20-24. The origin of paradoxical intention is traced to logotherapy through an examination of 3 shared characteristics. These characteristics are (1) a focus on achieving a lasting change in inner attitudes through the development of a fundamental confidence in the future and the gain of a proper perspective on the relative importance of different objects, (2) attention on influencing rather than understanding the self and on the concept of self-distancing, and (3) the use of humor to get patients to recognize the nonsensical nature of their fears and compulsions.

Lynch, T. D. (1990). Quantitative analysis of the use of humor in psychotherapy: The strategic humor model of Ericksonian psychotherapy (Doctoral dissertation, Union Institute, Ohio). *Dissertation Abstracts International, 51,* 3138.

Marcus, N. N. (1990). Treating those who fail to take themselves seriously: Pathological aspects of humor. *American Journal of Psychotherapy, 44,* 423-432. Presents a method of analyzing humor in which patients are made aware of their own smiling and laughing. Patients can then be led to see that their external life situation has predisposed them to experience an intrapsychic event. This event is the spontaneous emergence of antithetical ideation into consciousness that has, in turn, given rise to 3 beliefs: (1) the ir-responsibility (unaccountability), (2) the incongruity, and (3) the inconsequentiality of the production and nature of this ideation. Two vignettes of patients illustrate how foreknowledge of the 3 beliefs can aid the therapist in working through what might otherwise be intractable pathology.

Marek, W. K. (1989). A study on the correlation between expressive and receptive humor and between sense of humor and intelligence (Doctoral Dissertation, United States International University, California). *Dissertation Abstracts International, 50,* 1255.

Martin, J. F. (1983). Humor in therapy: An observational study (Doctoral dissertation, University of Tennessee). *Dissertation Abstracts International, 44,* 1245.

Megdell, J. I. (1984). Relationship between counselor-initiated humor and client's self-perceived attraction in the counseling interview. *Psychotherapy, 21,* 517-523. Videotaped 30 quasi-analogical initial counseling sessions between 30 31-66 yr old clients and 10 29-57 yr old counselors from 2 alcoholism counseling centers. Immediately following the sessions, clients rated degrees of attraction to counselors and recorded instances of counselor-initiated humor rated as humorous or not humorous. Results support the contention that counselor-initiated shared humor in an initial counseling session enhanced clients' attraction for counselors. (25 ref)

Megdell, J. I. (1982). Relationship between counselor-initiated humor and client's self-perceived attraction in the counseling interview (Doctoral dissertation, California School of Professional Psychology, San Diego). *Dissertation Abstracts International, 42,* 4584.

Mozdzierz, G. J., Macchitelli, F. J., & Lisiecki, J. (1976). The paradox in psychotherapy: An Adlerian perspective. *Journal of Individual Psychology, 32,* 169-184. Discusses the use of a paradoxical strategy in psychotherapy, drawing on examples from the practice of Adler. The paradoxical strategy consists of therapeutic interventions directed toward increasing social interest which are seemingly self-contradictory and sometimes even absurd. These interventions join rather than oppose symptomatic behavior while containing qualities of empathy, encouragement, and humor. Instead of creating forces and then counterforces, the paradoxical strategy seeks to join the force of the patient's symptom by moving in the same direction he or she is moving. 12 functions of the paradoxical strategy are specified. (28 ref)

Murgatroyd, S. J. (1987). Humour as a tool in counselling and psychotherapy: A reversal-theory perspective. *British Journal of Guidance & Counselling, 15,* 225-236. Examines the therapeutic use of humor in the light of reversal theory of M. J. Apter (1982). It is suggested that the use of humor needs to be related to the motivational task implicit in the therapeutic interaction.

Nagaraja, J. (1985). Humour in psychotherapy. *Child Psychiatry Quarterly, 18,* 30-34. Describes the use of humor and folklore in psychotherapy and presents some examples of humorous stories and anecdotes appropriate for psychotherapy. It is suggested that psychodrama, role playing, and Gestalt therapy are also related to the humorous approach to psychotherapy. The development of humor in children is discussed, and theories of the development of humor and its beneficial effects are noted. (4 ref)

Neto, D. A. (1984). O uso do comico na defesa contra a angustia em psicoterapia analitica de grupo (The use of humor as a defense against anxiety in group analytic psychotherapy). *Alter-Jornal de Estudos Psicodinamicos, 14,* 37-44. Discusses the basis of group analytic psychotherapy and the telling of anecdotes as means of expressing a defense against stress and anguish. In this type of therapy the size of the group is unimportant. The essence is the relationship, often a conflictual one, between the individual and the group. Perception of oneself and others depends on the maturity of group members. Verbalization in analytic group psychotherapy, as well as in individual psychoanalysis, may be a type of realization. The telling of an anecdote during the session has the same characteristics as a dream and can be considered from a manifest and a latent level. The symbolic representation of a myth in a therapeutic analytic group is an unconscious phenomenon. Due to the various defenses used, knowledge of myths and legends leads to a better understanding of group dynamics. (English abstract)

Nies, D. C. (1982). A role of humor in psychotherapy: Reduction of dating anxiety in males (Doctoral dissertation, Fuller Theological Seminary, School of Psychology). *Dissertation Abstracts International, 43,* 1993-1994.

Nisenholz, B. (1983). Solving the psychotherapy glut. *Personnel & Guidance Journal, 61,* 535-536. Each year there is a succession of new psychotherapies, ranging from dianetics to nude marathon therapy, each claiming to be uniquely different from its rivals and reporting almost perfect success rates. Suggestions to end this glut of psychotherapies include (1) establishment of a "Sigmund" for Best Psychotherapy of the year, (2) TV advertisements in which clients compare their therapist and the "Brand-X" therapist, or (3) a "psychotherapy olympics" in which competing theorists race to complete successful treatment of matched clients. (2 ref)

O'Connell, W. E. (1972). Frankl, Adler, and spirituality. *Journal of Religion & Health, 11,* 134-138. Reports a paper given by the author, then President of the American Society of Adlerian Psychology, at the 1970 Alfred Adler Centennial. It is contended that Frankl misunderstands Adler and is not justified in creating his "Third Viennese School of Psychotherapy." Specifically, Adler's will to power, social interest, and use of humor in therapy are misunderstood. By power, it is stated, Adler did not imply raw aggression or crass force, but rather self-esteem related to social interest. Social interest is not identical with social conformity, as Frankl argues. Frankl's "spirituality" is viewed as identical with Adlerian social interest a striving toward completion that has very little to do with the theological meaning of the term. While Frankl has attracted many clergy by employing this term, it is alleged that he has also misinterpreted Adler's theory and that logotherapy "offers no advances beyond traditional Adlerian psychotherapy." Frankl is seen as an orthodox tutor who lectures to people, while Adler wanted clients to discover themselves through social interaction.

O'Connell, W. E. (1971). Adlerian action therapy. *Voices: The Art & Science of Psychotherapy, 7,* 22-27. With the emphasis in action therapy being on behavior, how this form of treatment helps teach patients to have a sense of humor, greater self-esteem, and greater commitment to treatment is described.

Offen, J. R., & Burrough, L. P. (1987). The benign aspects of the strong superego: Theoretical and technical considerations. *Current issues in Psychoanalytic Practice, 4,* 35-45. Discusses the benign aspects of the superego and the capacities for love and humor as related to a strong superego from the perspectives of S. Freud (1974), R. Schafer (1960), and J. Sandler (1960). It is argued that Schafer points to the paradox that Freud identified the benign aspects of the superego as crucial and then neglected to formulate a theory; Freud also used the terms ego and superego interchangeably at times. Sandler stresses the patient's identification with the parents, which furthers formation of the patient's benign, strong superego. Clinical examples and 3 short cases are presented.

Olson, H. A. (1976). The use of humor in psychotherapy. *Individual Psychologist, 13,* 34-37. Notes that humor can be very helpful in therapy, e.g., to establish a therapeutic relationship, to build or rebuild a positive sense of humor in the patient (the therapist acts as a model), to demonstrate acceptance and respect for the client, or to help clients see that their problems may have more facets than they originally believed. Laughter helps the client to feel control over problems. The therapist must use humor with sensitivity and skill and never at the client's expense. (6 ref)

Papp, P. (1982). Staging reciprocal metaphors in a couples group. *Family Process, 21,* 453-467. Describes an approach to couples therapy based on defining the reciprocal positions of each spouse in relation to a central theme. These positions and the theme around which they are organized are crystallized into visible forms through staged metaphors, when studied in relation to one another, the metaphors provide a holistic view of the relationship and are used as an artifice for change. The group serves as a theatrical setting in which the marital relationships are "staged" and examined with humor and objectivity. An atmosphere of experimentation is created, which is necessary for carrying out unconventional tasks. (21 ref)

Pasquali, G. (1987). Some notes on humour in psychoanalysis. *International Review of Psycho-Analysis, 14,* 231-236. Investigates the reasons why humor in psychoanalysis is rarely written about, noting that the rare papers on humor approach the subject only, or mainly, from a theoretical point of view. Yet it is believed hardly imaginable that an analysis can be carried out without some humorous interchange between patient and analyst. Clinical examples showing both the patient's and the analyst's use of humor are given, and the meaning and function of humor are discussed. (French, German & Spanish abstracts)

Peterson, J. P., & Pollio, H. R. (1982). Therapeutic effectiveness of differentially targeted humorous remarks in group psychotherapy. *Private Practice, West Palm Beach, FL, 6,* 39-50. Video records of 5 sessions of a single therapy group of 6-11 22-34 yr old patients were scored for the occurrence of laughing, smiling, and talking. Successive 5-min intervals were also scored for therapeutic level through ratings derived from the Hill Interaction Matrix. Humorous remarks were categorized according to humor target: self, other in group, and generalized other. Results indicate that most humorous remarks were directed at some specific target and that over 50% of these remarks were negative in tone. Results also reveal that remarks targeted at others in the group tended to decrease therapeutic effectiveness; remarks targeted at individuals or institutions not presently in the group increased therapeutic effectiveness. Self-targeted remarks produced inconsistent effects. Findings are discussed in terms of their significance for a more general analysis of group humor as well as in terms of their more specific implications for therapeutic interventions. (10 ref)

Pinegar, P. W. (1984). Client self-exploration and humor in psychotherapy (Doctoral dissertation, Kent State University). *Dissertation Abstracts International, 44,* 3018.

Poland, W. S. (1990). The gift of laughter: On the development of a sense of humor in clinical analysis. *Psychoanalytic Quarterly, 59,* 197-225. Describes the components of the mature humor described by R. Sabatini (1921) and addresses the implications of the "gift" of humor. Four vignettes illustrate patients' gradual transitions from humorlessness or conflicted humor to more mature senses of humor. The development of humor in clinical analysis is discussed in terms of the (1) nature of words and the patient's development of humor, (2) analyst as an other in the analytic process and the patient's development of humor, and (3) analyst's own sense of humor and the patient's development of humor.

Poland, W. S. (1971). The place of humor in psychotherapy. *American Journal of Psychiatry, 128,* 635-637. Describes 2 cases in which humor furthered the development of insight during psychotherapy. It is suggested that before using humor, the therapist should evaluate the strength of the therapeutic alliance since humor can be destructive. When humor is integrated and spontaneous, however, it denotes a good therapeutic alliance and is a useful tool for the therapist's intervention.

Polivka, J. (1987). Cartoon humor as an aid in therapy. *Clinical Gerontologist, 7,* 63-67. Presents the case of a 55-yr-old widow in which humor was used by the psychotherapist to help the therapeutic process. (0 ref)

Post, J. (1966). Putting a lid on the id. *Psychiatric Quarterly, 40,* 472-481. An over-treated patient can be extremely seductive in leading a therapist down the garden path of primary process. By refusing to be seduced and by responding favorably only to healthy material, the therapist can help alter this maladaptive therapeutic posture. The active role in "untreating" includes conditioning techniques and the judicious use of humor.

Powell, G. S., & Gazda, G. M. (1979). "Cleaning out the trash": A case study in Adlerian family counseling. *Journal of Individual Psychology, 35,* 45-57. Presents the case history of a family's 9-session Adlerian counseling experience in which group support, encouragement, humor, conflict withdrawal, and child-rearing education helped family members to change their behavior. In addition, the family learned to implement many of these techniques themselves and to encourage each other in the process. It is also noted that the 4 traditional stages of counseling (establishment of rapport, assessment, interpretation, and reorientation) recurred throughout the focus of each session. (6 ref)

Prerost, F. J. (1989). Intervening during crises of life transitions: Promoting a sense of humor as a stress moderator. *Counselling Psychology Quarterly, 2,* 475-480. Discusses the humorous imagery situation technique, designed to promote a sense of humor in psychotherapy clients, while allowing for release of personal conflicts and anxieties. Methods of intervention using the factors of absurdity, incongruity, and exaggeration are discussed in promoting an adaptive sense of humor. The technique appears well-suited for normative crisis intervention.

Prerost, F. J. (1989). Humor as an intervention strategy during psychological treatment: Imagery and incongruity. *Psychology: A Journal of Human Behavior, 26,* 34-40. To promote the therapeutic benefits of humor, a treatment technique incorporating imagery procedures has been developed that can be used during psychotherapy. The humorous imagery situation technique permits the therapist to generate humor from imagery scenes. The humor generated assists in the resolution of personal conflicts and in the lessening of individual distress. The client is directed toward developing a lifestyle focused on using laughter to resolve areas of personal distress.

Prerost, F. J. (1988). Use of humor and guided imagery in therapy to alleviate stress. *Journal of Mental Health Counseling, 10,* 16-22. Describes the case of a 28-yr-old man, presenting with sleep difficulties, poor appetite, and a low tolerance for criticism on the job, to illustrate the use of the humorous imagery situation technique to relieve symptoms and promote better stress management.

Prerost, F. J. (1985). A procedure using imagery and humor in psychotherapy: Case application with longitudinal assessment. *Journal of Mental Imagery, 9,* 67-76. Developed the Humorous Imagery Situation Technique (HIST) to alleviate apprehension and reduce patient conflicts during therapy with mildly disturbed patients. The HIST allows for the therapist to assist in reviving a healthy sense of humor in patients, and has been used with 18-56 yr old patients exhibiting mild depression and anxiety. A longitudinal assessment of HIST use of a 19-yr-old female revealed an enhancement of self-descriptions during treatment and in a follow-up.

Prerost, F. J. (1984). Evaluating the systematic use of humor in psychotherapy with adolescents. *Journal of Adolescence, 7,* 267-276. Presents the humorous imagery situation technique (HIST), a procedure developed by the present author (1981) to use humor effectively in therapy within a guiding framework. The HIST integrates the directed daydream with the humor-producing elements of incongruity and is believed to be particularly useful in therapy with inhibited or isolated adolescents. The HIST procedure is reviewed, focusing on developmental factors and therapy assessments, and the successful treatment of a 16-yr-old girl is described. (33 ref)

Ravella, N. F. (1988). The serious business of humor in therapy. *Journal of Strategic & Systemic Therapies, 7,* 35-40. Notes that recent developments in the application of constructivist thinking to psychotherapy have created a context in which humor can be viewed differently from the past when the emphasis was on expressing painful feelings. This constructivist foundation permits the use of humor by the therapist for its therapeutic value. The influence of cybernetic thinking is mentioned as another element in the change in perspective over the past 30 yrs. An example of the use of humor to solve a problem of sexual disinterest is described.

Reisner, A. D. (1990). The use of cognitive and behavioral methods and neoanalytic conceptualization to treat a case of morbid fear of soiling. *Phobia Practice & Research Journal, 3*, 81-86. Presents the case of a 30-yr-old man whose phobia concerning fecal accidents was effectively and rapidly treated using cognitive behavioral therapy and a neoanalytic conceptualization. Along with conventional techniques for working with panic symptoms, the client was helped to see humor in his malady, which was seen as partly based on a reaction formation against anal sadistic impulses. Humor was used to facilitate insight and to promote desensitization to threatening material.

Reynes, R. L., & Allen, A. (1987). Humor in psychotherapy: A view. *American Journal of Psychotherapy, 41*, 260-270. Offers a perspective on the use of humor as both an assessment tool and as a therapeutic tool within the context of a psychodynamic approach to psychotherapy. While mindful of the potential difficulties that attend its introduction into the treatment situation, there is an attempt to balance this position through a consideration of the appropriate conditions and modes of operation under which a humor-enriched approach may be efficacious. It is concluded that proper employment requires an informed awareness of the risks and benefits along with the parameters for its use.

Riebel, L. K. (1985). Usurpation: Strategy and metaphor. *Psychotherapy, 22*, 595-603. Delineates rationales for therapists' joining client delusions, calling this process usurpation. It is suggested that usurpation is common to many forms of therapy. Acceptance, exaggeration, provoking, preempting, restraining, role-playing, humor, and prescribing the symptom (paradoxical intention) are described as sharing the general approach of entering, rather than opposing, client beliefs. Clinical vignettes illustrate how usurpation works to produce cracks in the patient's delusion. When the therapist goes along with the delusions and attempts to expand on it or take it to its logical end, the patient begins to doubt the reality of the delusion. It is emphasized that usurpation should not be employed by the inexperienced therapist. The practitioner must be able to establish a good alliance, judge if a client is ready to be invaded, create a suitable vehicle, foresee likely consequences, and refrain from acting out his/her own conflicts, frustrations, or hostility. Originally described for use with delusional clients, usurpation is placed in a continuum of techniques for use with mildly to moderately impaired persons. (47 ref)

Roberts, R. C. (1987). Psychotherapeutic virtues and the grammar of faith. *Journal of Psychology & Theology, 15*, 191-204. Presents a method for integrating secular psychotherapies into Christian practice (the virtues approach) that promises more fine-grained assessment of continuities and discontinuities between Christian theory and practice and secular theory and practice and more hope of a richly and distinctively Christian psychotherapy. Albert Ellis's (1977) therapy is examined as a test case. Three rational-emotive therapy (RET) virtues (equanimity, self-acceptance, and a sense of humor) are compared grammatically (structurally) with their Christian counterparts, and suggestions are made about consequences for Christian RET.

Roller, B., & Lankester, D. (1987). Characteristic processes and therapeutic strategies in a homogeneous group for depressed outpatients. *Small Group Behavior, 18*, 565-576. Identified the characteristic processes and therapeutic strategies that have been used with an open-ended homogeneous group of 80 depressed adult outpatients. Most Ss conformed to Diagnostic and Statistical Manual of Mental Disorders (DSM-III) diagnosis of dysthymic disorder. Ss met in groups of 5-15 each week; cotherapy was the mode of treatment for 20 of the 30 mo of treatment. Therapeutic strategies included humor and paradoxical intent. 25% of the Ss were prescribed medication, mostly tricyclic antidepressants or lithium carbonate. The majority of the group were considered successful in overcoming depression, as determined by achieving a modicum of success in at least 1 of 3 criteria: discontinuation of medication, obtaining a job, and establishing a positive relationship or friendship.

Roncoli, M. (1974). Bantering: A therapeutic strategy with obsessional patients. *Perspectives in Psychiatric Care, 12,* 171-175. Presents the thesis that the therapist, like Cervantes, can be a psychological humorist, assisting the obsessional patient to gain insight through the use of bantering. M. Cervantes is described is described as the forerunner of the psychological humorist, especially in Don Quixote. It is suggested that bantering is meant to be a caricature of the patient's behavior, a humorous exaggeration where the therapist appears both a benevolent and ridiculing authority. Bantering in therapy implies that the therapist is making an attempt to mobilize constructively his own feelings of exasperation and the patient's anger. When employing humor, the therapist takes the risk of appearing imperfect, fallible, and human. But he also gives the patient the license to behave imperfectly, fallibly, and humanly. (21 ref)

Rose, G. J. (1969). "King Lear" and the use of humor in treatment. *Journal of the American Psychoanalytic Association, 17,* 927-940. King Lear's Fool confronts the King with the reality the King wishes to deny and interprets the King's castration anxiety and its derivatives. The therapist, operating from a stable therapeutic alliance, may use humor to mobilize benign aspects of the superego, attack archaic elements of the superego, and support the ego. Humor may help lift repressions by utilizing negation and by fostering a favorable balance between the observing part of the patient's ego and the analyst. Humor may be useful in transmitting reality across ego boundaries in the right blend of distance and closeness. (27 ref)

Rosenheim, E., & Golan, G. (1986). Patients' reactions to humorous interventions in psychotherapy. *American Journal of Psychotherapy, 40,* 110-124. Explored the preference of patients for humorous or nonhumorous therapist interventions, 36 female hysterical, obsessive, and depressive patients (aged 22-47 yrs) were presented with 3 functional kinds of humorous interventions: emotional confrontation, anxiety reduction, and perspective development. Ss' reactions to humorous vs nonhumorous interventions were measured by having them listen and respond to 12 recorded simulations of psychotherapeutic interactions. Data indicate that personality make-up had a differential effect on the appreciation of humorous vs nonhumorous interventions. The functional type of humor had no effect on Ss' attitudes nor was there an interaction between type of humor and styles of personality. Ss consistently favored the nonhumorous interventions, but the degree of this preference varied according to personality style. Obsessive Ss stood out in their ardent repudiation of humorous interventions. Hysterical Ss rejected humor aimed at emotional confrontation and anxiety reduction but not humor aimed at perspective development, while depressive Ss exhibited the opposite pattern. Results suggest that the desirability of utilizing humor in therapy depends on a multiplicity of parameters. (27 ref)

Rosenheim, E. (1974). Humor in psychotherapy: An interactive experience. *American Journal of Psychotherapy, 28,* 584-591. Discusses the uses of humor as a psychotherapeutic technique. The use of a humorous orientation requires the therapist to be relatively free from defensiveness and ready for mutuality with the patient. Humorous exchanges during therapy can improve a patient's ability to perceive himself and his relations to others accurately, can serve as affect releasers for depressed, schizoid, or obsessive patients, and can help overcome the resistance of adolescent patients. It is concluded that humor is valuable in psychotherapy because its intrinsic qualities of intimacy, humaneness, and directness help the therapist and patient form a closer, more informal working alliance.

Ross, J. L. (1988). Lucy Ricardo as a model for strategic therapy: The great peach juice cure. *Journal of Strategic & Systemic Therapies, 7,* 44-47. Presents a case study that relates how a mother broke the pattern of escalating power struggles between herself and her 10-yr-old son by developing creative strategies using absurd humor of the dizzy Lucy Ricardo. The power that clients have to effect therapeutic changes in their own lives is also demonstrated.

Rule, W. R. (1977). Increasing self-modeled humor. *Rational Living, 12,* 7-9. Presents the idea that psychotherapy is education and such has implications for encouraging the production of self-directed humor. A quasi-experiment exploring a humor-based technique that combines Adlerian and Rational Emotive Therapy approaches is described. 10 students enrolled in a seminar kept a log of undesirable negative thoughts and feelings about self and others. They were instructed to use humorous exaggeration and to tape-record their statements. The self-modeled humor exercise had an effect on the self-monitored thoughts and feelings.

Ruvelson, L. (1988). The empathic use of sarcasm: Humor in psychotherapy from a self psychological perspective. *Clinical Social Work Journal, 16,* 297-305. A case is made for the therapeutic benefits of well-timed, prudently ventured sarcastic comments directed at persons in the patients' lives, including the therapist, who are experienced as failing them. Literature on use of humor in therapy is reviewed. The circumstances under which humor may be experienced empathically are suggested, as well as instances in which it may be contraindicated. Case vignettes of 2 female patients (aged 24 and 29 yrs old) illustrate how humor can be incorporated into an overall therapeutic style and be productive as well as pleasurable for both patient and therapist.

Salameh, W. A. (1993, September/October). Humor Immersion Training. *Humor and Health Letter,* pp. 1-4. Discusses different humor development modalities used in Humor Immersion Training (HIT) Workshops. Describes and illustrates the humor creation techniques of overstatement, understatement, incongruity, reversal, and wordplay. Offers practical suggestions for individuals wishing to expand their sense of humor.

Salameh, W. A. (1993, July/August). Clinical observations on teaching humor. *Humor and Health Letter,* pp. 1-5. Explores the persona projected by the psychotherapist in psychotherapy, and suggests the reevaluation of the traditional persona in favor of a more humorous and creative presence. Differentiates humor from its deformations of sarcasm, putdowns, racism, sexism, and ethnic slurs. Discusses various levels of humor absorption in different individuals and the differing perceptions of what is considered to be humorous by different persons.

Salameh, W. A. (1992). Humor, psychotherapeutic icons, and the missing link in psychotherapy. Abstracted in: J. Stora-Sandor (Ed.), *Proceedings of the 10th International Humor Congress.* Paris, France: Université Paris VII, International Society For Humor Studies. Reviews common patient complaints that psychotherapy is too complicated, that it is painful and confusing, and that psychotherapists are impersonal. Examines traditionally held psychotherapeutic icons that the therapist needs to be emotionally distant and is discouraged from taking creative risks that could lead to therapeutic breakthroughs. Proposes the term "Humorophobia" to describe therapists' fear of humor as a therapeutic tool. Suggests that humor is the missing link in the evolutionary process of psychotherapy to help bridge the aforecited gaps experienced by both therapists and patients. Discusses seven clinical humor techniques: humor to debunk the oppression of meaningfulness, humor to create a "fascia nova," humor to pin down semiarticulated feelings, humor to enliven psychotherapy, humor to seed new meanings, humor to deflate boredom and repetitiveness, and humor to illuminate the path of psychodynamic linkages.

Salameh, W. A. (1991). *Humor Immersion Training Manual.* San Diego, CA: Southern California Consulting Associates. Presents a hands-on systematic approach for developing one's sense of humor. Several humor development modalities are identified, with a review of the benefits of humor and some of the attitudinal blocks that can stunt the individual's sense of humor. Numerous humor development tools and exercises are offered throughout the Manual to help readers practice their humor development skills.

Salameh, W. A. (1990). Critical equations in launching a clinical practice. In E. Margenau (Ed.), *The Encyclopedic Handbook of Private Practice* (pp. 48-66). New York: Gardner Press. Reviews some of the factors that are deemed helpful for success in clinical practice, including operational and attitudinal factors. Discusses the concept of attitude redirection. Notes how the adoption of a humorous perspective can contribute to productive interactions with patients, colleagues, and other associates by carrying a soothing message of lightheartedness and alleviation. Reviews some of the myths and realities about psychotherapy. Comments on developing a comprehensive working alliance with patients that would include humor and would ultimately develop into a corrective emotional experience for the patient's benefit.

Salameh, W. A. (1989). Treating Achilles' heel: Differentiation of depressive states and clinical intervention with the depressed patient. In M. Yapko (Ed.), *Brief Therapy Approaches to Treating Anxiety and Depression* (pp. 64-105). New York: Brunner/Mazel. Examines how depression presents itself clinically in different patient populations, and analyzes the therapist's stumbling blocks in treating depressed patients. A specific eight-step program for clinical intervention with the depressed patient is presented including how humor can fit within this model. The use of humorous metaphors and indirect suggestions for treating depression is highlighted and illustrated with clinical vignettes. Espouses the viewpoint that productive treatment emanates from a reassociation of the patient's experiential life.

Salameh, W. A. (1988). Humor and personal freedom. In L. F. Nilsen & A. P. Nilsen (Eds.), *Proceedings of the Sixth (1987) Whimsy VI Conference* (pp. 257-259). Tempe, AZ: Arizona State University. Clarifies some of the clinical contributions that humor can make to the movement toward personal freedom and psychological openness. Describes how humor can be used to facilitate and expand patients' personal freedom in seven areas: freedom to act, freedom to feel, freedom to make mistakes, freedom to play, freedom to awaken unexpressed potential, freedom to unburden oneself, and freedom to create. Offers an illustrative clinical vignette for each type of freedom discussed.

Salameh, W. A. (1987). *Psychotherapeutic Humor: Applications in Practice.* A companion professional cassette program with the *Handbook of Humor and Psychotherapy: Advances in the Clinical Use of Humor.* Sarasota, FL: Professional Resource Exchange. Covers the multiple uses of humor in psychotherapy including the use of jokes, stories, and indirect suggestions. Describes how humorous stories can be productively developed and tailored to the patient's needs, and how clinicians can further develop their own senses of humor.

Salameh, W. A. (1987). Humor in Integrative Short-Term Psychotherapy (ISTP). In W. F. Fry, Jr. & W. A. Salameh (Eds.), *Handbook of Humor and Psychotherapy: Advances in the Clinical Use of Humor* (pp. 195-240). Sarasota, FL: Professional Resource Exchange. Provides a comprehensive theory of psychotherapy and how humor can be strategically used within this theory. Includes intervention recommendations, as well as sections on technique and pertinent uses, and clinical vignettes. Details the therapeutic strategy used within the Integrative Short-Term Psychotherapy (ISTP) process model that incorporates humor.

Salameh, W. A. (1986). Humor as a form of indirect hypnotic communication. In M. Yapko (Ed.), *Hypnotic and Strategic Interventions: Principles and Practice* (pp. 133-188). New York: Irvington. Explores the hypnotic qualities in humor, including guidelines for the effective framing of hypnotic and humorous stories. Various representations of the unconscious are surveyed, including a summary of how the unconscious is perceived in different psychological theories. The creative uses of absurdity are also considered, including the utilization of paradoxical humorous prescriptions as indirect suggestions. A group of nine indirect humorous suggestions are defined and illustrated with clinical vignettes. Structured hypnotic humorous experiences are identified, including a theory of psychotherapy that incorporates humor and specific hypnotic experiences that can be used by therapists to introduce humor into the therapeutic interaction.

Salameh, W. A. (1986). The effective use of humor in psychotherapy. In P. A. Keller & L. G. Ritt (Eds.), *Innovations in Clinical Practice: A Source Book* (Vol 5, pp. 157-175). Sarasota, FL: Professional Resource Exchange. Provides a model describing the effective uses of humor in psychotherapy and identifies therapist traits that help optimize the effective use of humor. Elucidates the Humor Immersion Training (HIT) system for creating humor, and defines several humor creation techniques. Lists resources and discusses strategies for adding humor to one's life. Concludes with the proposition that humor is an adaptive response in the face of life's adversities, symbolizing the courage to persevere.

Salameh, W. A. (1983). Humor in psychotherapy: Past outlooks, present status, and future frontiers. In P. McGhee & J. Goldstein (Eds.), *Handbook of Humor Research. Volume II - Applied Studies of Humor* (pp. 61-88). New York: Springer-Verlag. Reviews the history of the use of humor in psychotherapy and the available research data regarding the relevance of humor for the psychotherapeutic process. Identifies the therapeutic theories explicitly incorporating humor, and places the existing research on the therapeutic uses of humor within the larger context of psychotherapy research. Recommends future areas for humor in psychotherapy research relating to therapist factors, patient factors, matching factors, technique factors, diagnostic and assessment factors, problem definition factors, environmental factors, motivational factors, creativity factors, and outcome factors. A Therapeutic Humor Rating Scale is presented as a possible tool for rating the level of the therapist's humor. Twelve therapeutic humor techniques are defined, and each is illustrated with a brief clinical vignette. Ethical considerations relating to the use of humor in psychotherapy are discussed, including a detailed differentiation between therapeutic and harmful humor.

Salisbury, W. D. (1990). A study of humor in counseling among Adlerian therapists: A statistical research project (Doctoral dissertation, Union Institute, Ohio). *Dissertation Abstracts International, 50,* 5301.

Sands, S. (1984). The use of humor in psychotherapy. *Psychoanalytic Review, 71,* 441-460. Discusses the use of humor in psychotherapy, noting that humor is a form of emotional expression that psychotherapists rarely encourage or manipulate and usually leave to chance and spontaneity. A literature review reveals that, although many researchers have discussed the beneficial aspects of humor in psychotherapy, the literature is flawed by a vague sense of what humor is and a tendency to fit humor into an overly general philosophy about life or therapy. Humor is defined, and various forms of humor are identified and differentiated. Additional topics of discussion concern what makes something amusing, what happens in reactions to humor, and social aspects of humor. In psychotherapeutic considerations of humor, it is the patient's humor rather than the therapist's that is likely to be most useful to the patient; however, humor can be useful to the therapist in making him/herself less formidable to the patients, in testing aspects of the patient's condition, and in penetrating defenses of the patient. Since the effects of humor depend on contingencies that are often hard to control, therapists should use strategies involving humor with caution. (29 ref)

Saper, B. (1988). Humor in psychiatric healing. *Psychiatric Quarterly, 59,* 306-319. Examines the aphorism that "laughter is the best medicine" and reviews 3 claims regarding its benefits in treating physical and mental disorders. The extent to which the positive emotions of joy and laughter influence the physiological components of health and illness is considered. Individual differences in the personality of both the patient and therapist are discussed that may or may not enhance the efficacy of humor in treating mental or physical disorders. The wisdom and utility of incorporating humor into psychotherapy are analyzed.

Saper, B. (1987). Humor in psychotherapy: Is it good or bad for the client? *Professional Psychology: Research & Practice, 18,* 360-367. Although little systematic empirical research conclusively supports the contention that humor in, as, or with psychotherapy is beneficial, the past 15 years or so have witnessed a burgeoning advocacy of its use. Most of the literature advocating the use of humor as well as some of the research studies are briefly reviewed in this article. The latter are found wanting in terms of design, methodology, and definitive results. Employing a cognitive-behavioral or social learning model, we suggest a functional analysis to explore the complex nature of the interlacing components of the humor concept and experience as well as to expose the complicated mechanisms by which mirth may effect the significant ingredients of the psychotherapeutic process to produce positive change. Finally, specific humor strategies and techniques and their effects are briefly discussed. We conclude that deliberately bringing together humor and psychotherapy is not without its risks. As in the case of copulating porcupines, such a union, although potentially productive, should be consummated very carefully.

Schienberg,P. (1980). Therapists' predictions of patients' responses to humor as a function of therapists' empathy and regression in the service of the ego (Doctoral dissertation, California School of Professional Psychology, Los Angeles). *Dissertation Abstracts International, 40,* 4501.

Schimel,J. L. (1978). The function of wit and humor in psychoanalysis. *Journal of the American Academy of Psychoanalysis, 6,* 369-379. The use of humor in psychoanalysis has traditionally been viewed as thinly veiled aggression and as destructive or demeaning. The author urges a reconceptualization of the therapeutic use of wit and humor, suggesting that clinical judgment should replace blanket indictment. Humorous and/or metaphorical intervention can effectively cut through denial and manipulative use of affect and become a valuable means of multilayered communication for both analyst and patient. Case material is included.

Schnarch,D. M. (1990). Therapeutic uses of humor in psychotherapy. *Journal of Family Psychotherapy, 1,* 75-86. Since humor inherently offers the characteristic of multiple simultaneous levels of meaning and impact, it is a natural candidate for use in therapy. The use of humor in therapist-initiated interventions and by patients is described. The effect of humor in reducing anxiety and strengthening the treatment alliance with patients is compared with the use of therapist sarcasm, which generally has the opposite effect. Humor is discussed as an element in the private language of therapy, as training for marriage, and as a medium for tracking the course and progress of treatment.

Schwarz, B. E. (Winter, 1974-1975). Telepathic humoresque. *Psychoanalytic Review, 61,* 591-606. Contends that humor is intimately related to the subconscious and hence to the paranormal. Used tactfully and sparingly, it can be helpful in psychotherapy. 3 categories of what appear to be instances of telepathy and the paranormal allied to humor are presented: humorous situations from early parent-child relationships, physician-patient psychotherapeutic relationships, and strictly personal anecdotes. Numerous incidents in each category are presented and discussed briefly. (26 ref)

Scott, E. M. (1989). Humor and the alcoholic patient: A beginning study. *Alcoholism Treatment Quarterly, 6,* 29-39. Administered a questionnaire on humor to 80 men and 40 women applying for help at an alcoholic outpatient agency. Ss judged themselves as laughing often and were of the opinion that drinking increased their sense of humor (men more so than women). An overwhelming number endorsed humor as a desirable element in psychotherapy. Ss judged that a parent of the opposite sex laughed more often than a parent of the same sex.

Shaughnessy,M. F. (1984). Humor in logotherapy. *International Forum for Logotherapy, 7,* 106-111. Considers the role of humor and laughter in paradoxical intention and logotherapy. Situations, problems, and difficulties can be gently mocked and placed into perspective through paradoxical intention. Humor and laughter are effective in therapy because they also affect the organism. Whether humor can help individuals understand themselves depends on the degree of the humor's relevance, not on the degree of fun generated. It is contended that logotherapists can assist client sin their self-transcendental search and their search for meaning through the use of humor. (11 ref)

Sherman,M. H. (Winter, 1970-1971). Dr. Theodor Reik: A life devoted to Freud and psychoanalysis. *Psychoanalytic Review, 57,* 535-543. Reik met Freud when the former was 22 and orphaned. For the rest of his life he lived for the meaning that Freud and psychoanalysis were to give to his existence. Freud introduced Reik into the Vienna psychoanalytic society, sent him to Abraham for analysis, and gave him financial aid. Reik wrote on behalf of but also against Freud. The "question of lay analysis" was written by Freud to defend Reik against legal action. Reik's approach to psychoanalysis was anecdotal compared to the theoretical writings of other analysts. Reik's most creative effort was expressed in his work on psycho-analytic archeology. Reik had a great talent for dealing with the phenomenology of complex psychopathology. The major idiom in which Reik wrote was that of confession. Other areas explored by Reik included the emotional differences between men and women, the self-entrapment of the criminal, humor and Jewish wit, and the unconscious motivations revealed by great literary artists.

Shibles, W. (1991). Feminism and the cognitive theory of emotion: Anger, blame and humor. *Women & Health, 17,* 57-69. Argues that cognitive or rational emotive theory (RET) is one of the best theories of emotion to help advance an enlightened and humanistic feminism. Basic principles are presented to analyze emotion and show the contrast with feminist state-ments about anger, blame, freedom, and humor. RET is thoroughly humanistic, transcends gender exclusivity, and shows how to prevent and cope with negative emotions and how to create positive ones. RET may help women and men to achieve their goals in an effective, healthful, and humanistic way.

Solomon, K. (1982). *Counseling the Drug Dependent Woman: Special Issues for Men* (Tech. Rep. No. ADM 82-1219). Baltimore: University of Maryland. Discusses typical male socialization patterns and defensive maneuvers of men (labeling, intellectualization, confronta-tion, humor, verbal or physical assault, negation, "self-listening," and body language) and their consequences for male counselors who treat drug-dependent women. Methods male coun-selors can use to become aware of and identify their own masculine values and styles and rec-ognize their potential impact on the counseling process are suggested. Resources and ideas are included on how to conduct staff training sessions to help male counselors learn more about themselves as men, male and female gender roles, and the power dynamics that can interfere with communication between men and women. The author also discusses how the styles and orientations of male counselors can be both a drawback and a strength in providing services to drug-dependent women. A selected bibliography on the masculine gender role is appended.

Sonntag, N. (1985). Cartooning as a counseling approach to a socially isolated child. *School Counselor, 32,* 307-312. Describes the use of creating cartoon strips with grade-school-aged children as a counseling technique. An excerpt from the case study of a 7-yr-old 2nd-grade female is presented to demonstrate the application of this concept. At the beginning of counseling, the S had no friends either at school or in her neighborhood; through the course of counseling, the S made progress in playing with other children without becoming upset. This technique should be used in conjunction with more traditional counseling techniques. (14 ref)

Stanton, A. H. (1978). The significance of ego interpretive states in insight-directed psychotherapy. *Psychiatry, 41,* 129-140. Views insight as one of the most important therapeu-tic concepts, examines the effect of insight on the patient's self-image, and discusses the rela-tionship between insight and ego-interpretative states. These states include the artistic inter-pretive state, humor, sexual experience, the schizophrenic set, and the experience of being a patient in psychotherapy. The content of the various states of mind, their interpersonal re-quirements, and the construction and destruction are examined, and it is suggested that the insight-directed psychotherapeutic situation, since the patient takes part in it, is generally in-compatible with the schizophrenic set or significant parts of it. The benefit of understanding these states for both the patient and the therapist is discussed.

Sumners, A. D. (1988). Humor: Coping in recovery from addition. *Issues in Mental Health Nursing, 9,* 169-179. Explores the therapeutic possibilities of humor applied to the process of recovery from addiction. A theoretical framework for understanding humor is pre-sented, and the functions of humor in the 4 stages of recovery from addiction defined by S. Brown (1985) are outlined. Suggestions for using humor in the treatment setting are presented.

Humor is described as a means of coping with the stresses of the recovery process and is shown to be a valuable tool both for the recovering addict and for clinicians.

Sutcliffe, P., Lovell, J., & Walters, M. (1985). New directions for family therapy: Rubbish removal as a task of choice. *Journal of Family Therapy, 7,* 175-182. Presents a humorous satire of the task of rubbish removal in therapeutic terms. The removal of actual rubbish is discussed as a point around which to structure family therapy that can lead to gratification, healthy change, and child development gains.

Szafran, A. W. (1981). Humour, creativite et psychotherapie (Humor, creativity and psychotherapy). *Annales Medico-Psychologiques, 139,* 11-19. States that humor must be clearly distinguished from jokes and comedy. Humor presents the characteristics described by Freud for creative processes in general and has the ability to remove sexual and aggressive inhibitions on an intrapsychic level, which in turn allows the individual to struggle against social constraints. It is suggested that humor can be usefully employed in the framework of the corrective emotional experience of the psychotherapeutic relationship, since it can not only protect the individual against anxiety but also permit the narcissistic affirmation of the self toward the outside world. (28 ref)

Thomson, B. R. (1990). Appropriate and inappropriate uses of humor in psychotherapy as perceived by certified reality therapists: A Delphi study. *Journal of Reality Therapy, 10,* 59-65. Surveyed 56 reality therapists as to appropriate and inappropriate uses of humor in psychotherapy. Four themes emerged regarding the appropriate uses of humor: (1) the central importance of the therapeutic relationship if humor is to be used effectively, (2) the degree of spontaneity in the use of humor by both therapist and client, (3) the potential uses of humor in encouraging client change, and (4) the altered perception of self, others, and the environment derived from using humor appropriately in reality therapy. Ss' statements further suggest that the inappropriate use of humor may create an imbalance in the therapeutic relationship, block effective communication, and generate negative feelings among clients. Recommendations for the use of humor are outlined.

Thomson, B. R. (1986). Appropriate and inappropriate uses of humor in psychotherapy as perceived by certified reality therapists: A Delphi study (Doctoral dissertation, University of Georgia). *Dissertation Abstracts International, 47,* 90.

Van Den Aardweg, G. J. (1973). The factor "complaining," neurosis and homophilia. *Psychologica Belgica, 13,* 295-311. Explains neurosis by the central concept of autonomous self-pity, a repressed reaction to psychic traumatization in childhood that has priority over sex, anxiety, and aggression. 2 types of therapy are suggested: (a) self-observation and self-analysis to recognize the inner child of the past and (b) humor therapy. Homophilia (homosexuality) is defined as neurosis. Factor analysis of data from a homosexuality questionnaire administered to 51 homosexuals revealed 6 factors: (a) neurosis, (b) will to change, (c) character weakness, (d) mother-bind factor, (e) social extraversion, and (f) "lone wolf" pattern in childhood. Therapy was successful in 8 cases, partly successful in 18, and incomplete in the others. (English abstract) (34 ref)

Van den Aardweg, G. J. (1972). A grief theory of homosexuality. *American Journal of Psychotherapy, 26,* 52-68. Review of the literature indicates that male homosexuality is best correlated with the self-concept of being "inferior-pitiable." As a child the homosexual develops the self-image of being a weakling, which causes intense self-pity. This self-pity becomes autonomous by repression and is the source of an infantile longing for love from someone who is idealized as superior to the "poor me." It is suggested that unconscious infantile self-pity can be eliminated by the systematic application of a technique based on the curative value of humor and laughter. The patient learns to observe his inner child and then exaggerates the child's complaints until he sees how ridiculous they are. Laughing destroys complaining. 70 homosexuals have been treated by this method. Of 20 completed treatments 9 or 10 cases are considered as real and lasting cures, i.e., elimination of homosexual impulses, restoration of normal heterosexual feelings, and a basic change from childish emotionality to emotional maturity. (47 ref)

Ventis, W. L., & Ventis, D. G. (1988). Guidelines for using humor in therapy with children and young adolescents. *Journal of Children in Contemporary Society, 20,* 179-197. Discusses prominent characteristics of therapy with children and issues relevant to the use of humor in children's therapy. Applications of therapeutic humor are presented and discussed in the contexts of (a) psychodynamic psychotherapy; (b) the use of humor in behavioral treatments, predominantly of child phobias; (c) humor in family therapy; and (d) the purposeful use of games and stories. The therapist needs to bear in mind that because children do not have the same cognitive abilities as adults, there is more potential for the child to misinterpret the therapist's humor or experience it as a ridicule or a lack of seriousness about the child's problems. Therefore, the therapist should avoid directing humor at the client.

von Wormer, K. (1986). Aspects of humor in alcoholism counseling. *Alcoholism Treatment Quarterly, 3,* 25-32. Presents a systematic analysis of humor as a primary ingredient in successful work with alcoholics and their families. The resistance to and the relevance of humor in alcoholism treatment are discussed as well as the role of humor in group therapy. Practical illustrations are provided. It is concluded that humor can be introduced as a cheap and harmless equivalent for alcohol in facing the everyday cruelties of life.

Weddige, R. L. (1986). The hidden psychotherapeutic dilemma: Spouse of the borderline. *American Journal of Psychotherapy, 40,* 52-61. Describes the psychological reactions typically experienced by spouses of borderline patients, including self-doubt, reaction formation, undoing, reassessing the past, personalizing, denial, loneliness, displacement, projection, retreat, introjection, and defending the children. Psychotherapeutic implications and strategies concerning spouses married to individuals with borderline personality disorganization are discussed, focusing on husbands married to borderline wives. Elements of a supportive and educational psychotherapeutic process include dealing with the following issues: identifying the source of affect; diffusing the affect; maintenance of ego boundaries for the borderline; not criticizing the borderline's eccentric behavior; structuring visits to extended family; assisting the patient not to assume the role of therapist; helping the patient become the children's advocate; encouraging avocations and periodic retreats; the use of humor; and the discussion of options, escape maneuvers, and separation and divorce if initiated in the psychotherapeutic process by the spouse. (18 ref)

Weiss, H. (1984). Humor and imagination. *Hakomi Forum, Summer,* 25-28. Suggests that in hakomi therapy, character and all the behavior, experience, and problems attached to it are seen to resemble a role in a play. Humor with compassion in therapy can be a deep anthropological asset. It can facilitate discharging, create integration, and reenergize. Humor involves imagination on the part of the therapist. Examples are included.

Wells, M. (1983). Implicit frame crashing: A comprehensive psychological theory of humor and its application to a psychotherapy model (Doctoral dissertation, California School of Professional Psychology, Fresno). *Dissertation Abstracts International, 44,* 932.

Whitaker, C. A., & Keith, D. M. (1982). Terapia Familiare Simbolico-esperienziale (Symbolic-experiential family therapy). *Terapia Familiare, 11,* 95-134. Explains the techniques of symbolic-experiential therapy adopted by the authors as co-therapists to upset the pathological homeostasis that lies at the roots of many of the dysfunctional family's problems. The normal family is characterized by openness to change, the ability to play "as-if" games, and intergenerational solidarity combined with individual differentiation and independence. The dysfunctional family, in contrast, exhibits homeostatic rigidity and various unresolved stress situations, especially conflicts arising from the choice of 1 of the 2 spouses' families of origin as a family role model. In the family psychotherapy model under discussion, all members of a trigenerational family must participate in the therapy sessions, which the therapists conduct by playing grandparent and trainer roles, using the language of symbol and metaphor, free association, humor, and jokes. Therapists must also watch their own behaviors and attitudes toward individual members of the client family and the family as a whole. (This article was originally published in the handbook of Family Therapy, edited by A. S. Gurman and D. P. Kniskern [1982]). (11 ref)

Wilkins, R. (1989). The king and his fool. *Journal of Family Therapy, 11,* 181-195. Discusses the role of the Fool in Shakespeare's King Lear as that of an unsuccessful psychotherapist whose ineptitude was in large part responsible for driving Lear insane and hastening his death. Reasons for Lear's "therapeutic failure" are identified, and parallels are drawn with modern psychotherapeutic practices, especially the potentially dangerous misuse of humor, metaphor, paradox, and absurdity by inexperienced therapists.

Yampey, N. (1983). Acerca del humor y el insight (On humor and insight). *Revista de psicoanalisis, 40,* 1173-1181. Examines the psychodynamics and the semantic, clinical, and metapsychological aspects of humor as distinct from irony. Defined by Freud as one of the highest psychic functions, originating through the economical expenditure of affect, humor is a catalyst for positive change in the psychoanalytic process. It emerges when paranoid, depressive, or confusional anxieties are sufficiently overcome to set free the analysand's capability for tolerant self-observation. The development of humor in social history and literature is reviewed, and its ontogenetic roots, links with narcissism, and role in individual's insights into his/her psychic conflicts are discussed. Humor presupposes a positive relation of the Ego with internal objects; it facilitates mutual human understanding at both personal and global levels. (English & French abstracts) (0 ref)

Yeghicheyan, V. (1989). Langue maternelle et economie psychique (Mother tongue and psychic economy). *Psychiatrie Francaise, 20,* 130-131. Presents clinical cases of 2 patients whose mother tongue (MT) was other than French but whose basic elements were known to the analyst. Ss' decathexis of their MT had caused a regression favoring the death instincts. Through establishment of a reassuring setting (reminiscent of maternal protection) and by gradually leading Ss back to reinvesting in their MT through the healing medium of humor, the analyst restored Ss' erogenous masochism. (0 ref)

Young, F. D. (1988). Three kinds of strategic humor: How to use and cultivate them. *Journal of Strategic & Systemic Therapies, 7,* 21-34. Discusses 3 types of humor appropriate to strategic therapy: (1) Tactical humor is primarily reactive or responsive to the client system; (2) strategic humor mainly defines the roles of the players in a pattern and the payoffs of their interaction; and (3) systemic humor alters the context in which the pattern is understood and therefore the meaning and often the absurdity of its continuance. Each type of humor is discussed in terms of how to define it, when and how to use it, and how to cultivate or promote its development as a therapist or supervisor.

Index

R

S

Also Available

Handbook of Humor and Psychotherapy:
Advances in the Clinical Use of Humor

William F. Fry, Jr. and Waleed A. Salameh, Editors

"Humor is a seasoning for psychotherapy and its effective use is an indicator of the seasoning of the psychotherapist. . . .[This book] is a comprehensive organized compendium of how humor can be used constructively across schools of psychotherapy, and in individual, group, and family approaches. Fry and Salameh have collected the work of an array of European and American experts who cogently described important advances. Well written and well edited, this handbook is certain to be a standard reference. A sure-fire remedy for burnout."
-**Jeffrey K. Zeig, PhD,** Director, Milton H. Erickson Foundation

Table of Contents

Psychotherapeutic Humor:
Applications in Practice

Dr. Salameh's 40-minute tape provides an overview of psychotherapeutic humor and offers numerous examples of practice applications. The author presents clinical vignettes, anecdotes, and creative techniques for appropriately injecting laughter into your interactions with patients.

See Reverse Side For Ordering Information⸺▶

Order Form

Please send me:

_____ *Handbook of Humor and Psychotherapy:*
      Advances in the Clinical Use of Humor.
      $32.70 per copy (includes shipping).. _____

_____ *Psychotherapeutic Humor: Applications in Practice.*
      $11.95 per cassette ($7.00 if ordered with the book) (includes shipping)........ _____

_____ *Advances in Humor and Psychotherapy.*
      $38.70 per copy (includes shipping).. _____

          Florida residents, include 7% sales tax................................ _____

          Foreign orders (include an additional $2.00 shipping)......................... _____

          TOTAL (all orders must be prepaid)....................................... _____

❐   Check enclosed

Charge my ❐ MasterCard   ❐ Visa   ❐ Discover   ❐ American Express

Signature (Required if using credit card)_____

Card #_____ Expiration Date_____

Ship to:

Name_____
[Please Print]

Address_____

Address_____

City/State/Zip_____

Daytime Phone # (_____)_____

Order from:

Professional Resource Press
P.O. Box 15560
Sarasota, FL 34277-1560

Telephone # 813-366-7913
FAX # 813-366-7971

Would You Like Information On Our Other Publications?

For a copy of our latest catalog, please write, call, or fax the following information to the address and phone number listed below:

Name_____
[Please Print]

Address_____

Address_____

City/State/Zip_____

Telephone_____

Profession (check all that apply):

_____ Psychologist   _____ Mental Health Counselor
_____ Marriage and Family Therapist   _____ Psychiatrist
_____ School Psychologist   _____ Not in Mental Health Field
_____ Clinical Social Worker   _____ Other:_____

Professional Resource Press
P.O. Box 15560
Sarasota, FL 34277-1560

Telephone # 813-366-7913
FAX # 813-366-7971